Yesterday
Today
—and—
Forever

Rothman Foundation Series

Yesterday
Today
—and—
Forever

Exploring Contemporary Judaism
From the Perspective of Jewish History

VOLUME ONE

From the Creation to the Destruction of the First Temple

❧

Rabbi Mordechai Katz

FELDHEIM PUBLISHERS   *Jerusalem / New York*

Library of Congress Cataloging-in-Publication Data

Katz, Mordechai.
    Yesterday, today, and forever : exploring contemporary Judaism from the
perspective of Jewish history / by Mordechai Katz.
      p. cm.
    Includes bibliographical references.
    ISBN 0-87306-656-1 (hc.)
    1. Bible. O.T.—History of Biblical events. 2. Ethics in the
Bible. 3. Ethics, Jewish. 4. Orthodox Judaism. 5. Jews—History. I. Title.
BS1197.K285 1993
296—dc20   93-28277

First published 1993

Copyright © 1993 by the Jewish Education Program

FELDHEIM PUBLISHERS
POB 35002 / Jerusalem, Israel

200 Airport Executive Park
Spring Valley, NY 10977

Printed in Israel

In memory of

Maurice M. Rothman ז״ל

and

Golde N. Rothman ע״ה

לחמו מלחמות ה׳

*"who lived and fought
for Torah-true Judaism"*

❧ Jewish Education Program (JEP)

The Jewish Education Program, a project of Agudath Israel of America, was organized in September 1972, and since its inception has become a well-known, active force in the field of Jewish education. Its guiding principle, "Jewish power and Jewish pride through Jewish education," was formulated in response to what has become a Jewish tragedy of massive proportions, namely assimilation and its tragic by-products.

Under the guidelines of prominent *roshei yeshivos* and leaders in the field of Jewish education, and staffed entirely by *b'nei Torah* and yeshiva graduates, JEP relies almost entirely on the talents and efforts voluntarily contributed by capable young Torah students.

Some of JEP's programs include: Shabbatones, in which hundreds of children from various communities in the United States and Canada experience the beauty of Shabbos in a Torah-true environment; Release Hour classes for spiritually-starved public-school children; programs for needy Russian immigrants; *Ruach* and Seminar sessions for day-school students; *Chavruso* Big-Brother programs; high-school encounter groups; Holiday rallies; yeshiva and camp placement; and the publication of educational material for thousands of young people.

Through these and various other programs, JEP hopes to ignite the spark of Yiddishkeit deep within the hearts of these individuals, and turn it into a blazing fire. It hopes to instill within these youngsters a love of Hashem and His Torah and an understanding of Torah-true Judaism.

All royalties from this book will go to benefit JEP's various *Kiruv* projects, which have been instrumental in the placement of over 1,000 children into yeshivos, Hebrew day schools, and camps.

❦ Acknowledgments

If history teaches us anything, it is that no one person alone is responsible for notable achievements. There are always others whose major contributions helped see a project through to fruition, and if any credit results, they more than deserve to share in it.

Certainly, this *sefer* could never have been readied for publication without the selfless assistance of a number of very talented individuals, and I appreciate this chance to pay public tribute to the following:

Mrs. Chavie Aranoff and Mrs. Gabriella Bachrach, whose outstanding efforts in writing, editing, typing, and proofreading the manuscript played a very significant role in ensuring that it was ready to be submitted to the publisher.

Rabbi Eliezer Gevirtz and Messrs. Sandor Berkovitz and Bezalel Lerner, who reviewed the entire manuscript and made helpful corrections and suggestions.

Rabbi Yosef Chaim Golding, whose editorial expertise and invaluable guidance were, as always, essential in the preparation of this volume.

A supreme expression of gratitude is due to Harav Yisroel Belsky, *shlita*, Rosh Yeshiva, Yeshiva Torah Vodaath; Rabbi Shlomo Frankel, *shlita*; and especially the eminent historian Rabbi Joseph Elias, *shlita*, dean of the Rika Breuer Teachers' Seminary. Their willingness to take time from their busy schedules to ascertain that the material in this volume meets with the high standards of *da'as Torah* is most appreciated.

Special thanks to Mutty Salomon, Chaye Deitel, Hadassah Brown, Ruchie Koenig and Estie Zazulia for their invaluable technical assistance.

Mrs. Judi Dick, who assisted in editing and proofreading the manuscript, wishes to acknowledge her late parents, David and Mollie Lando, whose home was always open to those who seek Hashem.

The members of the Henry, Bertha, and Edward Rothman Foundation, who have so graciously sponsored this and other JEP volumes. May Hashem enable them to continue their most worthy work on behalf of Jewish education for many years to come.

In addition, I would like to thank my parents, Mr. and Mrs. Moshe Katz; my in-laws, Mr. and Mrs. Yitzchok Berger; my dear children; all the other members of my family; and, especially, my dear wife, Pessi, whose encouragement and support over the years have meant so much to me.

I would like to thank Yaakov and Yitzchak Feldheim for their interest and support in the publication of this work. I also would like to express my appreciation to the staff of the editorial, design, and typesetting departments at Feldheim Publishers for their skillful work.

Above all, my thanks to *Ha-Kadosh Baruch Hu* for enabling me to produce a work that, hopefully, will inspire others to take pride in their glorious past and strive, through mitzvos and *ma'asim tovim*, to help make the future even more auspicious for all *Klal Yisrael.*

Rabbi Mordechai Katz
Brooklyn, New York
Tishrei 5754

❧ Preface

זְכֹר יְמוֹת עוֹלָם בִּינוּ שְׁנוֹת דֹּר-וָדֹר שְׁאַל אָבִיךָ וְיַגֵּדְךָ זְקֵנֶיךָ וְיֹאמְרוּ לָךְ:

"Remember the days of old, consider the years of every generation. Go ask your father and he shall tell you; your elders and they shall speak to you about it" (*Devarim* 32:7).

We are commanded by the Torah to inquire about the past and to contemplate and study the events of previous generations. There is no more reliable teacher than past experience. To a Jew, forgetting is tantamount to denying his identity. The Jew lives very much in the present, but he understands himself on a basis of a continuity that stretches from Creation to ultimate Redemption. All past events contribute to his current situation, and direct him toward a purposeful future.

From the beginning of our history as a people we were assigned a unique role in world affairs. "You shall be unto Me a nation of priests, a holy people" (*Shemos* 18:16). Israel's very existence is defined by these words. The Jews were to live not only for themselves, but were to be God's model nation for mankind. They boldly proclaimed the creed of One Creator in the face of the polytheistic notions of the entire world around them.

When we study history, we find, repeatedly, how great nations such as Egypt, Assyria, Babylonia, Persia, Greece and Rome built up vast empires, but still collapsed one after another. They are now only a memory. In contrast, Israel passed through many crises — its land overrun by invaders; its independence lost; its population taken captive — yet the Jewish nation survived, whereas the other peoples perished. Why?

The answer is very simple. The Nation of Israel, alone among all nations, is not characterized solely by possession of territory or political status, nor by language or culture, but only by its God-given Torah. It was Torah which brought the Israelite nation into being in the first place, and the Jewish People survived only due to their continued adherence to the Divine teachings. This is the explanation of the uniqueness of Jewish history and the secret of Jewish survival. As Rav Saadyah Gaon expressed it, "Our nation is a nation only by reason of its Torah."

Rabbi Samson Raphael Hirsch, in his book of essays called *The Nineteen Letters*, summed it up as follows: "Other states, everywhere, in all the glory of human power and arrogance, disappeared from the face of the earth, while Israel, though devoid of might and splendor, lived on because of its loyalty to God and His Law. Could Israel, then, refuse to acknowledge the All-One as its God, or to accept His Torah as its sole mission on earth?"

This great truth is the theme of the last of the Five Books of the Torah. With untiring repetition, Moshe impressed upon his hearers before his death that faithfulness to the Torah was the essential qualification for their continued existence. Disloyalty to its precepts would result in destruction.

Through its thousands of years of history, the Jewish Nation has proved indestructible. Despots in their wrath and mobs in their hatred swore to annihilate it ... but it lives. We must "remember the days of old," how world empires appeared and vanished, nations rose and fell, but the Jewish Nation remained firm. It is only through the continuous study of our history, taught by unimpeachable sources like the *Tanach* and the Torah scholars, that we can gain insight into how we can surmount the problems of the present and face the challenges of the future.

❧ Introduction to the JEP History Series

This volume on Jewish history is the first one in the new JEP-Rothman Foundation History Series.

This *sefer* offers the English-speaking public a synopsis of the eras in Jewish history from the creation of the world to the destruction of the First Temple. Along with commentaries, it is replete with parables, stories, and the teachings of our Sages, that assist in understanding the chapters and subjects in Jewish history.

The work before us, which describes the earliest period in Jewish history, is the first of several that will, God willing, eventually cover the entire course of our history. Historic dates are listed according to both the Jewish and secular calendar.

There is no better way to teach the lessons gleaned from Jewish history than by showing how our Sages incorporated these lessons into their own lives. This *sefer* incorporates mitzvos, Jewish concepts, and ethics which we learn from these periods of time.

Included in this volume is a list of key people, places, and things at the end of each chapter, followed by footnotes listing the sources. A comprehensive glossary of Hebrew terms is included.

All Hebrew names and places have been transliterated into English (i.e., Moshe, not Moses) in order to make them consistent with, and to facilitate the studying of, the original Hebrew text.

The first time a specific Hebrew term is used in the book, it is transliterated into English and directly followed by its definition in parentheses, i.e., *lashon ha-ra* (evil gossip). At all other times it is simply italicized and its definition can be found at the end of the book in the Glossary.

❧ Foreword

This is a unique work. There exist source outlines of Jewish history; there exist books describing the mitzvos and practices ordained by the Torah; and there are books that seek to teach the outlook and character traits that the Torah demands of us. But until now there has not been a book that systematically weaves these three components together into "a thread that will not readily be broken."

The volume before us — the first one in a series that will cover the whole of Jewish history — outlines our history from the creation of the world to the destruction of the First Temple; and in connection with its personalities and happenings it discusses salient mitzvos (Shabbos, Pesach, *berachos*, etc.) as well as principles of thought (God's Providence, for instance) and of character (honesty and kindness to others, etc.). Each of the seventeen chapters is followed by a list of "Key People, Places, and Things," which serves as a summary of the chapter, and by footnotes listing the sources. These notes are primarily for the youth leaders and teachers who are sure to make use of this book as an excellent basis for their work with children of limited or no Jewish knowledge. However, this book is also of great value in the instruction of yeshiva pupils.

The general approach of integrating *Tanach*, *halachah* and *hashkafah* is exemplary; and so is the manner in which complex concepts are broken down and made intelligible to children. (Note, for example, the brief discussion of evolution in chapter 1.) The enormous effort that Rabbi Katz and his associates have put into this undertaking can readily be seen. May it be His will that they reap a plentiful and blessed harvest from it.

Rabbi Joseph Elias, Dean
Rika Breuer Teachers Seminary

Contents

Contents

CHAP. 10: The Jewish Nation Must Remain Holy

CHAP. 11: Yehoshua and the Conquest of Yisrael

CHAP. 16: King Shelomo's Reign and the Kingdom of Yisrael

🍎 Introduction to Chapters 1-4

The Torah begins not with the history of the Jewish People, but with the very creation of the world and the history of all mankind. The origin of the Jewish People must be understood against the backdrop of world history.

We begin with the history of creation, the story of early mankind, the destruction of the Flood and its aftermath. Because men had eliminated God from their lives, they found the meaning of life to be acquiring possessions and its purpose to be pleasure. Thus one people was introduced into the ranks of the nations which, through its history and life, would declare that God is the only cause of existence, and that the fulfillment of His will is the only goal of life. This group of people was the Jewish Nation.

The Jewish Nation began with the Patriarch Avraham. He was a man who, in his own personal life, had already fulfilled the ideal of the people that was to be. Avraham is introduced in the Torah with a Divine command telling him to leave his homeland. His willingness to follow Hashem without question or reservation earned for him the privilege of being the ancestor of a kingdom of priests and a holy nation. This obedience to God was to be the distinguishing feature which would elevate him and his descendants above the rest of mankind.

As the Biblical accounts show, he and his family – Sarah, Yitzchak, Rivkah, Ya'akov and his family — developed into a community who would offer loyal submission under the sovereignty of God.

The origins of the Jewish People are better known to us than are those of almost any other people, due to the account given in the Torah. This account is not just mere history but a lesson plan for life that illustrates to us how the Creator of the Universe forever guides His creations. We learn of the supreme devotion of our Patriarchs to the Almighty. Their shining characters, and their willingness to sacrifice everything to serve God, are worthy role models.

Early in their history, the Jews were a wandering people. The Divine plan was for the Jewish People to proclaim the sovereignty of God wherever they went. *Bnei Yisrael* were chosen to be the first servants of God and to lead the other nations to recognize His omnipotence.

Thus God declared, "I have known and loved him [Avraham] for he commands his children and his household after him, that they should keep the way of God to do kindness and justice, so that the Lord may bring upon Avraham and his family that which He has spoken."

Bereshis, the first book of the Torah, also relates God's punishment of the wicked, as in the episode of the Flood, and the destruction of S'dom. One learns of the great rewards bestowed by the Almighty upon those who walk in His path, as did our Patriarchs and Matriarchs. Their complete honesty, love of mankind, and eagerness to help other human beings stand as a living lesson for all of us. The Torah then focuses on the children of Ya'akov, who became the Nation of Israel.

Bereshis concludes with Yosef's brothers repenting for having sold him; Yosef settling his family in Egypt; and the death of Ya'akov and of Yosef.

CHAPTER 1

God, The Creator and Overseer of the World
From the Creation of the World Until after the Tower of Bavel
(Creation – 1998 / Creation – 1763 B.C.E.)

❦ HISTORY

CREATION OF THE UNIVERSE

The Torah (Bible) begins by describing God's creation of the heaven and the earth from nothingness. However, the world was still void and without shape or order. During the first six days, God shaped and made everything in the universe and placed them all in their proper functioning positions. The order of this Divine endeavor was as follows:

First Day — Creation of light and darkness.

Second Day — Creation of the heavens, by separating between the heavenly and earthly waters.

Third Day — Accumulation of the waters, allowing the dry land to be visible, and creation of trees and vegetation.

Fourth Day — Creation and placement in the sky of the sun, moon, and stars.

Fifth Day — Creation of sea life and birds.

Sixth Day — Creation of reptiles, animals, and man.

On the Seventh Day of Creation, God "rested" from His work, and sanctified the seventh day as the Shabbos, a day of rest.

LESSON I

Creation

The greatest phenomenon is the creation of the universe. Before that, nothing existed. At God's command, everything suddenly came into existence. This was the most spectacular of miracles, and the farthest removed from our experience or imagination. Thus, excepting God, nothing has intrinsic being; and the continued existence of all things is dependent solely on God's will.

A heretic once disagreed with a rabbi who taught that the world was created by God. "The world has existed forever and no one created it," said the heretic. The rabbi then asked the heretic to leave the room for several moments. When he re-entered, a beautiful painting hung on the wall. The heretic admired the painting and then asked who had painted it. The rabbi answered that he had spilled some paint onto a canvas and that the painting had taken shape by itself.

The heretic laughed mockingly and said, "That is impossible. Just by looking at the perfect design of the painting, anyone can tell that someone painted it carefully and purposefully."

The rabbi responded, "The same is true of the world. When examining how perfectly all its features exist and interact, anyone can tell that it was formed by an All-Knowing Creator."[1]

We take sight for granted, but we wouldn't if we considered the various components of the eye that make it possible: the pupil, acting as the shutter letting in light; the lens, allowing the light to focus properly on the retina, which in turn relays the message of what is seen to the brain via the optic nerve; the rods and cones, which account for color and black-and-white vision; the cornea, which protects the eye from damage; the tear ducts, which help remove foreign substances from it. The brain receives the image upside down, and must turn it right-side-up before the image registers. All of these parts and operations occur instantaneously so that man will be able to see and appreciate the world around him. A man who becomes blind will fully appreciate the wonder of vision since he realizes what he is missing.

The same, of course, is true of the processes of hearing, thinking, smelling, tasting, touching, eating, and breathing, among others.

Nature, and especially the human being, remain as testimonies to the fact that they have been created by a Superior Being.

In our times the theory that the world developed by itself has once again gained popularity, but this concept (called the "theory of evolution") is disputed and even discarded by many scientists. Evolutionists must explain from where the original matter came and where the first cell and atoms originated. They must explain reproduction, respiration, and excretion. Since they reject the idea of a Creator, they explain the development of all animate and inanimate objects in the world as being the result of pure chance.

The great teacher and Torah scholar, Rabbi Akiva, taught that just as the presence of a house testifies that it was constructed by a builder, and the garment testifies to the weaver, so, too, does the presence of the world testify to the fact that God, the Creator, formed it.[2]

Scientifically, it is logical and comprehensible to accept the fact that there is a Creator, a Being far above man's conception, Who caused and continues to cause all to be. All plant and animal life, all details of their composition and function, are of such complicated purposeful design that the theory of evolution which attributes them to chance is automatically disproved.

Even a child can perceive with his pure and simple "emunah" (faith) things that a non-believer may not. A gentile once asked a Jewish boy how the boy knew that God exists. The boy replied, "I live near the seashore. If I go there and see footsteps in the sand, I know that someone has been there. In the same way, whenever I look up and see the sun, the moon, the stars, and the wonders of nature, I know that God is there. Those are some of His imprints on the universe."

ETHICS I:

Pride as the Cause for Downfall

The Talmud tells us that the sun and the moon were originally created of equal size. However, the angels representing the moon complained to Hashem (God) that this was not a fair and practical arrangement, saying, "Is it possible for two kings to rule one country and share one crown?"

"You are saying that you and the sun cannot be of the same size," said Hashem. "Very well, since one of you must be subservient to the other, you will be the one to be diminished in size and power. The sun will continue to burn as brightly as it did when created, and will radiate light and warmth throughout the day. On the other hand, you will provide only a small amount of illumination during the darkness of the night."

The angel representing the moon was upset upon hearing this, and protested, "For having made a rational protest should I be punished and be made smaller?"

But Hashem with His everlasting sympathy and compassion, said comfortingly, "I will surround you with countless luminous stars which will add to your shine with their own twinkling brilliance. You will not be alone. Yet, because you tried to claim the superior position for yourself, your light will still be dimmed."[3]

How many of us, without necessarily realizing it, spend our lives pursuing honor and glory? How often do we want to be on top, to be better than everyone else? Yet, what we may not realize is that this striving for selfish superiority usually leads to bitter disappointment. Instead of seeking our own advancement at someone else's expense, we should be satisfied with what we have achieved.[4]

Why was man created on Friday afternoon and not earlier? So that, should he become pompous, he can be reminded that even the mosquito preceded him in the works of Creation.[5]

LESSON II

Shabbos

Hashem in six days created the world with all its beauty and perfection. However, an essential ingredient was lacking — Shabbos. All week long, man lacks a certain freedom. He is bound to the material world, and is a slave to its pressures. On the Shabbos, every man is a king ruling his own destiny. More than at any other time, the Jew can live as a Jew on the Shabbos. He divorces himself from everything else in the world and turns to God. The Shabbos is much more

than a mere day of rest from a hard week's work. It is a symbol of our belief in God's Creation. On Shabbos, the process of Creation stopped completely. Therefore, we emulate God's rest with our Shabbos.

Interestingly enough, the whole world observes a seven-day week. This is testimony that the entire world recognizes that God created the world in seven days. The whole week revolves around the Shabbos.[6]

In the account of Creation, the Torah tells us that "God finished on the seventh day." The commentaries ask an obvious question: If God rested on the seventh day, how could He have finished on the very same day? If He did nothing on Shabbos, then obviously He finished on the sixth day. The answer they give is that on the Shabbos God created "rest." On the seventh day, God added this dimension of tranquillity and harmony to the world. It was no longer in the process of change and therefore was able to partake of God's serenity. As such, it became holy and blessed. This explains why the concept of peace is so important on the Shabbos.[7]

❦ HISTORY

ADAM AND CHAVAH IN GAN EDEN

After God created man, whom He called Adam, He declared that it was not good for man to be alone. He brought all the animals and birds before Adam. Adam gave names to all of them, but could find no mate for himself among them. God then cast a deep sleep upon Adam and removed one of his ribs. He shaped, developed and completed the rib, forming it into a woman, and brought her before Adam. Adam called her Chavah. (This had been the original plan of Creation, but God made it so that Adam became a participant in his own development.)

God placed Adam and Chavah in the Garden of Eden, where they could eat from anything except the forbidden fruit of the Tree of Knowledge. However, Adam's wife, Chavah, fell under the influence of the crafty serpent and ate of the forbidden fruit and gave some to Adam as well. As a result, they were punished. They were forced to leave the Garden of Eden and begin life, as we know it, experiencing the hardship of toiling for their sustenance and the sufferings of childbirth. The serpent was also punished by having to crawl on the ground and eat the dust of the earth.

LESSON III

The Purpose of Man

Judaism believes that man has been endowed with the freedom to choose between right and wrong. In fact, that is why the formation of man was the ultimate climax of all Creation. Man is a miniature world containing all the elements found in the entire Creation.[8]

Man and his Shabbos was God's final creation. Each man contains a spark of the Almighty within him and is, therefore, able to recognize and serve God. He was created with the specific purpose of emulating God's righteousness on earth. He should not allow corruption, greed and violence to dominate over justice and kindness. Upon analysis of the Seven Noachide Laws, one can see that they serve as model rules for the world to follow:

1. Establish courts of law and order.

2. Do not blaspheme the Name of the Holy One.

3. Do not worship any form of idol or deity other than God.

4. Do not commit murder.

5. Do not commit adultery.

6. Do not rob or steal.

7. Do not eat an organ of a living animal.

These seven laws are intended to help man carry out his mission in this world and serve as a basis for morality and ethics. The prohibitions against idolatry and blasphemy teach man to worship and respect God, this being the foundation of the world. The prohibitions against murder, adultery, robbery and perversion of justice serve as the foundation of human morality. The prohibition against eating an organ from a living animal teaches man kindness towards lower creatures as well as control over his animalistic desires.

A gentile who fulfills these seven commandments because God commanded him to do so is called one of the *chassidei umos ha-olam* ("righteous gentiles of the world"). Such a non-Jew, although he never embraces Judaism, is deserving of life in *Olam Ha-Ba* (the World to Come). Eternal life awaits the pious non-Jew as well as the pious Jew.[9]

The first human being was created after all vegetation and animals had already been created. Hashem wanted Adam to find the world beautifully prepared for him. But there was another purpose, as well. It was also meant to serve as a reminder to Adam of the reason for his creation. Man was created in Hashem's likeness. He possesses the intellect and emotions necessary to comprehend Creation and serve the Master of the universe. Hashem then said, "If he fulfills My will, he will bear God's image and rule over the animals. However, if he fails, his Divine image will depart and the animals will dominate him."[10]

❧ HISTORY

KAYIN AND HEVEL

Adam and Chavah had two sons: Kayin, a farmer, and Hevel, a shepherd. Both Kayin and Hevel brought offerings of their produce to Hashem. Hevel was sincere in his offering and brought before Hashem from the best of his flock. Kayin was not generous and brought inferior produce. Hashem accepted Hevel's offering and a fire descended from heaven and burned it, but this was not so with regard to Kayin's offering. Kayin was greatly angered and highly embarrassed. While they were in the field, Kayin killed his brother, Hevel.

Asked by Hashem the whereabouts of his brother, Kayin replied, "Am I my brother's keeper?" Hashem punished Kayin for his actions. Kayin was cursed and as penalty was forced to wander over the face of the earth.

Adam and Chavah had a third son, Shes, as well as additional children. As each new generation reproduced, the numbers of mankind increased.

<u>LESSON IV</u>

The Choices of Man

Kayin and Hevel were of different character. Kayin chose to be a farmer even though the earth had just been cursed. Kayin's love of the earth and possessions drove him to constant labor. When Kayin had to bring an offering to God, he chose inferior fruit, for he did not want to give the best to Hashem. Hevel, on the other hand, chose a different profession. He did not wish to become a farmer, fearing the curse imposed after Adam had sinned. Each brother had a choice to make and each chose a different path. Hashem was aware of the motive behind each one's sacrifice. He accepted Hevel's offering, as he gave of the best. However, He was dissatisfied with Kayin's motives and his sacrifice remained unaccepted.

Instead of learning a lesson and rectifying the wrong, Kayin became angry at God. He vented his anger on Hevel and slew him. He took Hevel's body and buried it in the field. Hashem immediately appeared, to ask for his brother. Instead of admitting his terrible misdeed, Kayin brazenly replied, "Am I my brother's keeper?" Hashem announced to Kayin that he would never again obtain enjoyment from the earth. Since he had such drive and ambition for the land, he was punished by having to wander upon the earth. Eventually he would die in disgrace.

We see two people — each representing a completely different aspect of life. Hevel represented the person whose life was geared to fulfilling God's wishes and attaining *Olam Ha-Ba* by giving the best he had to Hashem. Kayin, on the other hand, is the prototype of the man who is attached to this world and invests the best of his time and talents to making his life a material success. His punishment was that he became a restless wanderer, finding no satisfaction in his life, for "he who loves money, shall not be satisfied with money." [11]

<u>LESSON V</u>

God Constantly Oversees the World

If one accepts the fact that God created the world, it makes no sense to assume that God then relinquished all contact with it. If the affairs of the world after Creation were of no interest to God, then what purpose would there have been in their creation to begin with? Would the Almighty have created such a wondrous, beautiful world if He intended to abandon it?

When one accepts the belief that God created the world, he also accepts the idea that Creation took place with a purpose. God did not form the world in a haphazard manner. Rather, He designed a universe in which each feature has its set purpose. At the apex of this plan is the human being, who alone among God's creations has the ability to know of and appreciate the Almighty's efforts.

Each man contains a spark of the Almighty within him and is, therefore, uniquely able to recognize and serve God. He was created with the specific purpose of emulating God's righteousness on earth.

God's wondrous miracle of Creation is not a dramatic one-time occurrence.

Rather, we look at God's Creation as a running spring that is ever-flowing and ever-giving.[12] Man is surrounded by unrecognized miraculous events. The fact that we constantly have food on our table is a clear indication that God is constantly providing for our needs. Farmers, on the whole, are of a religious nature because they realize how dependent they are upon the Almighty's bounty.[13]

The recent terrible drought and famine in Africa serves to remind us that food is not something that we receive automatically. It is something that comes from the hand of Almighty God, and He is able to withhold it when He chooses.

❧ HISTORY

NOACH AND THE FLOOD

There were ten generations from Adam until Noach, during which time two *tzaddikim* (righteous men), Chanoch and Mesushelach (Methuselah) lived. However, man turned to evil and practiced immorality and violence. Unfortunately, each succeeding generation's acts represented a moral decline from those of the previous one. Man deteriorated morally lower and lower, yet God refrained from punishing him. He waited, hoping that man would use his free will to repent from his wicked ways. The evil of the generation of Noach surpassed that of all previous generations, and God knew that the world as it existed had to undergo a drastic change. God decided to destroy all sinful beings by means of a flood. Only the righteous — Noach and his family — would be spared to rebuild the world.

Why did God command Noach to construct an ark which took one hundred and twenty years to build? This was all part of God's Divine plan. He wanted to provide mankind with one final chance to repent. Upon seeing Noach work so hard for so long a period of time, the people were bound to ask, "What are you doing?"

Noach could reply, "If we don't mend our ways, God will bring a flood upon the entire face of the earth. Let us repent before it is too late."

By prolonging the building of the ark, God gave humanity every opportunity to prevent the flood. Unfortunately, the message went unheeded.

Noach did as God instructed, and when the ark was completed, Noach, his wife, their three sons (Shem, Cham, and Yefes), and their son's wives entered the ark. They took with them seven pairs of every kosher animal and bird, and one pair of every other living creature. They also took into the ark all types of foods which would sustain the inhabitants during their stay in the ark.

On the seventeenth day of the second month of the Hebrew calendar, rain began to pour onto the earth, and large quantities of water erupted from the earth's interior. This inundation continued for forty days and forty nights and almost all living beings outside the ark drowned. The deluge was so great that almost six months elapsed before the waters subsided sufficiently for the ark to come to rest on the mountaintop of Ararat.

After almost three additional months, Noach released a raven from the ark to ascertain whether dry land had reappeared. The raven merely flew to and fro, waiting for the water on the surface of the earth to recede. Seven days later, Noach sent out a dove, only to have the dove quickly return to the ark, for it could find no resting place. After waiting another seven days, Noach again sent out the dove. This time the dove returned with an olive leaf in its beak, indicating that the waters were receding. Finally, on its third assignment seven days later, the dove did not return at all, and Noach knew that the land had at last begun to dry up. Noach was then able to remove the covering of the ark. Noach left the ark after his stay of one year and eleven days, or one full solar year. He offered sacrifices of gratitude to God for their survival.

God was pleased with Noach's sacrifices and He swore that He would never again destroy all of mankind by means of a flood. God placed a rainbow in the sky and told Noach that its appearance would always be the symbol of this promise.

ETHICS II:

Jealousy and Friction, Causes for Destruction

The Torah records two generations of sinners. The first was the generation of the Flood, which was destroyed and wiped off the face of the earth in 2105 B.C.E. (1656). The other was the genera- tion of the Tower of Bavel, 1765 B.C.E. (1996), who rebelled directly against God's authority as they attempted to build a tower, ascend to heaven, and conquer the heavens. The builders of the

Tower of Bavel were consequently dispersed throughout the earth, and divided into numerous groups, each speaking a different language.

Why did the generation of the Flood deserve such a severe punishment, while the generation of the Tower of Bavel was only dispersed and not destroyed?

The answer is given by the Midrash, which explains that the fundamental merit of the generation of the Tower of Bavel was peace. As wicked as they were, as rebellious and defiant towards God as they were, there was peace and harmony among them. Therefore, God saw fit to be lenient in their punishment. The generation of the Flood was not only rebellious toward God, but the people committed crimes against their fellowmen. Therefore, their punishment was more severe.[14]

It was Kayin's uncontrolled jealousy of his brother Hevel that prompted him to strike and kill him. His punishment was that he was forced to wander the earth and was eventually killed. That is why our Sages teach us that jealousy causes a person to leave this world. We must do everything in our power to maintain peace and harmony in our midst. The students of the great Rabbi Akiva were on a very high spiritual level. However, the lack of respect that they had for each other caused a terrible plague to take 24,000 from their ranks. Strife and hatred were also the causes of the destruction of the Second Temple. The people's lack of concern for each other and their constant divisiveness led directly to their punishment.

MITZVAH

Reciting the *Shema*

Because we realize that God oversees the world, it is incumbent upon every Jew to say the *Shema* in the morning and the evening. One must say the first sentence of the *Shema*, "SHEMA YISRAEL HASHEM ELOKEINU HASHEM ECHAD" (Hear, Israel, Hashem is our God and God is One) with deep concentration.

God wants His nation to accept upon themselves His kingdom and to proclaim His unity every day and every night. By saying *Kerias Shema* one reinforces the feeling that God is watching him. When saying the first sentence of *Shema*, one should place his hand over his eyes, to aid him in concentrating. One should also say this sentence out loud, and slightly elongate the end of the word *Echad*. When saying God's Name, he

should keep in mind that God was, is, and always will be the Almighty Ruler of the world. While saying *Echad* he should keep in mind that God is One Who reigns over all four corners of the universe.

Throughout the centuries, Jews have offered their lives for their faith, often proclaiming "*Shema Yisrael...*" with their very last breath.

While a Jew must believe in Hashem's oneness at all times, he is obligated to proclaim it verbally by saying *Shema* every morning and night. Reciting the *Shema* every morning is so important that it is stated, "The Garden of Eden with all its delights was created for those who pronounce the verse of *Shema* with the proper concentration."

❦ Key People, Places and Things

ADAM: the first person created in the world. He lived for 930 years.

BEIN ADAM LA-MAKOM: man's dealings with God.

BEIN ADAM L'CHAVERO: man's dealings with his fellowman.

CHAVAH: Eve, Adam's wife who was created from him.

DOR HA-PELAGAH: the generation that built the Tower of Bavel in 1996, intending to reach the heavens to fight against the Almighty.

EMUNAH AND BITACHON: faith in and reliance on God as the Supreme Ruler of the universe.

GAN EDEN: the Garden of Eden, where Adam and Chavah spent the first part of their lives until they were punished for eating the fruit of the Tree of Knowledge.

HASHEM, ELOKIM, RIBBONO SHEL OLAM, HA-KADOSH BARUCH HU: God, Almighty. The concept of God is embodied in a number of Hebrew terms, each emphasizing a different attribute of God, Who is an all-powerful Supreme Being. He is the Planner, Creator, and Eternal Master of all forces and life — One Who regulates all existence and gives it meaning.

HEVEL: Abel, son of Adam and Chavah, a shepherd who was killed by his brother, Kayin.

KAYIN: Cain, son of Adam and Chavah, tiller of the soil who killed his brother, Hevel, in a fit of jealousy. He was forced to wander for the rest of his years.

KERIAS SHEMA: the recital of the very important declaration of faith in the One and Only God.

MABUL: the Flood sent by God in 1656 to destroy the world because of man's wickedness.

NOACH: Noah, a righteous man who, along with his family, was saved from the Flood that destroyed the world.

SHEM, CHAM, YEFES: Noach's three sons who, along with their wives, survived in the ark. The Jewish nation descends from Shem (Semites).

NOTES

1. Bachyei Ibn Pekudah, *Chovos Ha-Levavos.*
2. Rabbi Akiva, *Osios D'Rabbi Akiva; Meshech Chochmah* cites *Midrash Temurah Vayikra* 19:18.
3. *Talmud Chullin,* 60b.
4. *Pirkei Avos,* 4:1.
5. *Talmud Sanhedrin,* 38; *Midrash Vayikra Rabbah* 14:1.
6. *Kuzari.*
7. Rashi, *Bereshis* 2:2.
8. Rav Chayim Volozhin, *Nefesh Ha-Chayim.*
9. Rambam, *Mishneh Torah, Hilchos Melachim,* 8:11.
10. *Bereshis Rabbah,* 8:12.
11. *Koheles* 5:9.
12. *Siddur, Birchos Kerias Shema.*
13. *Tosafos* in *Talmud Shabbos,* 31, quotes the *Yerushalmi.*
14. *Bereshis Rabbah,* 38:6.

CHAPTER 2

Avraham – His Love, Devotion and Sacrifice for God
(From after 1996 – 2100 / 1813 B.C.E. – 1676 B.C.E.)

The highest form of Divine worship that a human being can achieve is love of the Almighty.

When one truly loves someone, nothing that he does for that person is ever a burden. Rather, he has a good feeling about what he is doing. The capacity to love God is inherent, but the degree to which one feels and expresses his devotion is entirely the product of man's own initiative and choice.

❦ HISTORY

AVRAHAM — SPREADING THE BELIEF IN ONE GOD

The person who exhibited the greatest love and devotion for God was our patriarch Avraham (Abraham). He was born into a family of idol worshipers. Avraham's father, Terach, sold idols. Nonetheless, Avraham quickly came to the realization that mere man-made lifeless idols could not be the rulers of the earth. There had to be a superior force capable of creating the world and regulating all of nature.

Avraham gazed up at the sky and saw the glorious blaze of the sun. "This must certainly be the ruler of the earth," he said to himself, and began to worship the sun. But when night fell, the sun set and its dominance was taken over by the moon and stars. "Then the moon and stars must be the real powers," he now thought, and began worshiping them, only to realize at dawn that there must be a power superior to the sun, the moon, and the stars, and that His power must control all visible bodies. This power could only be an invisible, eternal, Almighty God Whom Avraham now worshiped.

Avraham transcended his pagan environment and recognized that the world is governed by one Supreme Being. Avraham was able to use his reason to see through the sham and falsehood of the values of his generation and understand the true purpose of Creation.[1]

One day, Avraham's father had to leave the idol store and placed Avraham in charge. A customer entered, looked around, and decided to purchase a particular idol. He approached Avraham to place his order. Avraham asked him, "How old are you?"

"Sixty years old," answered the startled customer.

"Aren't you, a sixty-year-old man, ashamed to worship an idol made only yesterday?" asked Avraham.

Upon hearing this, the would-be customer was so embarrassed that he left without his purchase.

Soon a woman entered the shop carrying a large tray filled with fine flour. She gave it to Avraham, explaining that she would like this flour to be offered as a gift to the idols. As the woman left, Avraham took a heavy stick and broke all the idols in the store except the largest one. He then took the heavy stick and placed it in that idol's hands. When his father, Terach, returned, he was aghast at the horrible condition of his store.

"What happened?" shouted Terach.

"A woman came into the store," explained Avraham, "and she brought a large tray filled with fine flour as an offering for the idols. After I placed it in front of the idols, an argument broke out among them. Each one wanted to eat from the flour. All of a sudden this big idol rose up, took that heavy stick and smashed all the other idols."

"Why are you joking with me?" screamed Terach. "You know these idols can't do that!"

"Ah-hah!" exclaimed Avraham. "Let your ears hear what your mouth is saying! Idols are only pieces of stone and wood. They have no power to even move. How then could they control the world? There is only one great Power in the world, and that is Almighty God in heaven!"

For this act, considered heretical at the time, Terach brought Avraham to the mighty King Nimrod to be tried and sentenced. When he was brought before King Nimrod, he was given a choice. Either he must worship Nimrod's great idol, or he would be thrown into a fiery furnace. To Avraham, however, it was not a question of choice. His answer was clear.

"I will never bow to a statue. I worship only God Almighty in heaven. I choose the flames of the furnace!"

Four soldiers seized Avraham and hurled him into the furnace. But something unexpected happened. No screams or cries of terror could be heard. The people looked at the furnace and saw the figure of Avraham making its way out of the furnace. When he emerged, Avraham had neither a mark nor a burn on him. It was a miracle performed before their very eyes, a miracle performed by God in defiance of their own gods. The people gasped in amazement.

Avraham's brother Haran was also tried by Nimrod and couldn't decide what to do. Should he bow down to the idol or be thrown into the furnace? He decided he would wait and see Avraham's fate. If Avraham came out alive, he'd be ready to follow Avraham. Otherwise, he would bow down to the idol. Finally, when he saw Avraham's escape, he also declared, "I will not worship the idol. Throw me into the furnace!" He was sure that the miracle that had happened to Avrohom would also happen to him.

Once again the doors of the huge fiery furnace were opened, and Haran was thrown inside. But this time the people assembled there heard screams as Haran was burned alive. He had depended on a miracle, but miracles happen only to those who have complete faith in God, as Avraham did. Haran's wishy-washy stand did not merit a miracle. One must be strong in his faith and ready to stand up for it wholeheartedly. Avraham's escape demonstrated to all the existence of God and the reward paid to one who fully believes in Him.

AVRAHAM — FOLLOWING THE WILL OF HASHEM

The Divine call came to Avraham to leave his homeland and to proceed to another land which Hashem would show him. Avraham journeyed toward the land of Kena'an (Eretz Yisrael), taking with him his wife Sarah, his nephew Lot, and all their possessions. They also took their many followers whom Avraham and Sarah had successfully brought closer to the ways of Hashem. Avraham reached the land of Kena'an and continued on until he arrived at Shechem. There Hashem appeared to Avraham in a vision and promised Avraham that the land of Kena'an would one day be the domain of his descendants. Avraham built a *mizbe'ach* (altar) to Hashem as a thanksgiving for these happy tidings.

A severe famine in Kena'an compelled Avraham to temporarily sojourn in Egypt. He feared that the Egyptians would be attracted to his wife Sarah and would murder him in order to take her. Therefore, as he approached the land of Egypt, he asked Sarah to tell the Egyptians that she was his sister. When they did arrive in Egypt, Sarah's beauty was greatly admired and she was taken into Paroh's royal household. However, when Paroh and his household were smitten with mysterious illnesses, he sensed that something was wrong. He learned that Sarah was really Avraham's wife and that his taking her had caused this punishment. Paroh asked Avraham to leave Egypt (Mitzrayim) with his family and possessions and Avraham complied.

Avraham and his wife, with their many possessions, returned to the city of Beis El in Kena'an. Because both Avraham and Lot had become very wealthy and had many flocks and herds, there was not enough pasture land for the herds of both men, and quarrels erupted between their herdsmen. Lot's shepherds allowed their flocks to graze on the land belonging to others. This was completely contrary to everything that Avraham taught and believed in. He feared people would confuse the shepherds of Avraham with the shepherds of Lot. This would result in *chillul Hashem* (desecration of God's Holy Name) since people would say, "Avraham preaches morality and Godliness to us, and his own shepherds are stealing." Consequently, Avraham realized the need to distance himself from Lot. To avoid conflict, Avraham suggested that he and Lot separate, and he offered his nephew the choice of where to settle. Lot chose the fertile, lush, well-watered plain of the Jordan (Yarden) and pitched his tents in the city of S'dom, infamous for the wickedness of its inhabitants.

LESSON I

Spreading the Word of God

A characteristic of extreme love and devotion is the desire to inspire this feeling in other people. Love for someone does not involve merely a private feeling, but it includes causing others to feel the same feelings of devotion for that individual.

Avraham best exemplified this characteristic. He did not keep his tremendous love and devotion to the Almighty merely to himself, his wife and immediate family. Avraham went out of his way to spread the belief in the One God and to impress upon everyone the kindness of God.[2]

When a civil war broke out between the five rulers in the south of Kena'an and four other kings, Avraham's nephew, Lot, was taken captive by the four kings. At the risk of losing his own life, and against tremendous odds, Avraham led his household in battle against the four kings. Not only did he obtain the release of his nephew, Lot, but he also freed the captives and recovered the possessions of the five kings who had been defeated. When they in turn sought to repay Avraham for his extreme efforts, he refused any rewards whatsoever.

Avraham's positive influence on others can be compared to the effect of a locomotive on the other cars in the train. Just as a locomotive has the power to pull other cars along on its route, so too, Avraham was able to persuade others to follow in his service to God. Unlike other righteous people of his time whose children quickly became reabsorbed in the idolatry of the generation, Avraham was able to transmit his values to his son Yitzchak. He was able to establish his teachings among his descendants, until they became a self-sustaining group, faithful to God. Thus, God said, "Avraham shall surely become a great and mighty nation...for I know him and that he will instruct his children and his household after him, that they keep God's way...."

LESSON II

The Reward for Love and Devotion to Hashem

We understand the far-reaching reward for a person such as Avraham, who lived in a period of idolatry and corruption but who, nevertheless, was able to stand up and publicly proclaim his belief in the One Almighty God. Avraham then dedicated his life to spreading the love and fear of God and was even prepared to die for his convictions.

Avraham is given the distinction of being called the "pillar of the world" not only because of his recognition of God, but also because of his extreme devotion and willingness to sacrifice everything for the sake of God. He devoted his entire life to the spreading of this faith and love of God. His son Yitzchak, and grandson Ya'akov, followed in his footsteps. Ya'akov's twelve sons then became the heads of the tribes of Yisrael (Israel), from whom the Jewish nation continued.[3]

Because of Avraham's own discovery of the true and only God, his complete rejection of idol worship, and finally his severely tested but undaunted devotion to God, he was logically chosen to be the one whose offspring would be the Jewish nation, the special standard-bearer of God's ideals in this world. Part of the Jews' basic faith is the belief in One God, and in having been chosen by God to be His special people who would follow His commandments.

The Jewish people are now spread all over the world, there exists diversity among us, and we speak a multitude of languages; still, Jews are bonded together as true brethren, forming one unique nation. It is a uniqueness that was given its permanent stamp by Divine command: "You shall be to Me a kingdom of priests and a holy nation."

One of the most important and basic principles of Judaism is its concept of monotheism. The Jews, with the belief in God and His unity, have disseminated this concept throughout the world.

ETHICS I

Kindness

Avraham, together with his wife Sarah, was known as a pillar of charity and *chesed* (doing acts of kindness). He dedicated his life to helping others, offering food and hospitality to wayfarers. This virtue of kindness permeated Avraham's character.

Charity, including hospitality, is one of the three pillars for which the world was created by God. Without loving-kindness, men could not live together in a functioning society.

It was the Almighty Himself Who provided the model for kindness and hospitality. It is because of God's kindness that we are provided with food, shelter and all the good things of life.[4]

When Avraham was recuperating after his circumcision, God appeared to him in order to comfort him. Once again, God set the example that all of us should follow — being involved in kindness and visiting the sick.

A pupil of Rabbi Akiva suddenly became sick. The scholars in the academy of Rabbi Akiva did not visit him. Some may have felt that this was not so important. Rabbi Akiva personally went to the home of the sick pupil, waited upon him, supplied him with all of his needs, and took a deep interest in his treatment. After he had recovered, the student said, "My master, you have saved my life."

When his pupils assembled shortly afterwards, Rabbi Akiva began his lecture by telling them, "Be advised that not visiting the sick is equivalent to hastening their death and shedding their blood."[5]

Man is required to emulate God. Just as God visits the sick, we, too, are required to visit the sick.

Avraham's tent was an open house for the poor, the needy and the wayfarers who sought a place to rest from their travels. Avraham provided free food and lodging to all who came to his home. His tent was known to have four doors, one on each side, so that from every direction the poor and the weary could easily gain entrance to his home.

When Avraham saw his guests, he was so pleased at the chance to perform the mitzvah of *hachnassas orchim* (hospitality) that he ran out to greet them. "Rest your weary feet and I will fetch some water and bread,"[6] he told them. Yet, when he returned, it was with a complete, sumptuous meal. Avraham was a living example of *"Emor me'at v'aseh harbeh* — Say little but do much."[7] Instead of making impressive promises, he quietly went about satisfying the needs of his guests.

One aspect of love and reverence for another is the desire to emulate his good traits. Avraham's great acts of charity and kindness were in themselves a means of emulating the Almighty. He recognized that it was because of God's kindness that we are supplied with all our needs and desires. Avraham copied God's generous ways, not out of any ulterior motive, such as the desire for wealth or greatness, but because he knew that this was the will of God and the right thing to do.

Another aspect of kindness we learn from Avraham is the obligation of caring for the deceased. When his wife, Sarah, passed away, Avraham sought to buy a proper burial plot in order to pay full respect to her departed soul. To bury Sarah, Avraham purchased a cave called *Me'aras Ha-Machpelah* for the large sum of four hundred shekels of pure silver. The *Me'aras Ha-Machpelah* was a unique place because Adam and Chavah had both been buried there; later Avraham, Yitzchak and Rivkah, and Ya'akov and Leah were also buried in this eternal resting place.

Today, the *Me'aras Ha-Machpelah* in Chevron remains a most holy site. Jews flock to it to offer prayers which we hope will, through the merits of our forefathers, be answered speedily.

In the following chapter, we discuss

how Avraham sent his trusted servant, Eliezer, to seek a girl for Yitzchak to marry who would be qualified to fill the gap left in the house of Avraham by the death of Sarah. The choosing of this special young lady would not be based upon her wealth, physical charms, or intellectual attainments , but rather on her character and the goodness of her heart. It would be her readiness to help others which would make her and Yitzchak fitting successors to Avraham and Sarah. The girl who would feel compassion not only for man, but also for weary and thirsty beasts, and in whose heart burned such a spark of the holy fire of human love as was kindled in the heart of Avraham and Sarah — she would be the maiden Eliezer would recognize as the heaven-sent spouse of Yitzchak.

The quality of *chesed* and concern for others is something we should also search for in our own families.[8] A wealthy Jew once visited a prominent rabbi, and proposed a match between his son and the rabbi's daughter. The rich man noticed that the rabbi seemed upset and asked the reason for his look of concern.

"A child in this town is dangerously ill, and I am worried about him," explained the rabbi.

"Is the child a relative of yours?"

"No," replied the rabbi.

"Then why are you so worried about a strange child?" asked the visitor.

Upon hearing this, the rabbi decided that his daughter should not marry into this man's family. Anyone coming from a family that showed so little concern for others could not be a desirable match for his own family.

In the same respect, David Ha-Melech did not allow Jews to marry within a certain group (Givon) because they did not practice kindness with one another.

MITZVAH

Blessings

Avraham's home was always open to strangers and wayfarers, whom he provided with food and lodging. After partaking of the meal, the visitors would thank Avraham for his hospitality.

"Oh, don't thank me," Avraham would reply. "It is God Whom you must thank, for He is the One who has given all this to you." He would then lead his guests in offering praises to God in acknowledgment of His favors for mankind.[9]

Berachos (blessings) serve to remind us that God is the source of all good fortune and sustenance, and they give us the opportunity to thank Him for His good will.[10]

The blessing is man's recognition that the earth and its fullness are God's. Man was put on earth to acknowledge that fact. Once he has done so, man is granted the right to make use of God's possessions.[11]

The benedictions are all worded in the present tense to show that all things are in a constant process of creation. God is the prime cause of the universe, and without Him there would be no life. As Creator of the universe, He is constantly at work creating and sustaining in accordance with His will.

The blessings recited before eating or

drinking are divided into six categories:

(a) *Ha-motzi* is recited over bread and rolls;

(b) *Mezonos* is recited over foods made from grains, such as cake and various noodle products;

(c) *Ha-etz* is recited over fruits grown on a tree;

(d) *Ha-adamah* is recited on vegetables grown from the ground;

(e) *Ha-gafen* is recited on wine and grape juice;

(f) *She-ha-kol* is recited over all foods that do not fall into the other five categories.

The blessing of *Besamim* is recited on fragrant smells from natural sources. One recites a special blessing on new purchases of significance, and on various special occasions.

A special blessing is recited when one returns from a dangerous trip or recovers from a dangerous illness.

(1) THE BLESSING AND PROCEDURE FOR WASHING HANDS BEFORE EATING BREAD:

A blessing is also made when one washes his hands before eating bread, to sanctify oneself as did the priests who washed their hands before eating the *terumah* (priestly portion).

When one washes his hands, he uses a cup that can hold at least 3.3 ounces of water. He must take the cup in his right hand, fill it with water, transfer it to his left hand and pour water twice over his right hand. Then the same procedure is repeated for the left hand. He then recites the blessing of *Al netilas yadayim*, dries his hands, and recites *Ha-motzi* over the bread.

(2) THE BLESSING AT THE END OF A MEAL:

Just as one makes a blessing before eating, so, too, must one do so after eating, thanking God for the food which He has given him. After most foods, the *berachah acharonah* (the concluding blessing) of *Borei nefashos* is said. There are several exceptions:

(a) The blessing of *Al Ha-michyah* is said after foods made of one of the five types of grain (wheat, barley, rye, oats or spelt).

(b) The blessing of *Al Ha-gefen* is said after wine or grape juice.

(c) *Al Ha-etz* is said after the five fruits with which Eretz Yisrael is blessed (grapes, figs, pomegranates, olives, and dates).

After eating bread, one recites *Birkas Ha-Mazon* (the Grace After Meals).

Grace After Meals contains four blessings: The first was composed by Moshe as a prayer of thanks for the good that God sustains us with. It was written in gratitude for God sending the *man* (manna). The second was composed by Yehoshua after entering Eretz Yisrael. The third was composed by King David and King Shelomo. The fourth blessing was composed by Rabban Gamliel the Elder in Yavneh, after the bodies of the victims in Beitar were found not to have decayed after many years, and were finally buried.[12]

Whenever one hears another recite a blessing, he should answer "Amen" at its conclusion. The "Amen" constitutes an endorsement and affirmation that the blessing is true, that the listener believes it, or that — where the blessing is in the form of a prayer petition — it should soon come to pass.

Just as the words of the blessing are to be said with devotion and concentration, so, too, the brief "Amen" is to be uttered with solemnity.

A person does not answer "Amen" after a blessing he recites himself (unless it is part of the formal structure of the prayer itself as in *Boneh Yerushalayim* in the Grace After Meals, or in Kaddish).

The Hebrew letters of "Amen" are the initials for *El Melech Ne'eman* — God, the Faithful King.

✌ HISTORY

AVRAHAM PERFORMS HIS BRIS MILAH

Since Sarah was childless, she suggested that Avraham take her maid, Hagar, as a second wife. When Hagar realized that she was pregnant, she no longer showed respect for Sarah. This bothered Sarah very much and she complained to Avraham. Avraham returned Hagar to Sarah's authority. Sarah dealt harshly with her, so Hagar fled. An angel of Hashem appeared to Hagar and told her to return to Sarah. He promised that the son she would bear, Yishmael, would be the founder of a great nation, the forerunner of a large segment of the Arab nations.

Avraham's name was originally Avram, and Sarah's was originally Sarai. When Avraham was ninety-nine years old, Hashem renewed the covenant with him and changed his name to Avraham, meaning "father of a multitude of nations." Hashem commanded Avraham to circumcise himself and all the other male members of his household. Since then, for all generations, every Jewish male child has been circumcised when he is eight days old. This has been the sign of the covenant between Hashem and Avraham and his descendants. Hashem also told Avraham that henceforth Sarai shall be known as Sarah, meaning, "princess for all."

Avraham promptly performed the great mitzvah of *bris milah* (circumcision). He circumcised Yishmael and every male member of his household. He then circumcised himself. All this was done by Avraham in the light of day without fear of what others might say or do.

AVRAHAM AND THE THREE ANGELS

As Avraham sat at the entrance of his tent hoping to greet visitors and welcome them, thereby performing the mitzvah of *hachnassas orchim,* three individuals appeared. Avraham ran to welcome them and proceeded to entertain them in a most hospitable manner. These "visitors" were actually *malachim* (angels) sent by Hashem to perform special duties in this world. One of the *malachim* informed Avraham that in a year's time his wife Sarah would give birth to a son. Sarah, who was almost ninety at the time, laughed at this seemingly unbelievable news. She was rebuked by Hashem for this slight indication of doubt. She should have believed wholeheartedly in Hashem's ability to enable her to give birth. Why was it so hard to believe? Is there anything that Hashem cannot do? Before the *malachim* left Avraham, the second *malach* carried out his assignment by healing Avraham from the pain he had incurred from his *bris milah.*

The time had arrived for the third *malach* to perform his task, the destruction of S'dom and Amorah. Hashem had decided that it would be improper not to inform Avraham of His intention to destroy the cities. When Avraham was informed by God of His intention, Avraham's *rachmanus* (mercy) was aroused. He approached Hashem with a prayer on behalf of the people of S'dom and Amorah. Avraham argued that the righteous should not be destroyed together with the wicked, and obtained Hashem's promise to pardon the entire condemned populace if even ten righteous people could be found among them. However, this was not the case, and the city was condemned.

The two *malachim* arrived in S'dom. The first one, the *malach* who had cured Avraham, was there to finish his assignment and save Lot and his family. The second *malach* was there to destroy the city. The two *malachim*, still outwardly mere human beings, were greeted by Lot and invited to stay in his house. When the word spread through the wicked city of S'dom, the entire city gathered around Lot's house. The evil men of the city tried to molest these visitors and were punished by Hashem with blindness.

The *malachim* then informed Lot of Hashem's intention to destroy the city. They told him to take his family and leave. Lot hesitated in leaving S'dom; he wanted to save all of his money. The *malachim* quickly grabbed Lot, his wife, and his two daughters, and placed them outside the city.

The *malachim* warned them not to look back at the destruction of the city. They were being saved only in the *zechus* (merit) of Avraham and, therefore, had no right to observe the punishment of others. They also warned them not to remain in the entire plain surrounding the cities. Lot pleaded to be allowed to remain in the area in a small town later known as Tzoar. Hashem granted Lot's request. Lot and his family found refuge in Tzoar.

Hashem then caused fire and brimstone to fall upon the cities of

S'dom, Amorah and the entire surrounding plain. The area was over-turned and destroyed. Lot's wife disobeyed the *malachim's* warning; she turned back and gazed at the destruction. She was punished and was turned into a pillar of salt.

ETHICS II

Showing Care and Concern for Others

Avraham understood the value of human life. When Hashem informed him that he intended to destroy S'dom, Avraham beseeched the Almighty to spare the city. The Torah describes in great length Avraham's prayer for the preservation of those wicked people. Avraham did everything in his power to obtain a reversal of God's decree.

Concerning Noach, the Torah states, "Noach was a righteous man, and wholehearted in his generation." However, some explain that had he lived during the lifetime of Avraham, the latter's righteousness would have outshone his.[13] Although Noach was a truly pious person, unfortunately, his piety never had any influence over others, except for his immediate family. We do not find one prayer uttered by Noach on behalf of the world about to be destroyed. Yes, he was pious, but it was a piety that affected only him and his family. Thus, Noach's character can be compared to silver coins which look impressive, but lose their luster when in the company of gold coins. Avraham was not only a pious per-son in his own right, but he stretched out his hand and helped others see the truth.

The Talmud relates that during a drought in the land, people came to the great Abba Chilkiya and asked him to pray to the Almighty for rain. He did so, but the rains still did not come until his wife also beseeched the Almighty with her prayers. Then the rains came.

When Abba Chilkiya was asked why his wife's prayers were answered faster than his, he responded that there was a time when some wicked people in his neighborhood were causing him a great deal of trouble. He wanted to pray to G-d that they should die. When his wife heard this, she questioned whether this was the proper thing to do.

"Why don't you pray instead that these wicked people repent? That way, they will not only stop sinning but will also have the opportunity to do mitzvos in the future." Abba Chilkiya followed his wife's advice, and those people did indeed repent. His wife's special care and concern to help the wicked improve gave her a special status before God.[14]

❧ HISTORY

THE BIRTH OF YITZCHAK (2048/1713 B.C.E.)

When Avraham was one hundred years old and his wife Sarah was ninety, a son, whom they named Yitzchak, was born. It was exactly a year after the angel had foretold the birth of their son. Avraham circumcised Yitzchak when he was eight days old, as Hashem had previously commanded him.

Until that time, Hagar and her son, Yishmael, were living in the household of Avraham. However, when Sarah had a son, she observed dismaying behavior from Yishmael and feared that he might prove to be a negative influence on Yitzchak, and she therefore urged Avraham to send Hagar and Yishmael away. Avraham was unhappy with the request, but Hashem appeared to Avraham and told him that he should follow Sarah's advice. Hashem then promised that Yishmael would also evolve into a large nation. Avraham took bread and water and gave it to Hagar and sent her and Yishmael away from his house. Hagar and her son wandered about in the wilderness for days. When it appeared that they might die from thirst, an angel appeared and showed her water and assured Hagar of her son's future.

LESSON III

The Ultimate Sacrifice (2085/1676 B.C.E.)

A characteristic of true love and devotion is the readiness to sacrifice one's life for that person. The best proof of faith and love of God is self-sacrifice in His service. Martyrdom is the ultimate expression of human loyalty and love of God, and has been accepted by countless Jews throughout the years who chose death over giving up their religion.

Avraham was a true servant of Hashem. In the course of Avraham's lifetime, Hashem had put before him ten very difficult challenges, which would demonstrate to the world his loyalty. Avraham passed these tests with flying colors; his sincere loyalty and devotion to Hashem had always carried him across any obstacles in the way.

The *Parashas Ha-Akedah* (2085) (the Biblical account of Avraham's willingness to offer his son to God, and Yitzchak's willingness to be sacrificed) represented the final and most difficult of the ten tests designed by God to demonstrate Avraham's worthiness of being the founder of the Chosen People. The difficulty involved in this task was that God was asking Avraham not to give up property or money, but rather to sacrifice a dream. For if Avraham were to kill his son Yitzchak, his visions of serving God as the ancestor of the Children of God would vanish into thin air. After all, he had been promised this son, and had to wait until he was a hundred years old and almost past hope of fathering him. Now he was being asked to not only give up this son, but to kill him with his own hands! This act was contrary to the very nature of all the *chesed* (kindness) that Avraham had always performed. It was almost like the acts that Avraham had fought against all his life, for he had constantly disputed those around him who had worshiped their gods by sacrificing their sons to them. And now Avraham was being asked to perform this very same murderous task by his own God!

Yet, Avraham did not question the command for a moment. He immediately set out to comply with God's request. To show his loyalty, he saddled his donkey himself rather than ordering his servant to do so, in order to save time. This way he could perform the command as quickly as possible.

The journey to the designated mountain was not an easy one. The way was riddled with obstacles set out by Satan to prevent Avraham's compliance with God's order. At first, Satan appeared in the guise of an old man, asking, "Where are you going?" When Avraham replied that he was going to pray to God, Satan demanded, "Then why are you carrying all those knives and pieces of wood?"

"We may stay a day or two," Avraham told him, "and with these utensils we will be able to prepare our own food."

Satan then said, "Don't try to fool me. You are the fool. It took you 100 years to have this son, and now you want to sacrifice him! This you were not commanded to do by God, for He would surely never give such a command. It must be your imagination. Don't do it."

Avraham realized that this was in reality an obstacle in his way to prevent his carrying out God's wishes, so he moved on. However, Satan persisted. This time he caused a large river to appear at a spot which Avraham and his retinue had to pass.

When Avraham came to the river, he remembered that he had never seen a body of water at this spot before, and realized that this, too, must be the work of Satan. He took his son Yitzchak with him and the two began to cross the river. They finally came to a point where the water reached their necks, and if they had gone any further they would certainly have drowned. At this moment, Avraham lifted his eyes towards heaven and prayed that he be allowed to continue and fulfill God's request. Immediately, the water disappeared and they traveled on.[15]

Finally, they reached Mount Moriah. Avraham took Yitzchak (who was already thirty-seven years old and who complied most willingly) and bound him on the altar that he had built. He took the knife and was about to bring it down upon Yitzchak when he heard a heavenly voice call out, "Stop, Avraham! I do not want you to kill your son. I wanted you to demonstrate that you were willing to follow My words wholeheartedly, and you have certainly done so. Now your awe of Hashem is certain."

It was now evident that Avraham was truly God-fearing and there was no need for the actual sacrifice of Yitzchak. Avraham found a ram caught by his horns in the trees and sacrificed the ram instead of Yitzchak. Hashem blessed Avraham that because of the *zechus* (merit) of this great deed he had performed, his descendants would become a great nation.

❧ Key People, Places and Things

AVODAH ZARAH: idol worship.

AVRAHAM: Abraham, founding father of the Jewish nation, who lived for 175 years.

BERACHOS: benedictions; blessings.

BIKKUR CHOLIM: visiting the sick.

BIRKAS HA-MAZON: Grace After Meals.

BRIS MILAH: the covenant of circumcision.

CHESED SHEL EMES: aid rendered in connection with burial.

GEMILAS CHESED: an act of kindness.

HACHNASSAS ORCHIM: hospitality.

HAGAR: princess of Egypt who was Sarah's handmaiden and who was later given in marriage to Avraham when Sarah was childless. She gave birth to Yishmael.

HALVAYAS HA-MES: attending a funeral.

HA-MOTZI: the benediction over bread.

KIDDUSH HASHEM: sanctification of God's Holy Name.

NETILAS YADAYIM: the ritual washing of the hands upon rising in the morning, after using the bathroom, or prior to eating bread.

MITZVAH: a Divine commandment (there are two categories: positive and negative precepts).

SARAH: Avraham's righteous wife who assisted him in all of his activities. She gave birth to Yitzchak at the age of 90, and lived for 127 years.

YIRAS HASHEM/YIRAS SHAMAYIM: the fear of God/fear of Heaven.

YISHMAEL: son of Hagar and Avraham, who was sent away with his mother in order that he should not be a bad influence upon Yitzchak. Yishmael was the ancestor of the Arabs.

YITZCHAK: Isaac, Avraham and Sarah's beloved son, born to them in their old age. He followed in his father's footsteps with extreme devotion to Hashem.

NOTES

1. Rambam, *Mishneh Torah, Hilchos Avodah Zarah*, Chapter 1.
2. Rambam, *Sefer Ha-Mitzvos*, 3.
3. Rambam, *Moreh Nevuchim*.
4. *Talmud Kiddushin*, 32b.
5. *Talmud Nedarim*, 40.
6. *Bereshis* 18:4,5.
7. *Pirkei Avos*, 1:15.
8. *Talmud Yevamos*, 79.
9. *Bereshis Rabbah*, 54:6.
10. Rambam, *Mishneh Torah, Hilchos Berachos*, 15:3.
11. *Talmud Berachos*, 35.
12. *Talmud Berachos*, 48.
13. Rashi, *Bereshis* 6:9.
14. *Talmud Ta'anis*, 23b.
15. *Midrash Tanchuma, Vayera*.

CHAPTER 3

The Patriarchs and the Matriarchs: Continuing the Legacy
(2085 – 2200 / 176 B.C.E – 1561 B.C.E.)

❦ HISTORY

ELIEZER AND RIVKAH

Sarah passed away (2085) and was buried in *Me'aras Ha-Machpelah*. Avraham wished to find a suitable wife for his son, Yitzchak. He therefore sent his loyal servant, Eliezer, back to his native land of Charan to find a girl from Avraham's own family.

Eliezer prayed that God give him a sign to show who would be the proper mate for Yitzchak. He met Rivkah at the well and realized that she was meant to be Yitzchak's wife. The kindness she extended to Eliezer, a total stranger, by giving him, as well as his camels, water to drink, was a clear indication to him that this girl was worthy to be the bride of Yitzchak. Rivkah left her parents' home and ventured forth with Eliezer to the land of Kena'an, where she married Yitzchak.

YA'AKOV AND ESAV

For the first twenty years of their marriage, Yitzchak and Rivkah were childless. They prayed to Hashem, Who answered their prayers, and were blessed with twin sons (2108). Esav, the elder, was a man of the field, a hunter; while Ya'akov, the younger, was a scholar.

Each parent had a favorite son. Yitzchak was misled by Esav. He showed him his affection, while Rivkah, perceiving the truth, preferred Ya'akov.

Avraham died at the age of 175 years (2123/1638 B.C.E.). He was buried by both of his sons, Yitzchak and Yishmael, in the *Me'aras Ha-Machpelah*.

Esav returned from a long session of hunting one day, clamoring for food. He saw Ya'akov preparing lentil soup and agreed to exchange his birthright for the soup. After all, what good was the birthright when he could trade it for some immediate pleasure? Ya'akov, however, had enough foresight to realize that as the *bechor*, the firstborn, he would have the opportunity to inherit the right to continue Avraham's heritage. This would bring him so much closer to Hashem, a prospect that meant little to Esav. To Esav, his lineage wasn't worth as much as a bowl of lentil soup!

YITZCHAK'S BLESSINGS (2171/1590 B.C.E.)

When Yitzchak had grown old and blind, he felt that the time had come to bless his eldest son. He therefore requested that Esav go to the field to hunt, and then prepare the game he captured, as a tasty dish, so Yitzchak could partake of it and then bless him. Rivkah, overhearing the conversation, dressed Ya'akov in Esav's clothing. She covered his hands and neck with goatskin to make them feel as hairy as Esav's, and sent him to Yitzchak bearing a tasty dish of young goat's meat and matzah which she had made.

Ya'akov's voice aroused Yitzchak's suspicions, but after feeling Ya'akov's hairy hands, which he was sure belonged to Esav, his doubts were allayed.

Yitzchak, now ready to bestow the blessings upon his son, called him forward. Ya'akov came forward and kissed his father. Yitzchak blessed Ya'akov, saying, "May Hashem give you from the dew of the sky and the fat of the land, and plenty of grain and wine. Nations shall serve you and kingdoms shall bow down to you. Those who curse you shall be cursed and those who bless you shall be blessed."

No sooner had Ya'akov left, than Esav returned and the truth was discovered. However, Yitzchak did not revoke his blessing to Ya'akov. Instead, he agreed to bless Esav as well and foretold that Esav's future descendants would live by the sword and would serve Ya'akov's descendants as long as the latter behaved properly. However, when the descendants of Ya'akov would stray from the path of the Torah, Esav's descendants would be free of this servitude.

Esav was very angered at Ya'akov's ruse and plotted to kill his brother as soon as their father died. To prevent this, Rivkah instructed Ya'akov to leave home and stay with her brother Lavan in Charan.

LESSON I

Following in the Ways of Our Ancestors

Yitzchak granted Ya'akov the blessing that all nations would come to serve the people who would emerge from his descendants. However, Yitzchak indicated that this blessing was contingent upon the Jewish people's adhering to God's commandments. Once the Jews abandoned the ways of the Torah, their enemies would gain superiority over them.

History has borne out this prediction.

When the Jews followed the Torah they enjoyed God's beneficence and were granted the presence of His Holy Temple. However, when they strayed from the proper path and refused to heed His warnings to repent, they suffered the loss of the Holy Temple and were reduced to living under gentile oppression in exile. Later, Jews tried to assimilate and become like the citizens of foreign countries, such as Greece, Rome, Russia and Germany. All attempts of the Jews to assimilate have been met by oppression, pogroms, and wars. It is only when Jews remember that they are Jews and are required to live according to Hashem's commandments, that they are successful and content.

❦ HISTORY

YA'AKOV FLEES FROM ESAV

Ya'akov was forced to run away from his brother Esav, who wanted to kill him; he fled to the home of his mother's brother Lavan in Charan. In his journey, Ya'akov reached Mount Moriah and slept there overnight. Hashem then appeared to Ya'akov in a dream and promised him that the land upon which he was then resting would be given to him and his descendants, and that he would return home under Hashem's protection.

Upon awakening, he vowed that when he returned safely to his father's home, he would offer to Hashem one-tenth of all of the possessions that Hashem would give him. This pledge later became the basis for the tithe given to the Temple, to the *kohen* (priest), and to the poor. Jews are expected to donate at least one-tenth of their income to charity.

MITZVAH

Tzedakah (charity)

The Torah teaches us that it is a positive commandment to give charity to the poor people of the Jewish nation.

The Rambam (Maimonides) lists eight levels of giving charity. Among them are the following:

I. The highest level of giving *tzedakah* is making someone self-sufficient so that he is no longer a financial burden on the community. This can be done by giving him a present, lending him money to establish himself in business, finding him a job, or taking him into one's own business.

2. The second level is giving *tzedakah* without knowing to whom one is giving and without the recipient knowing from whom he is receiving. This is done by giving money through an intermediary, such as a *gabbai tzedakah* (charity collector) in the synagogue.

3. The third level is when the donor knows to whom he gives, but the recipient does not know from whom he re-

ceives (e.g., sending money anony-mously).

A person should be happy about giv-ing *tzedakah*. It should be given in a way that causes the recipient the least amount of embarrassment and the greatest amount of happiness at the same time. Even if the person who is approached does not have money to give, he should still comfort the poor person with words, for the Talmud says that giving comfort is even greater than giving *tzedakah*.[1]

One should give at least one-tenth (*ma'aser*) of his income to *tzedakah*. He should be careful, however, to give within his means, i.e., one should not impoverish himself to the point that he must depend on others. However, even a poor person has a responsibility to give some *tzedakah*.

There is great merit in giving *tzedakah* in memory of a departed person, both for the donor and for the departed.

Some of the most worthy forms of *tzedakah* include: giving to poor brides (*hachnassas kallah*), giving to the sick, supporting children who learn Torah, and supporting *bnei Torah* (those who study Torah).

When both a man and a woman re-quest assistance, one must first give to the woman because it is more difficult for her to go collecting. The same applies when giving *tzedakah* to marry off poor orphans. One first gives to an orphaned bride and then to an orphaned groom.

The greatest type of *tzedakah*, and one of the greatest of all mitzvos, is that of *pidyon shevuyim* (the redemption of Jewish captives). If one has bought bricks to build a synagogue one is allowed to sell those bricks in order to raise money for such a purpose. A person who is able to redeem someone else, but does not do so, is guilty of committing many sins, among them: "You should not stand by while your friend's blood is spilled." (The only time we question whether or not to redeem a person is when the ran-som is an exorbitant sum and we fear that by paying it once, we will set a precedent for other Jews to be held for very high ransom.)

If all that the poor person requests is food to eat, one should give it immedi-ately without asking questions. How-ever, if the person requests a large amount of money or additional assis-tance, one has the right to inquire about him.

A person should do all in his power to avoid having to ask for charity, even if this means taking a job that he may feel is beneath his dignity.

When one pledges to give *tzedakah*, he must make sure to give it right away, for not fulfilling one's pledge is a very grave sin.

The Talmud states that the merit of the mitzvah of giving charity has the power to save one from death. "Charity length-ens the days and years of man."[2] The Talmud cites two incidents which sup-port this statement:

The great sage Shemuel once observed a workman carrying a load. When the load was opened, the worker found a venomous snake that had been cut in half by his sickle. If the snake had not been killed by the sickle, the man would most certainly have been bitten and would have died.

Shemuel inquired what the man had done to deserve being saved. He discovered that it was the practice in that town for portions of food to be collected from each of the workers and then equally distributed among them. Once, one of the people forgot his portion and had nothing to contribute. The man who was saved by the snake saw his fellow worker's predicament and therefore volunteered to collect the food that day. When he passed by that worker he put in his own food so it looked as if he was receiving a portion from the worker.[3]

The Talmud relates that Binyamin the Virtuous was in charge of the public charity chest. One year, when a drought plagued the town, a woman came to him and begged for assistance. Although Binyamin felt sorry for the woman, there was no money left. The woman cried in desperation, "If you don't help me, a woman and her seven children will surely die!" Binyomin could not bear the thought of this happening, and so, despite his own poverty, he gave her money from his own pocket.

Some time later, Binyamin became seriously ill and the doctors gave up hope of his recovering. Binyamin's proponents prayed fervently to the Almighty and exclaimed, "Lord of the Universe! You have said that whoever saves one Jewish life is regarded as if he has saved the entire world. Should then this virtuous and kind-hearted man, who saved the lives of a woman and her seven children, die in the prime of his life?" Immediately, the death sentence was annulled, and twenty-two years were added to Binyamin's life.[4]

❦ HISTORY

YA'AKOV, RACHEL AND LEAH (2185)

After Ya'akov had learned in the yeshivah of Ever for fourteen years, he arrived in Charan (2185). There he saw Lavan's daughter Rachel who had come to draw water at the well for her father's sheep. Ya'akov helped her by single-handedly removing the huge stone that covered the well. He then acquainted Rachel with their familial relationship and she quickly ran to inform her father of the arrival of their visitor. Lavan welcomed Ya'akov, who agreed to work as Lavan's shepherd for seven years in order to marry Rachel. Lavan consented, but after the seven years had elapsed, he tricked Ya'akov by substituting his elder daughter Leah in place of Rachel under the wedding canopy. His excuse for this deceitful breach of promise was that Leah was older and therefore should be married first. Ya'akov had no choice but to accept the situation. He soon married Rachel as well, on the condition that he would work another seven years for Lavan.

LESSON II

Overcoming Obstacles

Sometimes, difficulties seem to be a punishment, but they actually serve as a test by the Almighty. It would seem that the righteous are the ones who are being put to the test.

The Midrash[5] explains this with a parable: If you go to the marketplace, you will see the potter hitting his clay pots with his sticks to show how strong and solid they are. But the wise potter hits only the strongest pots, never the flawed ones. So too, God sends such tests and afflictions only to such people that He knows are capable of handling them, so that they and others can learn the extent of their spiritual strength. This applied to Avraham, Yitzchak and Ya'akov.

Ya'akov had the ability to learn how to improve himself despite all the obstacles that he faced in the house of Lavan. Ya'akov stayed in Lavan's home for twenty years. Not only did he not adopt this idol-worshiper's ways, but, instead, learned how to enhance his own service to Hashem.

The great Rabbi of Berditchev, Reb Levi Yitzchak, also understood the importance of overcoming all obstacles that might frustrate him from accomplishing his mission.

Reb Levi Yitzchak was once on a mission to raise funds for *pidyon shevuyim* (ransoming Jewish prisoners). After he had expended much effort and toil, he became frustrated because he did not achieve his goal. Reb Levi Yitzchak wondered if perhaps he was wasting his time trying to collect that money. Perhaps he should return home and continue his Torah study. Just then, he saw a thief being taken to jail.

He went over to him and said, "My son, look what troubles you have caused yourself by stealing. I hope this will be a lesson to you so that when you will be released from jail, you will not return to your evil ways. For you see, not only did you not get the money you stole, but you were also put in jail. Crime does not pay. You may as well give it up."

The robber responded, "If I don't succeed this time, I most certainly will succeed next time."

Reb Levi Yitzchak heard this and said, "Imagine! After all of his suffering, this thief has not become discouraged. What right then do I have to become discouraged? If I do not succeed in accomplishing God's mission today, then I will surely succeed tomorrow."

A Jew must never let obstacles discourage him from fulfilling his obligations. We must remember to learn from our ancestors, who, despite all troubles and difficulties, refused to give up, and ultimately accomplished their goals.

ETHICS I

Honesty

Ya'akov was renowned for the trait of extreme honesty. He made a special point of practicing honesty throughout his life, even in the potentially corrupting environment of his uncle Lavan's home. When taking care of Lavan's sheep, he watched them as if they were his own. He naturally did not take any of the sheep for himself, even though Lavan would probably not have noticed the loss.

Our Rabbis learned from and emulated Ya'akov's admirable traits. They recognized that one must be honest at all times. Even if one feels that no one is noticing his deception, God is always watching.

In a *mikveh* (ritual bath), the saintly rabbi known as the Chafetz Chaim once saw a person using an article that belonged to someone else. The Chafetz Chaim went over to him and whispered, "A person who washes himself with something that does not belong to him ends up dirtier than when he started."

Rabbi Shimon ben Shetach was a great Sage who showed the importance of honesty in his business dealings, thereby earning a good reputation for religious Jews. He set the proper example for relations with men and God. Needing a donkey for his travels, he bought one from an Arab. At the time, neither he nor the Arab noticed that the donkey carried a small package in its saddle. Some time later, one of Rabbi Shimon ben Shetach's students found the package. When he opened it, he was amazed by what he found.

"It is a diamond, Rebbe!" he exclaimed. "A perfect diamond! It must be worth a fortune. Sell it, and you will never want for money. Imagine all the mitzvos you will be able to do with the money!"

Rabbi Shimon ben Shetach shook his head. "I may be able to perform many mitzvos with the money, but I will never be able to cancel the demerit that will be mine if I keep property that belongs to another. No, I will return the diamond to its rightful owner, the Arab."

"But, Rebbe," protested the student, "why not keep the diamond? The Arab will never know of his loss!"

"Possibly. But God will know what I have done. I did not buy the diamond and so it is not mine. If one claims to be a good Jew, he must be truthful at all times."

Rabbi Shimon ben Shetach was true to his word, and returned the diamond to the astonished Arab.

"It's hard to believe that anyone could be that honest," said the Arab. "The Jews must truly have wonderful laws. Blessed be the God of Rabbi Shimon ben Shetach!"

Rabbi Shimon ben Shetach's exceptional adherence to the laws created a tremendous *kiddush Hashem* (sanctification of God's Holy Name) and should remind us of the need to fulfill all of God's laws with equal zeal.[6]

LESSON III

The Greatness of the Matriarchs

Our first Matriarch, Sarah, had worked with her husband Avraham both in helping the poor and needy, as well as spreading the word of God to the women of her time. In practically all the trials and sacrifices in which Avraham gave proof of his knowledge of God, his trust in God, his loyalty and obedience to God and his love of man, he was in close association with Sarah. Nearly all of them would have been impossible for him if Sarah had not been the faithful companion of his long wanderings, and if she had not shared all his activities as his faithful comrade.

Because of her outstanding righteousness, God bestowed upon Sarah special personal qualities. In fact, we are told that in terms of prophecy she was even greater than her husband, Avraham. She advised Avraham that Yishmael (his son by Hagar) should be sent away. She was correct in viewing Yishmael as a potentially bad influence upon her own son, Yitzchak.

The Torah lists Sarah's age at the time of her death as being one hundred years, and twenty years, and seven years. Why was it necessary for the Torah to divide the years of her life into three separate segments?

Each separate number indicates to us the following about Sarah: When she was one hundred, she was as free of sins as at the age of twenty. When she was twenty, she had the same innocent beauty as she had at seven, for she did not do anything wrong or immoral.

When Avraham eulogized her, he did not mourn excessively because he realized that her death, as sorrowful as it was, was not a tragedy, for Sarah had lived a full and rewarding life. She had accomplished much during her stay on earth, and her good deeds were countless. The comforting realization that she had lived a fulfilling life made the loss much easier to accept.

Rivkah was chosen to be the wife of Yitzchak because of her extreme kindness. When Eliezer, the servant of Avraham, and his attendants, came to the well while on a mission to find a wife for their master's son, Yitzchak, they met Rivkah. Eliezer asked her for a drink of water. Not only did she offer to provide him and his camels with water, but she made sure that his needs would be taken care of first so that he should not have to drink with the animals. In addition, she made sure to draw enough water so that the animals would be completely satisfied. Can one imagine how much water must have been needed to satisfy the thirst of all those camels? Yet Rivkah provided all this because she was a person of genuine kindness.

Rivkah also had keen insight in understanding her sons, Ya'akov and Esav. She realized that although Esav was closer to Yitzchak, he did not deserve his father's blessings. Rivkah did everything possible to make sure that it was Ya'akov who received his father's blessings rather than Esav.

Although Ya'akov was supposed to marry Rachel, for whom he had served Lavan seven years, he was tricked into marrying her older sister, Leah. Despite the fact that Leah knew that she was not as beloved as Rachel, and suffered much, nevertheless she praised God for everything she received. She was the one who named her sons, and in each case, the name made reference to the good that God had bestowed upon her. We learn from Leah these traits, of always being satisfied, and blessing God for what He has given us.

The Maggid of Mezritch was once asked by one of his students how it is possible to fulfill the injunction of our Sages, "A man is obliged to utter a blessing to God upon hearing bad tidings just as he does upon hearing good tidings."

"Go and find my disciple, Reb Zusya," the Rebbe answered his student. "He will explain the *mishnah* to you."

He went searching for Reb Zusya and when he found him, could not believe the utter poverty in which he lived. Reb Zusya lived in a decaying hut that the student was even afraid to enter.

Reb Zusya responded to the question posed to him. "I am most surprised that our Rebbe should have sent you with this question to me, of all people. A question like this should surely be put to a person who at some time had experienced

something bad. I'm afraid that I cannot be of any help to you since no evil has ever befallen me, even for a moment. Thank God, I have had only good things happen to me from the day I was born through today, so how could I know about anything evil?"

At last the student understood the obligation to bless God upon hearing bad tidings just as one blesses Him upon hearing good tidings. A man should rejoice in his lot to the point that he does not consider anything that befalls him to be a misfortune.

ETHICS II

The Importance of Not Embarrassing Anyone

We see the greatness of Rachel, in that she did all in her power to spare her sister embarrassment. Although Lavan had agreed to allow his daughter, Rachel, to marry Ya'akov in exchange for seven years of labor, Lavan had nothing of the sort in mind. Ya'akov was aware that Lavan might try to trick him, and he gave Rachel a secret code so that he would know his bride was Rachel. However, when Rachel learned that her father was planning to substitute Leah instead, she revealed these codes to Leah. She felt that she could not let her sister be humiliated. So Rachel, who had waited seven long years to marry Ya'akov, sacrificed her chance for happiness simply because she did not want to see her sister shamed. This act of utter selflessness is a lesson to us all. Because of it, she was rewarded by God; Sha'ul (Saul), the first king of Yisrael, was her descendant. This trait of acting selflessly, rather than embarrass-

ing someone else, has always been characteristic of the Jewish people.

The importance of not embarrassing anyone is clearly evident in the Talmudic story of Mar Ukva and his wife.[7] Mar Ukva was one of the great rabbis of the ancient Jewish community in Babylonia. He was preoccupied not only with the study of the Torah but also with the dispensing of charity in his community. It was of the utmost importance to him that no poor person be embarrassed by accepting charity. He therefore distributed it secretly by leaving it in a crack in the door, or wherever else it could be found by the needy individual. But the latter never knew who had left the money. Mar Ukva wanted to be sure that the poor gave their thanks to God for His beneficence.

Once, Mar Ukva's wife came to meet him at the yeshivah, and the two went home together in the evening. As they made their way home, Mar Ukva secretly dropped off money at several homes of poor people. At one particular house, the recipient was most curious to find out who his benefactor was. He stood watch at the door and saw a man and woman approaching. When Mar Ukva realized that someone was at the door he quickly ran away with his wife. They sought to hide from the man, but the only place that was available to them was a huge baker's oven. Although the fire was out, the bricks of the oven floor were still very hot, and Mar Ukva burned the soles of his feet. His wife, who was not affected by the heat, told him to put his feet on hers. There they stayed until they considered it safe to come out and return to their home, without being seen by the poor man.

Mar Ukva and his wife went so far as to risk being burned in a hot oven rather than embarrass a poor man for accepting charity.

The commentaries on the Torah state that when God chose Moshe to be the leader who would take the Jews out of Egypt, Moshe delayed his acceptance of that position for seven days. He did not want to be exalted above Aharon, his older brother. Moshe finally consented to go to Egypt to ask for the release of the Jewish people from bondage only when God said to him, "When Aharon sees you, he will be glad in his heart."

The Torah relates that Chavah sinned when she ate a fruit from the forbidden Tree of Knowledge; however, the Torah does not state the name of that tree. Why was it not identified? Had the tree been identified, people might have said, "This is the tree through which the world was afflicted." God did not wish to embarrass any of His creations, and He even spared an inanimate object from shame. How much more so should we be careful not to embarrass another human being.

At the Passover Seder of the great *Gaon* (Talmudic genius) Rabbi Akiva Eiger, one of his guests accidentally spilled some wine onto the tablecloth. Noticing his guest's embarrassment, Rabbi Akiva Eiger discreetly shook the table so that his own cup also spilled over. "Something must be wrong with the table. It's not standing properly," Rabbi Eiger then explained, making his guest feel more at ease.

❧ HISTORY

YA'AKOV AND HIS FAMILY LEAVE LAVAN

Leah gave birth to Ya'akov's first four sons (Reuven, Shimon, Levi and Yehudah). Bilhah, who was the handmaiden of Rachel, became Ya'akov's wife and bore two sons, Dan and Naftali. Zilpah, the handmaiden of Leah, also became Ya'akov's wife and bore him two sons, Gad and Asher. Thereafter, Leah gave birth to Yissachar and Zevulun and a daughter named Dina. Then Hashem answered Rachel's prayers and entreaties for a child and she subsequently gave birth to a son whom she called Yosef.

With Hashem's help, Ya'akov became very wealthy. However, he noticed the jealousy of Lavan's sons and the cool attitude of Lavan himself, and he decided it was time for him to leave. Consequently, he took his wives, children, and flocks while Lavan was away, and began the journey homeward. Before they left, Rachel, without Ya'akov's knowledge, stole her father's idols. She reasoned that in this manner she would be able to prevent her father from worshiping them.

Upon discovery of Ya'akov's departure, Lavan and his men pursued him. Hashem appeared to Lavan and warned him not to harm Ya'akov. When they met, Lavan upbraided his son-in-law for having left so hurriedly and accused him of stealing his idols. Ya'akov denied the theft and unwittingly declared that anyone who had taken the idols would die. Lavan's search proved fruitless and the two parted company after concluding a peace treaty.

Upon his return trip to his homeland in Kena'an, Ya'akov received word that Esav was approaching with four hundred men, and was preparing to do battle with him. Ya'akov divided his people into two camps. He prepared to meet his brother in three different ways: He sent a gift to appease Esav; he prayed to God for assistance; and he prepared for war. The night before his encounter with Esav, Ya'akov had to fight Esav's *sar* (heavenly messenger). Although Ya'akov was injured in the struggle, he emerged victorious. He then received the blessing that thereafter he would be known as Yisrael, and was given a promise of safety.

When the two brothers finally met after so many years, Ya'akov and Esav embraced and cried on each other's shoulders. God's promise of a safe return trip home had been fulfilled.

YA'AKOV RETURNS TO KENA'AN

After the return to Kena'an, the prince of Shechem kidnapped Ya'akov's daughter Dina, and no one in the city protested this outrageous act. Dina's brothers, Shimon and Levi, rescued her after punishing the perpetrators of the crime as well as those who had quietly allowed it.

When Ya'akov and his family returned to Kena'an, Rachel died while giving birth to her second son, Binyamin. Rachel was not buried in *Me'aras Ha-Machpelah*, the burial place of all the other Patriarchs and Matriarchs. Instead, she was buried where she died, on the road to Beis Lechem (Bethlehem). Ya'akov erected a monument on the site, which became a place for all Jews, throughout the centuries, to pray to God.

Rachel also had the distinction that her son, Yosef, had two tribes descend from his sons, Efrayim and Menashe.

LESSON IV

The Greatness of the Patriarchs

The Jewish people were chosen by God primarily because of the merit of the Patriarchs. The Torah thus states, "Only in your fathers did God delight, and He loved them and chose their children after them, namely you, above all people."[8]

The world stands on three pillars: Torah, *avodah* (worshiping God), and *gemilas chesed* (acts of kindness and charity). Each of the Patriarchs symbolized one of these three pillars. Avraham symbolized *chesed*, dedicating himself to helping others. He dug wells for wayfarers; offered them lodging; stood over his guests and served them himself; and risked his life to rescue others. Avraham helped the people not only with food and lodging, but assisted them spiritually as well. The descendants of Avraham are full of compassion and Godliness, implanted in them by the first Patriarch.

Under Avraham's intensive tutelage, Yitzchak spent his entire youth exclusively in the study of God's ways. Yitzchak had attained such perfect devotion to God and full maturity of wisdom that he was prepared to give his life for the sake of God. He was the symbol of *avodah*.

Ya'akov was the symbol of Torah. He had learned for many years at the feet of Shem and Ever and later on for an uninterrupted span of fourteen years in the yeshivah of Ever. With the strength of Torah he was able to impart to all of his children the beauty of God's ways. It was for this reason that he was chosen to be the father of the entire nation, dedicated to serving God. Because he learned Torah for such a great length of time, he acquired a great inner strength that enabled him to overcome many obstacles.

One such struggle occurred on his journey from Charan back to Kena'an, prior to his meeting with Esav. Ya'akov found himself alone and a man wrestled with him until daybreak. (This "man" was the *Sar* of Esav.) When the man saw that he could not defeat Ya'akov, he struck him in the hollow of his thigh, and Ya'akov's hip was dislocated as he wrestled. The man then said, "Let me go, for day is breaking."

Ya'akov replied, "I will not let you go unless you bless me."

The man asked him, "What is your name?" and he answered, "Ya'akov."

The man then said, "Your name shall no longer be Ya'akov. From now on it shall be Yisrael, for you have been great with God, and you have prevailed against man."

The *Sar* with whom Ya'akov wrestled symbolized all the forces of evil in the world, and the fact that Ya'akov finally won the battle showed that he had enough spiritual fortitude to give his children the power to eventually vanquish evil. Thus, Ya'akov was worthy that his children should be God's vehicle to ultimately overcome the evil of the world and return all things to good.

In this episode, however, Ya'akov was wounded in his left thigh. This symbolizes the partial victory of evil and the many persecutions that Ya'akov's children would have to endure as a dedicated people. Ya'akov accepted both the responsibility and its consequences, merely asking for a blessing to give his children the strength to endure.

It was at this time that God gave him the name Yisrael. The name indicates that his children would be "great before God" and would survive to carry the banner of God's teachings to mankind.

❦ Key People, Places and Things

BILHAH AND ZILPAH: handmaidens of Rachel and Leah, who also became the wives of Ya'akov; each bore two sons.

ELIEZER: Avraham's faithful servant who was sent to find a suitable wife for Yitzchak.

EMES: truth.

ESAV: Esau, Ya'akov's twin brother, who sought to kill him.

GID HA-NASHEH: the nerve part of the thigh where Ya'akov was injured. That part must be removed from slaughtered animals and cannot be eaten by a Jew.

HACHNASSAS KALLAH: giving charity to a poor bride or groom.

LEAH: Lavan's elder daughter, who was Ya'akov's first wife. She was the mother of six sons and a daughter.

MA'ASER: a tithe.

PIDYON SHEVUYIM: ransoming Jewish captives.

RACHEL: Lavan's younger daughter, who was Ya'akov's favorite wife. Mother of Yosef and Binyamin. Buried in Beis Lechem, rather than in the *Me'aras Ha-Machpelah.*

REUVEN: Reuben, Ya'akov's oldest son.

RIVKAH: Rebecca, pious wife of Yitzchak, who did not have any children for the first twenty years of their marriage and then bore the twins, Esav and Ya'akov.

SHEKER: a lie; a falsehood.

TZEDAKAH: charity.

YA'AKOV: Jacob; Yisrael; Israel, the third of the Patriarchs, who persevered despite all of the trials and tribulations he endured. His sons became the tribes of Israel.

YA'AKOV'S CHILDREN: Reuven, Shimon, Levi, Yehudah, Yissachar, Zevulun, Dan, Naftali, Gad, Asher, Yosef, Binyamin, and Dina.

YEHUDAH: Judah, the fourth son and the leader among the brothers.

NOTES

1. *Talmud Bava Basra*, 9b.
2. *Talmud Shabbos*, 156b.
3. Ibid.
4. *Talmud Bava Basra*, 11.
5. *Bereshis Rabbah*, 55:1.
6. *Talmud Yerushalmi, Bava Metzia, perek* 2.
7. *Talmud Kesubbos*, 67b.
8. *Devarim* 10:15.

CHAPTER 4

The Trials and Tribulations of Ya'akov and His Sons
From the Sale of Yosef to the Death of Ya'akov
(2216 – 2309 / 1545 B.C.E – 1452 B.C.E.)

❦ HISTORY

YOSEF AND HIS BROTHERS

Ya'akov's favorite son was Yosef, for whom he made a multicolored cloak as a sign of distinction and royalty. Yosef told his brothers of his dreams that indicated that he would rule over them. As a result, Yosef's brothers were jealous and began to hate him.

Ya'akov sent Yosef to see how his brothers were faring while they tended their father's flocks. When they saw him approaching in the distance, they decided to act against him. They judged that because Yosef reported to Ya'akov against them, he was unfairly endangering their future. Since Yosef was putting them in jeopardy, they reluctantly decided to kill him and then conceal their act by saying that he had been eaten by a wild beast.

Reuven, Ya'akov's oldest son, convinced his brothers not to kill Yosef but rather to cast him into a pit. Immediately thereafter, the brothers noticed a caravan which "just happened to be passing by." They withdrew Yosef from the pit and sold him to the caravan that was headed south to Egypt (2216/1595 B.C.E.). Yosef was then seventeen years old.

ETHICS I

Do Not Suspect Your Fellow Jew

God determined that Yosef deserved the harsh treatment he received from his brothers, because he had judged them harshly. Much of what he innocently said, such as reporting his dreams, aroused their jealousy. He made the additional error of mistakenly accusing his brothers of a crime. When Yosef saw his brothers eat the meat of an animal that seemed to be alive and moving (although it had just been slaughtered properly), he ran to their father, and accused them of committing a serious transgression. In his readiness to condemn his brothers, he disregarded a major Jewish principle — that one should judge every person in a favorable light.

The following is an example from the

Talmud of judging another person favorably:

There was once a person who worked for someone for three years. At the end of this period, on the day before Yom Kippur, he approached his employer. The worker explained that he felt it was time to return to his family and he would like his wages for the years of devoted labor.

The employer replied, "I am sorry, but I have no money at the moment."

"Then I'll accept my wages in land or in livestock or even in housewares," decided the worker.

The employer shook his head solemnly, "I'm sorry, but I possess none of those either."

The dejected worker wordlessly set out on his way home with empty pockets.

Right after the *Yamim Tovim* (Holidays), the employer took the worker's wages and three donkeys laden with food, drink, and delicacies, and went to the worker's home.

After he paid him his wages and they had partaken of the delicacies the employer had brought, the employer asked the worker, "What did you think when I told you I had no money to pay you?"

"I thought maybe you had just been offered some goods at a bargain price and had spent all your money purchasing these wares."

"And when I told you I had no livestock or land, what did you think?"

"I thought maybe you had rented them to people," answered the worker.

"And how did you understand that I had no produce or housewares?" was the next question.

"Well, I figured you couldn't give me produce because you hadn't yet given *ma'aser* (tithes) from them. As for the housewares, I assumed you must have donated all your property to the *Beis Ha-Mikdash* (Temple)," he explained.

"Yes, yes! That's exactly what happened," exclaimed the employer. "You have judged me favorably. May Hashem always judge you favorably!"[1]

❧ HISTORY

YOSEF IN PRISON; PAROH'S DREAMS; YOSEF'S BROTHERS IN EGYPT

Yosef was sold into slavery as punishment for his having suspected his brothers wrongfully. Although he was a righteous and good person, he still erred and was punished for it. We must remember that the actions of the righteous are judged more strictly than those of other people.

In Egypt, instead of becoming a slave toiling in the fields, Yosef "just happened" to be sold to Potifar, an officer of Paroh, who then put him in charge of his household. When Yosef rejected Potifar's wife's advances, her false accusations sent him to prison.

In prison, there "just happened to be" two royal officers of Paroh, awaiting word of their fate. One night, each had a dream that he revealed to Yosef. Yosef interpreted the dreams to mean that the butler would be pardoned by Paroh and restored to his position. However, the baker would be executed. Subsequently, Yosef's interpretations proved correct.

Two years passed. Paroh had two unusual dreams. In one, he saw seven lean cows devour seven well-fed cows, and still remain lean. In the other, he saw seven thin ears of grain swallow seven full ears of grain, and still remain thin. Paroh was disturbed by these dreams, and was not put at ease by any of the explanations offered by his advisors. It was then that the chief butler, recalling Yosef's ability to interpret dreams, told Paroh of Yosef's talent.

Yosef was immediately summoned before Paroh. Paroh told him that he had had a dream which no one could satisfactorily interpret and that he had heard that Yosef was capable of interpreting dreams. After proclaiming that it was not his own wisdom with which he interpreted dreams, but rather it was Hashem Who would interpret the dream for Paroh through him, Yosef proceeded to listen to Paroh's recounting of his dreams and to interpret them.

He explained that Paroh's two dreams were actually conveying the same message from Hashem. The seven well-fed cows and the seven full ears of grain represented seven years of economic prosperity for Egypt. The seven lean cows and the seven thin ears of grain symbolized seven years of severe economic depression resulting in a severe famine, which would follow the prosperous years. The seven years of famine would be so devastating that the seven good years would be forgotten. Yosef then advised Paroh to accumulate and store food during the first seven years for use during the second seven years. Paroh, realizing Yosef's abilities, appointed him as his second-in-command and Viceroy over Egypt.

Just as Yosef had predicted, the seven bountiful years ended and the seven years of famine began. This forced Ya'akov to send his sons to Egypt, the only country that had stored food during the years of plenty. Yosef recognized his brothers upon their arrival in Egypt, but he concealed his identity from them. He wanted to test them to see whether they regretted their previous behavior towards him. Under Yosef's orders, the brothers were accused of spying. The brothers now remembered with regret their treatment of Yosef. They attributed the pain and suffering that they were enduring to Divine punishment for their mistreatment of their brother.

Yosef held Shimon hostage and forced the brothers to return to their home and bring Binyamin, the one son who had remained at home with

Ya'akov, to Egypt. Ya'akov reluctantly agreed to allow Binyamin to travel to Egypt, only after Yehudah personally guaranteed his safe return.

When the brothers returned to Egypt with Binyamin, Yosef had his servants "frame" Binyamin, by putting Yosef's silver goblet in Binyamin's sack, making it appear as though the latter had stolen it. The brothers felt devastated at the thought that Binyamin might be thrown into prison. Yehudah offered his own life in return for the safe release of Binyamin. Seeing their strong sense of commitment to each other's safety, Yosef revealed himself to his brothers. He comforted them and told them that it was Divine Providence that he had been sent to Egypt so that the family would be kept alive during the years of famine. Yosef gave his brothers a plentiful supply of food and wagons to return to Kena'an and bring their father, Ya'akov, to Egypt.

After twenty-two years (2238/1523 B.C.E.), Yaakov was united with his beloved son Yosef. Ya'akov came to Egypt with his entire family of seventy people. Ya'akov and Yosef embraced after having been separated for so many years. Yosef took care of the needs of his brothers and their families. He assured them that they could live peacefully away from the Egyptians in Goshen, an area that had fertile pasture land for their flocks.

LESSON I

God Judges the World

Although what befell Yosef seemed at first to be a great tragedy, it turned out to be a farsighted plan of the Almighty, which was later beneficial to the family of Ya'akov.

Whatever happens in this world is planned and controlled by God. Some may occasionally question this statement. "If God controls everything," they ask, "why do certain unfortunate things happen? What is the reason for this?" Often we may not be able to perceive the reason behind certain events. However, this does not mean that there is no explanation. What we lack is the ability to see events in total perspective from the vantage point of hindsight. What might seem

tragic today may prove to be fitting tomorrow. Life is like a puzzle with all the pieces scattered about, and we seem unable to fit them together into a logical form. However, God designed the puzzle and it is He Who will eventually link together all the pieces into a perfectly comprehensible whole.

The events of Yosef's early life probably seemed very tragic at the time they occurred. He was his father's favorite son, and yet he was thrown into a pit by his jealous brothers, seemingly doomed to die. Then, in apparent coincidence, they noticed a caravan of travelers which "just happened" to take him to Egypt. There, instead of becoming a menial slave toiling in the fields, he "just happened" to be sold to an important member of Egyptian society. Then again Yosef's fate seemed to take a downward turn when he was unjustly thrown into jail. At this point, an observer might have thought that Yosef was being punished for no obvious reason. However, it was in jail that Yosef "just happened" to meet and interpret the dreams of the butler and the baker. This eventually led to his becoming second-in-command to Paroh, which in turn led to the immigration of the children of Ya'akov to Egypt. It was in Egypt that Yosef was able to support his family and keep them alive even during the terrible famine. So what seemed to be a series of unreasonable hardships for Yosef finally resulted in the sustainment of the Jewish nation. God's Divine Hand had been in command of the situation throughout, and His Divine plan finally became clear in retrospect.

If one were to look at a beautiful tapestry, what would he see? On the front side, it is an intricately woven, beautiful piece of art, drawing together threads of different lengths and colors, to create an inspiring picture. But when you turn the tapestry over, you see a hodgepodge of many threads, some short and some long, some smooth and some snipped and knotted.

Similarly, God's plan has a pattern into which all of our lives fit. It requires that some lives be knotted and twisted with suffering, and some to be cut short, while others extend to impressive lengths because the pattern of the Creator requires it.

From our view, reward and punishment from God may seem arbitrary and without reason. Many times, history proves otherwise. Every twist and knot seems to have its place in a great design that adds up to a work of art. The story of Yosef and his brothers illustrates this point.

LESSON II

Teshuvah (Repentance)

Yosef's conduct towards his brothers when they came to buy food in Egypt is puzzling. For what purpose did Yosef falsely denounce them? How could he ignore their plight and their hunger? How could he cause his father such worry through threats to Shimon and Binyamin?

One thing is abundantly clear. Yosef cannot be accused of being driven by a desire for revenge. Though Yosef's brothers suspected that he would hate them, Yosef avoided all acts of vengeance. Had he wanted to, he could easily have ordered all his brothers killed. That he did not do so indicates that he aspired to a different goal.

What then was Yosef's motivation? Yosef's brothers were guilty of a grievous injustice towards him. The spiritual honor of the House of Ya'akov could be restored only if this wrong were righted. How could this injustice be atoned for?

The answer is that the brothers must do teshuvah, repentance. How is teshuvah accomplished? In its true form, it takes place when one is confronted with the same temptation to which he had previously succumbed. If one withstands the test and resists this time, he has fully repented.

How, then, could the brothers of Yosef do *teshuvah*? If they discovered Yosef's identity and showed him their regret, this would not be true *teshuvah*, for they might be penitent only out of fear for their lives. No, the only way they could achieve true *teshuvah* would be for them to face the same situation as they had previously faced, and failed. They had to show that they would not allow their father's favorite son to be lost this time.

To accomplish this, Yosef had Binyamin brought to Egypt and accused him, and only him, of stealing his goblet. Now the brothers had a valid excuse for leaving their youngest brother to his fate. They could easily claim that they had no choice but to surrender Binyamin, for how could they fight the entire Egyptian army? However, they steadfastly refused to abandon Binyamin. If he were taken prisoner, they declared, they would all go with him. This, in addition to their previous statements of concern, showed Yosef that they were truly sorry for what they had done to him, and that they would never allow something like it to happen again. It was then that they achieved true *teshuvah*, and Yosef felt that the time was right for him to reveal his true identity.

Teshuvah is a very difficult concept to understand, yet repentance is crucial to all God-fearing Jews. Although *teshuvah* cannot really be defined in precise terms, it consists of three parts. A person who wants to do *teshuvah* must:

(1) acknowledge that he has sinned;

(2) take his wrongdoing to heart and truly regret what he has done; and

(3) commit himself to not repeat his improper activity. The best proof of true and genuine repentance is if the person can overcome his temptation when he is faced with similar circumstances.

Often, those who have erred, regardless of the degree of their transgression, mistakenly hesitate to do *teshuvah* because they feel that their Creator is not interested in the efforts of sinners. However, God readily accepts the *teshuvah* of those who truly regret their sins, and He eagerly awaits their repentance.

A person who does *teshuvah* is considered in the eyes of God as if he had never sinned. Furthermore, our Sages tell us, "In the place where those who do *teshuvah* stand, even the completely righteous cannot stand."[2] People who have done *teshuvah* are, in a sense, greater than those who have never sinned, for they have had to work very hard to change their ways.

Rabbi Yisrael Salanter once went to a shoemaker to have his shoes repaired. The hour was late and darkness had already descended. Noticing that the candle was burning out, Rabbi Yisrael realized that the shoemaker might have trouble repairing the shoes in the dim light, and he suggested that perhaps the man could wait to do it until the next day.

"Do not despair," the shoemaker replied. "I can work very well by candlelight. As long as the candle burns, it is still possible to fix the soles."

Rabbi Yisrael immediately realized the significance of the shoemaker's words. As long as the candle burned, he could still repair what was broken. And as long as the spark of life still flickers in a person, that person can still repair his sinful ways and mend his soul. One can never resign himself to spiritual doom.

❦ HISTORY

YA'AKOV'S BLESSINGS

Ya'akov had reached the age of 147, and the end of his days was approaching. He sent for his son Yosef and made him promise that he would bury him in Kena'an, the resting place of his fathers, rather than in Egypt. Some time later, Yosef was informed that Ya'akov was ill, and Yosef visited him with his two sons, Efrayim and Menashe. Ya'akov told Yosef that Efrayim and Menashe would be counted among Ya'akov's own sons — each would be considered head of a *shevet* (tribe) like Reuven, Shimon, and the others. Yosef brought these sons closer to his father and Ya'akov kissed and hugged them.

Ya'akov stretched out his right hand and placed it on [the younger son] Efrayim's head and his left hand on [the elder son] Menashe's head. Ya'akov then blessed his two grandchildren. Yosef saw that his father's right hand was placed on Efrayim's head and thought there was a mistake in identity. Yosef lifted his father's hand and explained to his father that Menashe was the oldest and, therefore, Ya'akov's right hand should be on him. Ya'akov refused to change the position of his hand, predicting that though Menashe would become a great tribe, Efrayim would be even greater.

ETHICS II:

The Blessings of Harmony

Parents who bless their sons say, "May you be like Efrayim and Menashe." Why are sons specifically compared to the two sons of Yosef? One reason is that Efrayim and Menashe shared a most admirable trait, one that we hope our sons will emulate: their mutual lack of envy towards one another. Though Menashe was older than Efrayim, and the blessing he was granted was not as great as Efrayim's, still Menashe bore no ill will towards his younger brother.

A great Sage once commented on the fact that God's Name is written in many *siddurim* with two *yud*s. However, if one *yud* is higher than the other, then it is not the Name of Hashem. The reason for this is that the two *yud*s must not be rivals and must consider themselves equal, and only then do they symbolize Hashem. Similarly, two *Yidden* (Jews) can evoke Hashem's spirit only when they work together harmoniously, and not when one considers himself above the other. Egotism can lead to destruction.

The relationship between Moshe and his brother, Aharon, is another example of harmony, mutual love, and respect for one another. When Hashem chose Moshe to be the leader who would take the Jewish people out of slavery in Egypt, Moshe hesitated. He felt that his older brother, Aharon, should be given this honor. It was only after the Almighty assured Moshe that Aharon would be happy for him and would escort him to Paroh, that Moshe agreed to go. Throughout the *Chumash*, wherever details are related concerning Moshe and Aharon, there is no hint of any degree of envy or rivalry between Moshe, the younger brother, and Aharon, the older brother.

Rivalry and hatred can only cause the downfall of *Bnei Yisrael*. It is when the Jews are united and accept each other as equals that they will thrive and flourish, bringing credit to Hashem and His Torah.

❦ HISTORY

YA'AKOV'S LAST DAYS

Ya'akov called all his sons to his bedside. He spoke to each of his sons and blessed them. These famous blessings are known as *Birchos Ya'akov*, the blessings of Ya'akov, full of prophecies about the future of each tribe and the description of each tribe's special attributes and characteristics.

Ya'akov commanded all of his sons to bury him in the *Me'aras Ha-Machpelah*, which Avraham had purchased from Efron the Hittite following the death of his wife, Sarah. Ya'akov finished commanding his sons, and returned his soul to his Maker (2255/1506 B.C.E.).

MITZVAH

Prayer

A Jew recites prayers at three intervals during the day. These three prayers were established by our Patriarchs. Avraham, who was like the "rising star" of the Jewish nation, established the morning prayer, *Shacharis*.

Yitzchak, who continued in the ways of his father, established the afternoon service, *Minchah*.

Ya'akov, who had to overcome great difficulties and experienced many dark days, established the prayer of the night, *Ma'ariv*.

It is a positive commandment to pray every day to God, as it says, "You should serve Him."[3] How does one serve God? Through prayer! Now there are no prophets, no priests, no sacrifices, no Temple. What procedure do we have, to worship God? We have only prayer.

It is important for us to realize that it is not for God's sake that we pray. Rather, the purpose of prayer is to give us a chance for introspection and self-analysis. Prayer makes us realize that God is the only One Who can and does provide us with all our needs. We must always remember to be humble before the Almighty and to thank Him for what He grants us.

Prayer involves much more than simply worshiping God or requesting our daily needs. It is one of the important means that we as human beings have of establishing a personal relationship with the Almighty. Prayer makes it possible for man to pour out his heart before God without any intermediaries. No matter how unimportant one thinks he is, he is always welcome to communicate directly with the Almighty.

Rabbi Ze'eira stated in the Talmud: "A man may have a loving friend, but if he persistently asks him for favors and assistance, the friend rebuffs him. But the Holy One, blessed be He, appreciates a man more when he pleads, invokes and prays. The Lord even invites man, as it were, to pray to Him."[4]

Prayer is also a refuge from disappointment and despair. As both Rabbi Yochanan and Rabbi Elazar said, "Even if a sharp sword rests on a man's neck, he should not desist from prayer [for it is never too late for God's salvation]."[5]

Our Sages instituted that ideally our prayers be recited in Hebrew. Most of the prayers are phrased in the collective "we" and refer to each person's membership in the Jewish nation. Once we learn to pray for the greater good of all, we become more deserving of a positive response to our own personal pleas. We also learn to request intelligent and meaningful things.

There is no better means of approaching God than through prayer, for in the very hour that Yisrael prays, and praises God, lifting their eyes and hearts toward heaven, the Holy One, Blessed is He, looks down upon them, embraces them, and is overjoyed to hear their voices.[6]

The one Hebrew book that is perhaps most familiar to every Jew is the *Siddur*, our book of prayers from which we *daven* (pray) every day. The *Siddur* is a

priceless treasure that has served the Jewish people for more than a thousand years. It is universal among Jews. Wherever one travels throughout the world, in any synagogue he may enter, he will find that the *Siddur* is essentially the same. The prayers have not been substantially changed since the *Siddur* was first circulated in the year 858 C.E., during the Gaonic period.

The word *Siddur* is related to the word *seder*, which means "order." The *Siddur* has all the prayers arranged in a special order. If one looks at the table of contents in a *Siddur*, one finds a long list of prayers for every occasion. Those prayers recited most often, *Shacharis* (morning), *Minchah* (afternoon), and *Ma'ariv* (evening), are found at the beginning of the *Siddur*. They are followed by the services for the Shabbos and the Holidays. The rest of the *Siddur* is devoted to prayers recited on special occasions, e.g., *Hallel* — a service of praise and thanksgiving, recited on *Yom Tov, Rosh Chodesh* (the first day of the new Hebrew month), and Chanukah.

(1) What are the different categories of prayer in the *Siddur*?

PRAISE — We praise God as the Creator of heaven and earth and declare that His Holiness and His Presence exist in all parts of the universe. We declare the power of God to do whatever He wills, and we testify to His loving-kindness.

THANKSGIVING — Jews all over the world recite prayers of thanksgiving every day. We thank God for the blessings of life and for the blessings He grants us personally. We also thank Him for giving us the Torah and providing us with food, clothing, shelter, and all the rest of our many needs.

REQUEST — Many people think that the only time it is necessary to pray to God is when they want something special. This attitude is wrong. We should not take our daily well-being for granted. Without God's constant kindness, we could not survive for a moment. Therefore, our requests and prayers are always needed for peace throughout the world, especially for the Jewish people. We ask Him to teach us to care for our fellow-men and to bless us with a happy and healthy life, one devoted to Torah and Jewish ideals. We ask for the privilege of witnessing the return of all Jews to the Land of Yisrael, the coming of *Mashiach* (the Messiah), and the rebuilding of the *Beis Ha-Mikdash* (the Holy Temple).

We also pray for all our personal needs. When we do so we reinforce our knowledge that we are dependent on G-d for everything we require and can only succeed by His blessing and grace. A person must never be tempted to say, "My power and the strength of my hand provided me with all I possess."[7]

(2) Why are the prayers of the *Siddur* written in Hebrew?

Although the Halachah states that an individual is permitted to recite the prayers in any language, it is most important that a synagogue or congregation does not deviate from the practice of conducting its public prayers in Hebrew, the sacred tongue. The main reason is that the Hebrew language is *lashon ha-kodesh* (the holy language). When God spoke to the prophets, He spoke in Hebrew. There are hidden meanings and special merits that are attached to Hebrew words.[8] Another reason for this is

that our prayers link our thoughts and desires with the yearnings of Jews all over the world. We therefore pray in Hebrew since we want our prayers to be international for the good of Jews wherever they are. We use the historic Hebrew language that unites all Jews in all countries, throughout the generations. Not only does it tie the simplest Jew ever closer to Israel, where Hebrew is chiefly spoken, but it enables a Jew to feel at home in any synagogue in the world, even when he speaks a language different from that of the other worshipers.

Historically, when a Jewish community severed its bond with the Hebrew tongue in public prayer, it ultimately led to the total disappearance of that community through assimilation and intermarriage. The reason for this is that a total estrangement from the Hebrew language usually also represents estrangement from the Torah and all other classical Jewish sources. It means the loss of understanding of Jewish concepts and values, best conveyed through the original Hebrew text.

(3) How can one pray if one does not understand the meaning of the words? Isn't it hypocritical to utter Hebrew words that one does not fully understand? Doesn't the Talmud teach us that he who prays should concentrate on what he is saying?

It is important for the people of a congregation to invest time and effort to master Hebrew reading and its meaning. If there are members, however, who cannot read, then it is best to have prayer books available with the Hebrew on one side and translation on the other. They will then be able to say the Hebrew prayers, and at the same time study the translation and slowly learn the meaning of the prayers. Eventually the Hebrew words will become more under-standable. If a person recites prayers of which he does not fully understand every word, he can still direct his thoughts to his Father in heaven.

LESSON III

The Righteous Are Rewarded

Ya'akov's entire life was turbulent. During his early years, he had problems with his brother, Esav. Because of the threat to his life, he was forced to flee from his parents' home. He had to live in the house of Lavan for twenty years. Upon his return to Kena'an, he had to prepare to battle his brother, Esav. Ya'akov lost his beloved wife Rachel at an early age. He then suffered the agony of the separation from his son Yosef for twenty-two years.

In contrast to his early years of wanderings and tragedy, Ya'akov's final years were ones of peace and contentment. He lived to be reunited with his son Yosef and to see him become the second most powerful leader in Egypt.

We often find pious people enjoying the final years of their existence on this earth, after they had earlier gone through much uncertainty and suffering. This was certainly true of Sarah, whose final thirty-seven years on this world were her happiest, for it was then that she experienced the joy of raising her son Yitzchak. The closing years are ones of peaceful reward for the righteous. However, for the wicked, the process is reversed. Often their early years are spent hoarding temporary pleasures, while their final years are spent in abject misery as a result of their recklessness.[9]

If one examines the Torah, he will find that nowhere does the text use the ex-pression, "And Ya'akov died." Why was the word "death" not used in connection with Ya'akov?

Actually, there are two deaths that can be associated with a person. One is his physical death — the cessation of his bodily functions — and this death occurs to everyone sooner or later. The other possible death is the end of one's influence and impact on the world. In the case of many, both deaths occur simultaneously. They have accomplished little of lasting value on this earth, so when they pass away, neither their memory nor their life's work lingers on. This was not the case with Ya'akov, though. True, he no longer functioned physically after the age of 147. However, he had achieved so much during his years of existence that his influence and his example are felt even today, as if he were still alive. He helped found the still thriving nation of Yisrael. His noble traits and his devotion to God are guides for us all. Therefore, Ya'akov can be considered more a part of this world than many who are actually alive today.[10]

Rav Yehudah ben Bava was also one who realized that one's life's work can survive his death. Rav Yehudah ben Bava lived during the days of Roman oppression, when the government decreed that the granting of semichah (rabbinical ordination) was forbidden under penalty of death. Nevertheless, Rav Yehudah ben

Bava assembled five of his disciples, and when hidden from view, secretly ordained them. However, just as he had finished doing so, his disciples heard the footsteps of the Roman soldiers coming to kill them.[11]

They began to make their escape, and shouted to their mentor, "Quick, run for your life, or you will be killed by the enemy!"

Rav Yehudah ben Bava refused. "I am an old man. You run and save yourselves, but I will stay. I have completed my life's work, and even if the Romans do kill me, they cannot kill my accomplishments. The words of God's Torah will live on!"

Soon afterwards, the enemy soldiers did indeed catch up with Rav Yehudah ben Bava. They so riddled him with spears that his punctured body resembled a sieve. However, his disciples escaped to transmit Torah to others, and in this way, Rav Yehudah ben Bava continues to live with us today.

It should be our goal in life to survive in this world even after death. For, though we must all die physically, if we accomplish something worthwhile during our lives, the achievements of our existence will live on.[12]

❦ HISTORY

YA'AKOV'S DEATH AND BURIAL IN KENA'AN

Ya'akov's death was mourned not only by his sons and family but by the Egyptians as well. They mourned for Ya'akov for seventy days. Yosef, together with his brothers, and their households, received Paroh's permission to go to Kena'an to bury Ya'akov. Yosef and his brothers did as they had been commanded; they buried Ya'akov in the *Me'aras Ha-Machpelah* in Chevron.

On their return to Egypt, Yosef's brothers, now afraid that Yosef would seek vengeance against them, sought his pardon for their past misdeeds. However, Yosef reassured them that he had no vengeance in mind. Yosef calmed them and told them that he would support them and their children. Before Yosef's death, he made *Bnei Yisrael* take an oath to take along his coffin with them when Hashem would return them to the Promised Land. Yosef died at the age of 110 and was temporarily buried in Egypt.

🐛 Key People, Places and Things

BA'AL TEFILLAH (CHAZAN): the cantor, leader in prayer.

B'EZRAS HASHEM: with the help of God.

DAN L'CHAF ZECHUS: to judge others favorably.

GAM ZO L'TOVAH: "Everything is for the best."

HASHGACHAH: Divine Providence.

MA'ARIV: the evening prayer service.

MINCHAH: the afternoon prayer service.

PAROH: Pharaoh, ruler of Egypt, who asked Yosef to interpret his troubling dreams. He then made Yosef his Viceroy.

SHACHARIS: the morning prayer service.

SIDDUR: the prayer book.

TESHUVAH: repentance.

YOSEF: Joseph, Ya'akov's favorite son, envied by his brothers who sold him into slavery. He eventually became Viceroy of Egypt and thus was able to help his family during the years of famine.

NOTES

1. *Talmud Shabbos,* 127b.
2. *Talmud Berachos,* 34b.
3. *Devarim* 11:13.
4. *Talmud Yerushalmi, Berachos, perek* 9:1.
5. *Talmud Berachos,* 10.
6. *Midrash Koheles.*
7. *Devarim* 8:17.
8. *Shulchan Aruch, Aruch Chayim* 101, *biyur halachah.*
9. *Bereshis Rabbah,* 66:4.
10. *Talmud Ta'anis,* 5.
11. *Talmud Sanhedrin,* 14.
12. *Aruch Ha-Shulchan, Aruch Chayim* 156, quotes the *Yerushalmi.*

❦ Introduction to Chapters 5-8

This section reviews the history of the Jewish people through the years of their oppression and slavery in Egypt (Mitzrayim). It describes the greatness of Moshe and Aharon as messengers chosen by Hashem to lead the Jews out of Egypt. It shows Moshe's exceptional character, especially his faith, persistence, modesty and superb leadership abilities when he brought his people forth from slavery. This spectacular liberation came to the Jewish nation in its hour of greatest need. The dramatic account of the splitting of the Red Sea and the giving of the Ten Commandments are among the most outstanding incidents in the Book of Shemos.

The miraculous redemption of the Jewish people from slavery showed how, in the end, by a mighty revelation of Divine justice, it was not the oppressor who triumphed but the oppressed. It impressed upon the Jewish people that they did not survive as a result of their own power, but through the benevolent protection of Hashem. As soon as they realized this, they were ready for the revelation of the Divine Will at Mount Sinai.

After the Jews left Egypt, what alone saved them from splitting up into tiny fragmented groups and being swallowed up by the surrounding peoples was their willingness to accept the Torah. Had they not exclaimed, "All that the Lord has spoken we will do," the world would have soon forgotten the name of Yisrael. Its story would have resembled the many streams which flow a short distance and disappear in the sands. The Torah that was transmitted from God to His people was the possession which united them, provided them with cohesiveness, and gave them strength.

The giving of the Torah at Mount Sinai was the event which gave guidance and direction to the Jews' service of Hashem. In essence, the Torah became the national constitution of the Jewish people. The laws of the Torah became the fundamental principles that shaped the daily lives of the Jews. Unlike other nations of the world, we do not depend on land or state for our survival, but rather on the Torah itself. It was Torah which brought the Jewish nation into being; it is the Torah which has kept it alive. This is the explanation of the uniqueness of Jewish history and the secret of Jewish survival.

CHAPTER 5

The Exodus from Egypt
From Egyptian Slavery to the Crossing of the Red Sea
(2332 – 2448 / 1429 B.C.E. – 1313 B.C.E.)

❦ HISTORY

SLAVERY IN EGYPT

After Yosef's death, many Jews started to socialize with the Egyptians and disperse from their secluded section in Goshen to every city in Egypt (Mitzrayim). This made it easier for them to assimilate into the Egyptian culture. However, the Egyptians scorned them and forgot everything that Yosef had done for Egypt. The Egyptians initiated a policy of oppression and the enslaved Jews were forced to build fortresses and storage cities for their Egyptian overlords.

One of the worst types of cruelty was heaped upon the Jewish slaves. Their male babies were thrown into the river and even into fire. Sometimes they were used as mortar in place of brick.

LESSON I

Assimilation: Cause for Jewish Suffering

When the sons of Ya'akov first came to Egypt, they indicated that they intended to make their stay there a temporary one. However, they soon changed their attitude. Since Egypt was a flourishing nation full of riches, many Jews forsook their own community for the general population of Egypt. They put themselves in danger of losing their separate Jewish identities and of forsaking the God of their fathers. It was because of this attempt to assimilate that they were punished. Instead of accepting them as equals, the Egyptians turned on them and treated them as slaves. They could no longer make the mistake of forgetting that they were Jews, for the Egyptians would not let them.

Despite the lessons of Egypt, Jews have continued their attempts to assimilate, and have continued to be punished for them. The Jews in the days of Esther were faced with annihilation at the hands of Haman. Why? Because they had attended King Achashverosh's banquet where they mingled with the gentiles, showing a desire for non-Jewish influences and pleasures. It was only due to their repentance that God saved them. Similarly, the Jews at the time of the second Beis Ha-Mikdash (Temple) were often influenced by Greek concepts and pastimes (Hellenism), and were in danger of forsaking their Jewish ways. They were punished with foreign domination, and it was only when the Maccabees reminded them of their separate Godly, national consciousness that they were able to regain independence.

Those who think that they can blend easily into gentile society are deluding themselves. The results can often be disastrous, as the Jews have learned all too frequently.

It is customary for parents to bless their sons with the blessing, "May you be like Efrayim and Menashe." Why are our sons compared specifically to the two sons of Yosef? One reason was mentioned in Ethics II of the previous chapter. Another is that because they were the only two heads of tribes who were born in exile (outside Eretz Yisrael), and despite the corrupting influence and temptations that the secularism of exile can offer, they remained as true to God's principles as Ya'akov himself.

Therefore, in praying that their sons should become like Efrayim and Menashe, parents ask God to protect their offspring from the pitfalls of assimilation and to help them remain loyal and steadfast Jews.

The classic example of loyalty to one's religion and one's people, is, of course, Moshe, who was raised from infancy in Paroh's palace. He followed the example of Menashe and Efrayim and did not allow himself to be influenced by his surroundings.

Many times throughout our history, the Jewish people suffered tremendous catastrophes. They kept looking for reasons why God allowed this to happen. The reason is often all too clear. Whenever we try to imitate and emulate the gentiles around us, God sends reminders — sometimes tragic ones — that despite the fact that we live in exile, we are still God's Chosen People and are expected to live accordingly.

❧ HISTORY

MOSHE'S BIRTH DURING THE PERIOD OF PAROH'S EVIL DECREE (2368/1393 B.C.E.)

Paroh was concerned about the rapidly increasing Jewish population. Taking a drastic approach, Paroh ordered the midwives to kill all male infants at birth, but they refused. One of the midwives who refused to obey was Yocheved, wife of Amram and mother of Aharon and Miryam. Yocheved was rewarded for her courage by giving birth to a very special son. She hid him from the authorities as long as she could but then had no choice but to place the baby boy in a basket and set it upon the bank of the Nile River under Miryam's supervision.

Paroh's daughter came to bathe in the waters of the Nile and saw the basket. She realized it contained a Hebrew child and, touched with pity, decided to adopt him. Miryam came forward and received the princess' permission to find a nurse for the infant. She returned with Yocheved, under whose care the boy was later taught the traditions of his ancestors. The boy was taken to the royal palace, and was named Moshe, which means "drawn from the water."

MOSHE IN PAROH'S PALACE

Although he lived in the royal palace, Moshe went out to be among his fellow Jews and observe their suffering. He once noticed an Egyptian taskmaster savagely beating one of the Hebrew slaves. He killed the Egyptian and buried him in the sand. The next day, Moshe intervened in a quarrel between two Israelites. One of the two demanded to know what right Moshe had to judge others, and tauntingly asked whether he intended to kill them as he had already killed the Egyptian. It became instantly clear to Moshe that his deed was known and hence his life was in danger. Moshe therefore fled to Midyan. There he came to a well, where he protected the seven daughters of Yisro from unfriendly shepherds. He was welcomed by Yisro, who hired him to tend his sheep. Moshe soon married Yisro's daughter Tzipporah, who bore him two sons, Gershom and Eliezer.

During Moshe's stay in Midyan, Paroh died. His successor continued the oppression of the Jews with even greater severity and they cried out to God to save them.

Moshe became Yisro's shepherd. Not content to let the sheep wander off, Moshe ran after every stray sheep and treated it as he would his own. When a lamb strayed from the flock, he brought it back on his shoulders, carrying it as one would a child. God decided that one who exhibited such compassion for small creatures was fit to lead His Chosen People. It was then that Moshe saw an extraordinary sight — a bush that was on fire but was nevertheless not consumed. As Moshe turned to gaze at this wonder, God addressed him for the first time and informed him that he was to be a special messenger to bring the Jews out of slavery in Egypt, into the Promised Land.[1]

ETHICS I

Compassion

Moshe was chosen to be the leader of the Jewish people because of his exceptional compassion and concern for others.

One hint of Moshe's unique leadership capabilities is given by the Torah's statement that, as a young man, Moshe went out to his brethren and looked at their burden. This was no mere once-over glance. Rashi (a major commentator on the Torah) explains that Moshe directed his heart and mind to share the experiences of his fellow Jews. Although he himself enjoyed the privileges of a palace upbringing, he empathized with the plight of those Jews who were treated like slaves. This quality of concern for others helped make Moshe an outstanding leader.

As noted above, these same attributes were visible as well when Moshe later became Yisro's shepherd. He exhibited this personal concern for both man and animals.

Compassion for other people has characterized our greatest rabbis. Rabbi Chaim Soloveitchik, the Rav of Brisk, was supplied by the community with wood to heat his house. When the treasurers found that the expenses were inordinately great, they launched a brief investigation. The inquiry elicited the fact that all the poor men in the town were taking wood freely from the unlocked timber shed in the Rabbi's yard, and the shed was immediately locked. When Rabbi Chaim heard of this, he refused to take any more wood for himself. He could not enjoy the warmth, knowing that his brethren were freezing in their homes. The wood bin was unlocked and remained open for everyone.

A man once came to Rabbi Baruch Ber Leibowitz and asked him to pray for the recovery of his wife. Ten years later, Rav Baruch Ber met that person and asked him about the welfare of his wife. The man answered his inquiry and then found out that throughout the entire ten years, Rabbi Leibowitz had not stopped praying for his wife's well-being.

LESSON II

Every Person Has a Choice

An important lesson can be learned from Moshe and Yosef. We know that every man has the ultimate choice of whether or not to serve God according to his ability and circumstances. Despite the environment in which they lived (Yosef was Paroh's Viceroy; Moshe was raised as a prince in Paroh's palace), they chose to cling to God and the Jewish people. There is a Talmudic dictum: "Everything is in the hands of God, except the fear of God."[2]

Although a person's actions may be influenced by his heredity and environment, neither of these absolutely determines his actions. The veracity of this was proven by Onkelos, nephew of the Roman Emperor, who chose to convert to Judaism. Despite the fact that he was raised in a royal family, and one which despised the Jewish nation, he was attracted by the beauty and teachings of Judaism and decided to convert.[3] His uncle, the Emperor, did not look upon this kindly, considering it a threat to his own paganism. Onkelos went on to become a great scholar who wrote the renowned Aramaic translation of the Bible that bears his name.[4]

Akiva grew up as an ignorant shepherd. Until the age of forty, he had no knowledge of Judaism and didn't even know the *Alef-Beis*. Despite these shortcomings, when he finally set his mind to studying and learning, to which he dedicated his whole life, he eventually became the renowned Torah scholar and leader, Rabbi Akiva.[5]

❧ HISTORY

MOSHE AND AHARON APPEAR BEFORE PAROH

After Hashem appeared to Moshe and told him that it was time for the Jews to be redeemed from bondage, Moshe was hesitant to deliver the message to Paroh. Why would Paroh listen to him, especially as Moshe had a speech impediment? He was told that his brother, Aharon, would be his spokesman, and that Paroh would refuse to let the Jews go until God had inflicted severe punishment upon the Egyptians.

As commanded by Hashem, Aharon cast down his rod before the Egyptian leader and it turned into a serpent. However, the Egyptian magicians were able to duplicate this feat. Even though Aharon's rod then swallowed the magicians' rods, Paroh remained unimpressed.

THE FIRST THREE PLAGUES

The first plague was now brought upon Egypt. After warning Paroh of what was to happen, Aharon followed Moshe's instructions and waved his rod over the Nile River. All of the waters in Egypt turned to blood. The fish died, and this created an unbearably foul odor. The Egyptians, faced with a lack of water, were forced to beg for water from the Jews, for the plague had no effect upon the Jews' water. The plague continued for seven days. Since the miracle was again duplicated by the Egyptian magicians, Paroh retained his stubborn attitude.

Similarly, Paroh ignored the threat of a plague of frogs. Just as he had done before, Aharon stretched his hand over the Nile and soon frogs swarmed over the land. Paroh pleaded with Moshe to stop the plague's effects and promised to capitulate and allow the Jews to leave. As soon as Moshe prayed to God, the plague ceased; however, Paroh balked and refused to fulfill his promise.

Aharon then struck the dust with his rod and the dust turned into lice, which swarmed over man and beast. This time, the Egyptian magicians were unable to do likewise and they were forced to admit the superiority of God's power. Nevertheless, Paroh's heart remained hardened towards the Jews.

ETHICS II

Displaying Gratitude

The Torah records that Moshe called upon his brother Aharon to initiate the first three plagues upon the Egyptians: blood (*dam*), frogs (*tzefarde'a*), and lice (*kinim*). Why did Moshe rely upon his brother for these acts when he was the leader chosen by Hashem to confront Paroh? Why did he not bring about these three plagues himself?

The answer lies in Moshe's appreciation for past favors. All three of the above-mentioned plagues involved some slight ingratitude to the forces that had aided him in the past. For instance, the plague of blood caused the waters to become unusable. These same waters of the Nile had once save Moshe's life, for it was on their shores that Moshe's mother hid him from Paroh. Similarly, the plagues of frogs and lice were produced from the ground. This same dust of the earth had once protected Moshe by hiding from view the Egyptian taskmaster he killed. Because the waters and the earth had proved beneficial to him, Moshe showed his gratitude by not starting plagues involving them. Therefore Hashem ordered Aharon to bring about these plagues.

Gratitude is one of the pillars that sustains human society. By being grateful, one rewards those who have aided him. He shows that he recognizes their efforts and does not take them for granted. How many individuals simply expect assistance from their parents, teachers and friends? How many demand something from others as a matter of course and then don't bother to thank them when assistance is given? If they would stop and think of all the favors they are receiving, the care and sustenance provided by their parents, the wisdom imparted by their teachers, the kindness shown by their friends, then their uncaring attitudes would surely be different. How would they cope if all these helpers were not there?

Rabbi Levi Yitzchak of Berditchev was one who made his feelings of gratitude very clear. When he arrived at a small town one evening, he found himself without lodgings. He was forced to wander from house to house seeking shelter. Since no one knew who he was, he was turned away from each home. There remained only one rather run-down residence and Rabbi Levi Yitzchak was not optimistic about his being accepted there. Nevertheless, he knocked at the door, and when it was opened, he repeated his request for a night's lodging.

"Well, I am only a poor man with few furnishings," was the reply. "But if you wouldn't mind staying in a poor man's home, it would be an honor for me to welcome you."

Rabbi Levi Yitzchak gladly accepted the invitation and thanked the man profusely when he left the next day.

Some years later, when Rabbi Levi Yitzchak had become known far and wide as a saintly sage, he again paid a visit to that town. The townsfolk, who were now aware of the identity and fame of their visitor, gathered before him and competed for the honor of having this Torah leader lodge with them. But Rabbi Levi Yitzchak shook his head.

"I will stay with the poor man at the edge of town, if he will allow me to," he announced. "He extended himself for me the last time and it is to him that I must express my everlasting gratitude. Once someone performs a favor for you, you must never forget it."

Naturally, we should express our ultimate gratitude to the One Who created us and supplied us with all our needs and happiness: the Almighty. We can never take for granted the benefits that Hashem provides. It is for this reason that we pray to Him daily, and recite blessings over the food that we eat. Thus we will never forget His unceasing kindness.[6]

❦ HISTORY

THE REMAINING SEVEN PLAGUES

Moshe warned Paroh that swarms of wild animals (*arov*) would invade the homes of the Egyptians, while the land of Goshen, where the Jews lived, would be unaffected. Paroh remained obstinate. However, the devastation caused by this fourth plague convinced him to agree to let the Israelites sacrifice to God — in the land of Egypt. Moshe, however, demanded that the Jews be allowed to make a three-day journey into the wilderness to offer sacrifices, to escape any harassment by the Egyptians. Paroh yielded, but as soon as the plague was halted, he again refused to let the Jews leave.

Subsequently, Moshe warned Paroh that murrain (*dever*) — a cattle plague — would devastate Egypt (again sparing Goshen) if Paroh would not capitulate. Paroh refused to budge and the murrain struck with full fury, causing the Egyptians' cattle to die while the cattle of the Jews was not harmed. Still, Paroh remained unmoved.

For the next plague, Moshe sprinkled ashes towards the heavens, in Paroh's presence. The ashes turned into dust and this caused an epidemic of painful boils (*shechin*) to erupt among man and beast alike. Paroh's magicians were likewise affected, but Paroh did not change his mind.

After this, Paroh was told that if he did not relent, Egypt would be hit by a torrent of hail (*barad*) which would be catastrophic for the crops and the remaining cattle. He was advised to shelter both people and animals to save them from death. Some of the Egyptians heeded the warning and shielded themselves and their cattle. Then Moshe stretched his rod towards the heavens, and a terrible storm with thunder, lightning and hail raged over Egypt (except for Goshen), killing man and beast and destroying crops. (The hail was of an unusual nature: each piece was composed of fire on the inside and ice on the outside, and was as huge as a boulder.) This time, Paroh openly acknowledged his error, but when the storm ceased, his heart once more turned to stone.

Some time later, Moshe warned Paroh that on the following day a plague of locusts (*arbeh*) would destroy Egypt's crops. At this juncture, Paroh's advisors urged him to let the Israelite men depart. However, Moshe and Aharon insisted that the women, children, and flocks also be allowed to leave. Paroh refused to listen. The next day Moshe extended his rod, and an east wind carried into Egypt a swarm of locusts which devoured the country's vegetation. After witnessing this disaster, Paroh admitted his error and begged Moshe and Aharon to pray for the removal of the plague. They complied, and a strong west wind drove the locusts into Yam Suf (the Red Sea). However, once again Paroh reneged on his agreement.

The next plague Moshe brought was total darkness (*choshech*) which descended upon the Egyptians for six days. For three of these days they were unable to move about at all. Only the Israelites were granted light. The resulting nightmarish chaos proved too much for Paroh to cope with, and he offered permission to all Israelites — men, women, and children — to leave, provided the flocks and herds were left behind as surety that the Israelites would return. Moshe rejected this stipulation, and Paroh forbade him to appear again in the royal presence. Moshe replied that there would be one final, devastating plague, one that would cost all Egyptian firstborn sons their lives (*makas bechoros*). Moshe and Aharon then departed for the last time.

LESSON III

Why the Necessity for Egyptian Enslavement?

Let us understand what was happening to the Jews in Egypt. Many had left Goshen and dispersed among the Egyptians. The Egyptians then turned on them, enslaving them in a most cruel and inhuman manner. For years, the Jews suffered under the yoke of Egyptian taskmasters. It might seem that this was for no purpose, yet one should realize that to make steel, iron ore must be smelted in a furnace at a very high temperature. The resulting product has solid strength. Egypt was like the smelting furnace, from which the children of Ya'akov emerged a tested but stronger nation, with their faith in the Almighty intact. Their suffering brought them to the realization that their lives and future happiness depended on God and no one else.

Despite the tragedy and hardships of slavery, the Jews still retained their singular identity as Hebrews. They did not change their Hebrew names, their language, nor their style of clothing. In all the years of enslavement, there were no instances of permanent assimilation and intermarriage with the Egyptians. It was there, amidst hostile neighbors and crushed by cruel tyrants and taskmasters, that the descendants of Ya'akov merged into a unity of everlasting brotherhood.

Yet, after so many years of torturous slavery, they did not have the morale, nor were they at the spiritual level, to become God's Chosen Nation. God had to do something miraculous to take His people out of both physical and spiritual bondage.

❧ HISTORY

THE KORBAN PESACH

God informed Moshe that deliverance was near. But first the Jews were commanded to sacrifice a lamb. Its blood was to be smeared on the lintels and doorposts of each house as a sign that it was inhabited by Jews. That night, as well as in future generations, besides the roasted sacrifice, they were supposed to eat only unleavened bread with bitter herbs. In the future, this festival was to be observed annually as Pesach, a permanent reminder of the deliverance from Egypt. Only unleavened bread was to be eaten for seven days. In the future, the *korban Pesach* (Passover sacrifice) was to be offered in the *Beis Ha-Mikdash* (Holy Temple).

Exactly at midnight, God killed all the Egyptian firstborn, both man and animal. Paroh and his fellow Egyptians rose in the middle of the night in terror. They then insisted that the Israelites leave, just as God had predicted. The Egyptians were no longer speaking from a position of power, but from one of subjugation.

The Israelites left in such haste that their unleavened dough had no time to rise. (To commemorate this, Jews have been commanded to eat unleavened bread, or matzah, on Pesach ever since.) There were six hundred thousand men between the ages of twenty to sixty who began the journey, with their wives and children. They also carried a large supply of gold and silver, which the Egyptians had given them. The Jews were commanded to bring a Pesach sacrifice every year on the fourteenth day of *Nissan.* They were also commanded to redeem their firstborn male children in all future generations, and to wear *tefillin* "for a sign on your hand and for a memorial between your eyes" to remind them of the salvation from Mitzrayim.

MITZVAH

Pesach

The Torah states that all Jews are obligated to go up to Yerushalayim, the city of God's Holy Temple, three times a year — Pesach, Shavuos, and Sukkos. On Pesach we thank God for freeing us from slavery in Egypt. On Shavuos we thank God for giving us the Torah that made us into the Jewish nation. On Sukkos we thank God for the Clouds of Glory which protected the Jewish people during their years in the wilderness. We also thank the Almighty for Eretz Yisrael and its bountiful produce.

God established special times during the year for His nation to remember the miracles and goodness that He has bestowed upon them. He commanded us to keep these holidays so that we can come closer to Him and fully appreciate our Creator. These holidays are celebrated with feelings of happiness and gratitude to the Almighty for all that He has done.

The first of the three major Festivals is called Pesach. It starts on the fifteenth day of the Hebrew month of *Nissan* and lasts for eight days (outside of Eretz Yisrael). It celebrates the liberation of our ancestors from Egyptian slavery. We observe the Pesach Seder on each of the first two nights in the Diaspora (only once in Israel). At this special service, we retell the story of the exodus from Egypt (as stated in the Torah). We eat matzos instead of bread throughout the entire eight days, since all foods containing leaven are forbidden.

The three positive precepts which apply to the observance of Pesach nowadays are:

(1) Disposing of all leaven foodstuffs no later than the morning of the fourteenth day of the month of *Nissan*.

(2) Eating matzah on the first night of Pesach. On the second night it is required *mi-d'Rabbanan* (Rabbinically).

(3) Relating the story of the exodus from Egypt on the night of *Pesach*.

(The following laws are abridged, and one whose knowledge is not adequate must continue to learn and consult for in-depth instruction.)

(1) GETTING RID OF THE CHAMETZ IN OUR MIDST

Chametz is a product of one of the five types of grain (wheat, barley, spelt, rye and oats) remaining in contact with water for a period of time, normally eighteen minutes, before baking. The Torah forbids eating or deriving any benefit from *chametz* on Pesach, or even possessing it. If a small amount of *chametz* is mixed with other food particles, one cannot eat the entire mixture. Therefore, only foods produced under strict rabbinical supervision can be used. For example, cake, cookies, cereals, macaroni products and coffee substitutes such as Postum are usually made with grain, and therefore cannot be used on Pesach, unless prepared in a special way for Pesach.

Products that were never fit for animal consumption, such as chemicals, shampoos, laundry detergents, etc., can be used on Pesach.

There are two methods of disposing of *chametz*:

(a) *biyur chametz* — actual destruction of the *chametz* in one's possession or removal of it from one's possession

(b) *bittul chametz* — renouncing one's title to the *chametz* in one's possession. By Rabbinical decree one is required to use both of the above methods.

Throughout the month preceding Pesach, we clean our house thoroughly to make sure that there is no *chametz*. On the night before Pesach, one makes another thorough search for *chametz* in one's house, preferably with the light of a single candle (not a torch or a *Havdalah* candle) or with a flashlight. Every room is searched thoroughly, as are the pockets of one's clothing, one's place of business, basement, garage, automobile, locker, etc. Any *chametz* that has been found is put away until the time prescribed for the burning of the *chametz* on the following morning.

Preceding the search for *chametz*, one recites a special blessing. In order to make sure that some *chametz* is found and that the blessing has not been made in vain, it is customary to place ten pieces of bread throughout the house, before starting the search. After the search is complete, we renounce ownership of the *chametz*.

The following morning, the leftover *chametz*, and any other *chametz* that was found, is burned. A more inclusive version of the declaration renouncing ownership of the *chametz* is said, including all *chametz* ("whether I have seen it or not seen..."). All this should be done before five-twelfths of the day have passed.

If one has valuable *chametz* which he does not want to destroy, he can sell his *chametz* to a non-Jew. This is customarily done through a competent rabbi who acts as his agent. Since the laws of selling *chametz* are very complex, we rely upon a rabbi to take care of the transaction for us. Immediately after Pesach, the rabbi buys it back.

(2) THE MITZVAH OF MATZAH AND SEDER

There is a Biblical commandment to eat matzah on the first night of Pesach.

For the rest of Pesach no bread may be eaten, and matzah is eaten in its stead. Some authorities hold that each time one eats matzah, he is fulfilling a mitzvah. Matzah is made from one of the five types of grain, kneaded with water and immediately baked. The Torah says that one should eat *matzah shemurah* (commonly known as *shmura matzos*). These matzos, according to most customs, should be supervised from the time of harvesting. (For at least the Seder night(s) of Pesach, one should try to obtain matzah that has been under supervision from the time the grain was cut. If necessary, supervision from the time the grain was ground is sufficient.)

Although machine-made matzos are generally acceptable for Pesach use, there are various opinions concerning the suitability of using machine *shmura matzos* for the mitzvah of matzah on the Seder night(s) of Pesach.

Egg matzos or any matzos kneaded with any liquid other than water should not be eaten on Pesach unless there are special mitigating circumstances. In such a case, a rabbi should be consulted.

(3) HOW DO WE CONDUCT THE SEDER?

The Seder is the religious festive meal which takes place on the first night of Pesach (first two nights in the Diaspora). The word *seder* means "order," and the ceremony is so called because there is a set order of service.

The food for the Pesach meal should be prepared and set in place so that one can begin the Seder right after nightfall, upon returning from the synagogue. The reason we begin the Seder promptly is to be certain that the children will be awake and able to ask the Four Questions. This allows the father to answer their questions, thereby fulfilling the commandment of relating the story of the exodus from Egypt. We use beautiful tableware at the Seder, to symbolize that we are free men and members of spiritual royalty. We also recline during the meal as a symbol of this. In many homes, it is the custom for married men to wear a white robe (known as a *kittel*) at the Seder.

One of the main purposes of the Seder is, as the Haggadah states, "A person is required to consider himself as though he personally went out of Egypt." The Seder night, as well as the entire Festival of Passover, is not merely a commemoration of past historical events (as indeed are all our holidays), but is for us to relive the exodus from Egypt. Just as God redeemed our ancestors from slavery and became their King, so can we utilize the experience of the Seder and what it represents to proclaim our own redemption from the shackles of this transitory world and accept upon ourselves the Kingdom of Heaven.

The Seder plate (*ke'arah*) is placed before the master of the house. It consists of three matzos, *maror* (bitter herbs), *chazeres* (romaine lettuce), *karpas* (greens), *charoses* (a mixture of nuts, apples and wine), and two cooked or roasted foods like a shankbone and an egg. Also, a plate of salt water is left on the table.

The three matzos represent the three categories of Jews — *Kohen*, *Levi*, and *Yisrael*. The *karpas* represents the numerical value of sixty myriads of Israelites who were oppressed with heavy and arduous work in Egypt. The bitter herbs represent the bitterness of slavery suffered in Egypt. It can be represented by either romaine lettuce (which must be carefully examined and cleansed of worms and bugs), freshly ground horseradish, or endive.

The *charoses* mixture is to recall the mortar which our forefathers were forced to work with in Egypt. The shankbone symbolizes the *korban Pesach*, (the Passover sacrifice brought in the Temple). It also symbolizes the "outstretched Hand of God" which He displayed to the Jews of Egypt when He took them out of slavery.

During the course of the Seder we drink four cups of wine, symbolizing the four Divine promises of redemption found in the Torah. If one cannot drink wine, then grape juice is permissible. We read the story of Pesach, the Haggadah, to fulfill the commandment of the Torah, "You shall tell your son on that day." Most important in retelling the story of the exodus from Egypt is showing the two contrasting parts: the bitterness of slavery and the joy of redemption and freedom, discussing the great miracles the Almighty performed.

The special commandments of eating matzah and drinking the four cups of wine are performed while reclining in one's seat. Besides eating the bitter herbs to remind us of the bitter slavery suffered in Egypt, we also make a sandwich of two pieces of matzah with the *maror* inside.

After we finish the meal, the last thing eaten is a piece of the middle matzah, the *afikoman*. Nothing may be eaten after the *afikoman*. In many homes, it is the custom to hide the *afikoman* to keep the children awake. It is also an educational tool that arouses their curiosity, so that they ask questions, thus giving parents the opportunity to tell the children the story of the exodus from Egypt.

❦ HISTORY

THE EXODUS FROM EGYPT (2448/1313 B.C.E.)

When the Jews left Mitzrayim, the Almighty led them with a pillar of fire by night and a cloud by day. As soon as the Jewish people left Egypt, Paroh regretted releasing them. He assembled his whole army, consisting of huge numbers of soldiers and chariots, and pursued the Israelites as far as Yam Suf (the Red Sea). The Egyptians were soon at the heels of the Jews, who were cornered — with no place to go but into the sea. As the Jews were standing at the shores of Yam Suf, watching their enemy draw closer by the minute, they were petrified. Under specific orders from Hashem, Moshe stretched out his rod so that the sea would split.

A man by the name of Nachshon ben Aminadav, imbued with faith in Hashem, stepped forward and jumped into the waters of the Red Sea before they split, fully confident that it would. At the very moment that the waters reached his neck, the sea parted, and the Israelites were able to walk through on dry land. It was their unwavering faith in God that led directly to the miracle that saved the Jewish people.

This is but one of the many examples of Jews standing at the edge of disaster, watching the enemy approaching, and yet, because of their faith in Hashem, surviving intact. The Nefesh Ha-Chaim explained that when in danger, we should have complete faith that Hashem will protect us.

The Egyptians followed them into the sea bed but were thrown into confusion by God. Their chariot wheels became stuck in the wet sand. Then Moshe stretched out his hand over the sea again, and the waters began to flow over the Egyptian army, drowning them, along with their chariots and horses.

LESSON IV

The Miracle of the Red Sea

There are always those who will deny the existence of miracles. They claim that the works of Hashem are simply natural phenomena. This was the attitude that many non-believers assumed in regard to the splitting of the Red Sea. It was caused by an earthquake, they might claim; it was just a freak accident of nature.

To forestall any such beliefs, Hashem magnified the miracle of Yam Suf (the

Red Sea). He split not only the Red Sea, but also all the waters in the world.[7] Even water that was in a cup gravitated to two separate sides! Because of this, no one could deny that the splitting of Yam Suf was a true miracle, a true act of God, just as were all the plagues in Egypt.

A song of triumph, *"Az Yashir"* was sung by Moshe and the Children of Yisrael, in which they praised God's infinite power in destroying the enemy. This song of praise is recited every morning in our prayers, as a testimony to the great miracles God performed when taking us out of Egypt. Every Jew has to regard the miracles done for our ancestors as of direct relevance to us. Every Jew must look upon himself as if he had been delivered from Egypt.[8]

LESSON V

The Importance of Miracles at the Time of the Exodus

The reason that God does not always perform obvious miracles or punish someone immediately after the commission of a sin is that, if He were to do so, man would lose his free will. He would be performing like a robot, manipulated to act in a specified manner. If a Jew were immediately rewarded for observing God's commandments, his reasons for doing them would not be for the purpose of serving God, but rather for the immediate reward. Likewise, if a person were punished every time he committed a sin, he would be like a conditioned animal, performing more like a robot, than like a human with free choice. This is not the man God wished to create. Therefore, punishment and reward cannot always be automatic.

One of the few times that the Almighty deviated from this was when He took us out of slavery in Egypt with spectacular and wondrous miracles. He did so at that time so that the Jews would realize that the Almighty is capable of doing anything and that we owe our allegiance solely to Him.

These miracles were necessary to show the world, and especially the Jews, that God does exist! They now had a clear demonstration that reinforced their belief in God. God introduced Himself to *Am Yisrael* (the People of Israel), showing His power and His might. This is what is referred to as God's "outstretched Hand." This was meant to teach the Jews to have faith in God and to observe His commandments. That is also the reason why throughout the Torah and many of our prayers, reference is made to: "I am the Lord your God, Who took you out of the land of Egypt, from the house of bondage." This theme runs throughout the Bible and our lives.[9]

❧ *Key People, Places and Things*

AFIKOMAN: a piece of the middle matzah, eaten at the conclusion of the Seder, which symbolizes the *korban Pesach.*

AHARON: Aaron, Moshe's older brother, who accompanied him when they appeared before Paroh.

AMRAM: Moshe's father.

ARBA KOSOS: the four cups of wine which are drunk during the Seder, two before and two after the meal.

ARBA KUSHYOS: the Four Questions, asked by the youngest at the Seder.

AVADIM: slaves.

BECHIRAH: free will.

BEDIKAS CHAMETZ: the search for *chametz* conducted on the night before Passover.

BITTUL CHAMETZ: the nullification of possession of any bread or *chametz.*

CHAMETZ: leavened grain products. During Passover all leavened grain products must be excluded from the Jewish home.

CHAROSES: a mixture of apples, nuts and wine, into which the *maror* is dipped st the Seder. It is intended to remind us of the mortar and bricks that the Jewish slaves had to make.

ESER HA-MAKOS: the ten plagues that God brought upon the Egyptians.

HAGGADAH: the narrative recited at the Pesach Seder which recounts the Exodus from Egypt and extols the miracles of God Who redeemed the Jewish people from Egyptian bondage.

HAKARAS HA-TOV: displaying gratitude.

KARPAS: celery; any of several vegetables dipped in salt water at the Seder.

KOS SHEL ELIYAHU: the special cup set aside for the prophet Elijah. Since it is questionable whether one needs four or five cups of wine at the Seder, the *kos shel Eliyahu* is the extra cup.

KRIAS YAM SUF: the miraculous splitting of the Red Sea.

MAKAS BECHOROS: the plague of the death of the (Egyptian) firstborn.

MAROR: the bitter vegetable (for example, lettuce or horseradish) eaten at the Seder to remind us of the bitterness of slavery.

MATZAH SHEMURAH: unleavened bread made from wheat that has been meticulously guarded from the time of its harvest.

MECHIRAS CHAMETZ: the selling of the *chametz.*

MIRYAM: Moshe's sister, who watched her infant brother in his basket on the river and then suggested to Paroh's daughter that she find a Jewish woman (Yocheved) to nurse him.

MITZRAYIM: Egypt, the land where the Jews were enslaved.

NACHSHON BEN AMINADAV: the courageous man who jumped into the Red Sea before it split.

NES (NISSIM): miracle(s).

PAROH: Pharaoh, the wicked ruler of Egypt who enslaved the Jews, persecuted them and steadfastly refused to let them go despite all the plagues that descended on his land.

SEDER: the order of the Pesach night ceremony which recalls the Exodus from Egypt and the liberation from bondage.

YOCHEVED: Moshe's mother.

NOTES

1. *Shemos Rabbah,* 2:2.
2. *Talmud Niddah,* 16b.
3. *Talmud Avodah Zarah,* 11.
4. *Talmud Megillah,* 3.
5. *Talmud Kesubbos,* 62b.
6. Rambam, *Mishneh Torah, Hilchos Berachos,* 1:3.
7. Rashi, *Shemos* 14:21.
8. Haggadah.
9. Ramban, end of *Parashas Bo.*

CHAPTER 6

The Emerging Nation – Preparation for Receiving the Torah
(2448/1313 B.C.E.)

❦ HISTORY

THE JEWS' SONG OF PRAISE (SHIRAH) TO THE ALMIGHTY

After Hashem split the Red Sea, a song of triumph was sung by Moshe and the Children of Yisrael in which they praised Hashem's infinite power and thanked Him for destroying the enemy. This song of triumph, known as "*Az Yashir*," also contains praises which refer to the future, to the great and final deliverance which we will experience in the time of *Mashiach*. It is interesting to note that after the splitting of the sea, when the Jews arrived safely at the shore, the angels in heaven attempted to begin their song of praise. The Almighty refused to grant them permission. "How can I let you sing," He said, "while My creatures are drowning? My mercy includes all beings. Only after My sons say *shirah* will you be allowed to follow suit."

Bnei Yisrael, on the other hand, were given permission to say *shirah* because they had actually experienced miracles and were obliged to thank and praise Hashem.

The women did not sing *shirah* together with the men. Miryam, Moshe's sister, took cymbals in her hand and sang the *shirah* to the women, who repeated it. This was done in the same manner in which Moshe and the men had recited it.

THE JEWS AND THE MANNA

After crossing the Red Sea, the Jews continued marching southwards through the wilderness to a place called Marah (bitterness), so named because of its bitter waters. The people were thirsty and complained to Moshe. God showed him wood and instructed him to throw it into the waters to make them sweet. The Israelites refreshed themselves and then moved on.

Proceeding inland, they entered the wilderness of Sinai one month after their departure from Egypt. The food they had brought with them from Egypt was soon depleted. They became hungry and wished that they had died in Egypt. Hashem made it known that He would cause bread and meat to rain from the heavens for them and would test whether they would obey His law. In the evening, quails came to the camp, and in the morning, the ground was covered with manna. The manna's taste was dependent upon each person's wishes. The Israelites were commanded to gather no more than an *omer* (a measurement of approximately four pints) of manna per person every day. However, on the sixth day, a double portion was to be gathered to provide food for the Shabbos, when no work was permitted. An *omer* of manna was placed in an earthenware jar and kept before the Holy Ark in the *Mishkan* as a testimonial to Hashem's kindness to the Jews in the desert.

LESSON I

The Almighty, Provider of All Our Needs

Every morning, the manna fell from the heavens at the command of Hashem. Every Jew was ordered to collect only a set amount of manna; no amount was to be left over and no extra amounts were to be taken. Whatever manna was left over began to rot and serve as a breeding place for worms. The reason for this was that those who took more than they were told to were exhibiting a lack of faith in Hashem. Hashem had said that this certain amount of manna would be sufficient and that the manna would appear daily. Those who took more indicated that they did not trust His word. They did not believe that the manna would reappear the next day, as they were told.

The Talmud relates that the students of Rabbi Shimon bar Yochai once asked him why the manna had to fall every day. Why couldn't the Almighty cause enough to fall at one time to last for an entire year?[1]

Rabbi Shimon bar Yochai answered by means of a parable about a king who supported his son with a sizeable allowance that he gave him only once a year.

Consequently, the son came to visit his father once a year when his allowance was exhausted. The king, therefore, decided to change his method and provide his son with a daily allowance. In this way, the son had to come visit his father every day.

Similarly, the Almighty provided His children with manna on a daily basis. The head of the family would then worry, "What if no manna will fall tomorrow. What will my children eat? They might perish from hunger." Thus, *Bnei Yisrael* constantly directed their thoughts and prayers to heaven.

After the construction of the *Mishkan* (Tabernacle), Hashem commanded Moshe to tell Aharon to place an *omer* of manna in an earthenware flask and deposit it in front of the Holy Ark. It was to serve as a remembrance of the miraculous manner in which Hashem sustained *Bnei Yisrael* in the desert.

The manna in that flask never melted nor decayed; it remained eternally fresh. The flask was preserved in the *Mishkan* and later in the *Beis Ha-Mikdash* until the time of King Yoshiyahu, who concealed it together with the other precious vessels of the *Beis Ha-Mikdash* before the Temple's destruction. In the future, the prophet Eliyahu will return the flask of manna to its rightful place near the Holy Ark.

The manna serves as an important lesson that it is the Creator alone Who provides food for all creatures. A person's livelihood is in essence gathering the portion that has been decreed for him on the past Rosh Hashanah when everyone's income was determined for the entire year. In our daily prayers, we recite the psalm *"Ashrei"* three times a day. It contains the fundamental verse, *"Pose'ach es Yadecha...* (You [the Almighty] open Your Hand ...)" which must be said with great concentration, for it is the Almighty Who provides us with all of our needs. The Almighty has a tremendous surplus of food in store for us, as He demonstrated with the manna. We must always remember to pray to the Almighty that He bestow upon us His bountiful blessings.

❧ HISTORY

THE JEWS IN THE DESERT

The Jews traveled through the desert to reach the land of Kena'an. At various times during their travels, they complained to Moshe. At Refidim, the people again quarreled with Moshe, complaining about a lack of water. At Hashem's bidding, Moshe struck a rock on nearby Mt. Chorev with the staff he had used in Egypt, and streams of water gushed forth, allowing the people to drink to their hearts' content. The place where this miracle occurred was called Massah-Merivah.

At Refidim, Amalek attacked the Israelites who, led by Yehoshua, fought back. While the war raged, Moshe ascended to the top of the hill holding his staff. He was accompanied by Aharon and Chur, the son of Miryam. Whenever Moshe kept his hands raised, attracting the Jews to look upward to heaven in supplication, the Jews were victorious. When his arms tired, they supported them. The battle lasted until sunset, and Amalek was decisively defeated. Moshe was told to record this incident and impress its occurrence upon Yehoshua, who would lead the Israelites into Kena'an. Because of their treachery in attacking Yisrael, the tribe of Amalek is to be totally destroyed and its memory eradicated.

LESSON II

Forgetting about Hashem's Protection

After the Jews left Egypt, they began journeying through the wilderness. Soon, they began complaining to Moshe that they would have been better off if they had died in Egypt rather than in the desert. One of their complaints was the lack of water to drink. Hashem responded by telling Moshe to hit a rock, which caused water to flow from it.

We can well imagine that Hashem's patience was sorely tried by this incident. Hashem had performed miracle after miracle for the Israelites, and the only way they saw fit to thank Him was to complain! In fact, they said they would rather have died in Egypt. Consequently, Hashem caused Amalek to attack them, as punishment for their not having had full faith in Him.

This is similar to a father who put his son onto his shoulders to protect the boy from the dangers of the road. The two traveled for a distance, and then a man passed them.

"Have you seen my father?" the boy asked the stranger.

Upon hearing this, the father became angry and said, "I have been carrying you all this way, and you didn't even appreciate it, or realize I was there!" As a result, the father threw down his child, and the boy began walking by himself. A moment later, a dog came and bit him.[2]

In the case of *Bnei Yisrael*, the dog was the tribe of Amalek, who attacked the ungrateful son (*Bnei Yisrael*) of the unappreciated father (Hashem).

The Jews certainly have much for which to be eternally grateful to Hashem. It would be extremely disastrous for us to be unappreciative and complain to Hashem about what we do not have. If we should take such an attitude, the dogs of punishment could swiftly be upon us.

ETHICS I

Modesty

One of Moshe's outstanding qualities was his modesty. Anyone else might have leaped at the chance to become the powerful leader of the Jewish people, but Moshe declined the honor several times before he finally agreed to accept. He actually believed that he was not worthy of this great honor and that others could fill the post much better than he. It was, however, because of his humility and lack of arrogance that Hashem considered Moshe fit to be a leader of Yisrael.

When the Almighty spoke to Moshe for the first time, He did not appear to him from the lofty peaks of a mountain. He chose to appear to Moshe from a thorn bush, a seemingly insignificant creation. Hashem thereby wanted to point out that even the humblest of men

can make history if filled with God's spirit. In addition, Hashem demonstrated that He empathized with the Children of Yisrael, who were at that time suffering as lowly slaves. So He appeared in a thorn bush, to emphasize His understanding of their plight.

The Midrash states that when Hashem decided to give the Torah to the Jews, all the angels representing the mountains of the desert vied with each other for the honor of being the site for this great event. Each considered itself the most fitting setting for the giving of the Torah. Only one mountain, Mount Sinai, did not make any such claim. It felt itself unworthy of being selected for such greatness. Yet, when Hashem made His decision, He chose Mount Sinai, a lowly site, for the transmission of the Torah. In this manner, God demonstrated to all of mankind the importance of modesty and humility, in contrast to overbearing self-confidence and pride. This is certainly the path preached in the Torah.

Modesty has been a leading characteristic of many great rabbis throughout the ages. Once, the renowned Torah giants Rabbi Akiva Eiger and Rav Ya'akov of Lisa were traveling together to a certain town by horse-drawn coach. As they approached the town, they noticed a large group of Jews, apparently waiting to honor the visitors. A few people began pushing the coach. Rabbi Akiva Eiger, noting the crowd, immediately assumed that they had come to pay tribute to Rabbi Ya'akov. He therefore slipped out of the coach and began to help push the coach to its destination. At the very same time, Rabbi Ya'akov came to the conclusion that the crowds had gathered to honor Rabbi Akiva Eiger, so he, too, slipped out of the coach and joined in pushing it. When the coach reached the crowd, the people were amazed to find it empty and the two Torah giants themselves walking alongside and pushing it! It was then that the people learned that each man had considered only the other worthy of honor, while feeling that he himself could not be the cause of any tributes. Naturally, this display of modesty by both rabbis only made the populace respect them all the more.

❦ HISTORY

PREPARATIONS FOR MATAN TORAH

On the first day of the third month (*Sivan*) after they had departed from Egypt, the Jews arrived in the wilderness of Sinai and camped in front of the mountain. On the second day Moshe ascended the mountain and heard the voice of God instructing him to remind the people of how He had delivered them from Egypt. If they obeyed Him, they would be transformed into a "kingdom of priests and a holy nation." Moshe descended from the mountain and repeated God's words to the Elders and to the people. A united nation responded, "All that the Lord has spoken we will do!"

Moshe reported these words to Hashem and was told that God would manifest His presence in a thick cloud and speak to him before the entire assembly of Jews. That way, His Divine mission would never again be doubted. The people were to prepare themselves for three days, in anticipation of the great event of the acceptance of the Torah. They were not to touch the boundaries placed around the mountain, under penalty of death.

MITZVAH

Sefiras Ha-Omer

It is a positive commandment to count seven complete weeks from the day the Jews brought the *omer* sacrifice. The counting begins from the second night of Passover and continues every night thereafter until Shavuos, which is the fiftieth day.

The purpose of freeing the Jewish nation from Mitzrayim was to give them the Torah, an event which took place fifty days later. Just as a slave counts the days left until he is to be completely freed from his master, so, too, do we count how many days have passed from Pesach until the giving of the Torah, which took place fifty days later.

(1) Each night from the second night of Pesach through the night preceding Shavuos, one must count the *omer*. The blessing "...*al sefiras ha-omer*" is recited before the counting.

(2) In counting the *omer*, one counts the days and the weeks. For example, on the 32nd day, one says, "Today is thirty-two days which is four weeks and four days to the *omer*." One must understand what he is saying in order to fulfill the mitzvah of counting the *omer*. If one does not understand Hebrew, he should count the *omer* in a language that he does understand.

(3) For thirty-three days during the period of *sefiras ha-omer*, it is customary to observe certain aspects of mourning.

This is to commemorate the tragic deaths of Rabbi Akiva's students during this time (in about 130 C.E.). Therefore, weddings, concerts, parties at which there is musical entertainment, and taking haircuts or shaving are generally prohibited during this period.

(4) There are different customs concerning when this thirty-three day period of partial mourning is observed.

(a) Some observe this period from the second day of Pesach until Lag Ba-Omer (the thirty-third day of the *omer*) and all mourning ceases on Lag Ba-Omer. It was on this day that the plague that had killed thousands of Rabbi Akiva's students suddenly stopped. It has therefore been observed as a day of joy ever since. All festivities usually forbidden during the days after Pesach are permitted on Lag Ba-Omer.

(b) Some begin the mourning period on the first day of *Rosh Chodesh Iyar* and observe the mourning period until the morning of the third day of *Sivan*, except for Lag Ba-Omer.

(c) Some observe mourning for the entire *omer* period.

(5) If Lag Ba-Omer falls on a Sunday, the custom is to permit haircuts on Friday in honor of Shabbos.

(6) Weddings are permitted on Lag Ba-Omer.

❦ HISTORY

THE NATIONS OF THE WORLD REFUSED THE TORAH

A Chosen People is really a choosing people. We chose to become God's

People and accepted all the responsibility that comes with it. In order to give all of mankind the option of living according to the Torah's precepts, Hashem first offered the Torah to each nation in the world.

Hashem first approached the nation of Edom and asked, "Will you accept the Torah as the basis of your lifestyle?"

"What does the Torah contain?" asked the Edomites.

"One commandment is, 'You shall not kill.'"

"No killing?" was the response. "But our entire existence is based on the permissibility of killing. We kill to live, and live to kill! If the Torah forbids killing, we cannot accept it."

God then asked the nation of Yishmael if it would be willing to receive the Torah. "What does the Torah contain?" asked Yishmael.

"The Torah states, 'You shall not steal.'"

"If that is so," replied Yishmael, "then we cannot possibly accept the Torah. If we cannot steal, then we will starve. Take the Torah and give it to some other nation."

And so it went, down the line. Nation after nation refused to accept the Torah, for they could not agree to live according to its laws. Finally, God approached the nation of Israel: "Will you accept My Torah?"

The Jews' response of "*Na'aseh v'nishma*" ("We will observe and we will hear") was immediate and enthusiastic.

LESSON III

The Mission of the Jewish People

The Torah makes it clear that man was created for a specific purpose: To emulate God's righteousness on earth. God then chose one specific nation to especially pursue this mission. The Chosen People would act as God's model nation on earth, demonstrating to the rest of mankind how to behave properly. This nation was the Jewish people.

By becoming God's Chosen People, the Jews accepted certain responsibilities. On an individual level, they would have to:

(a) accept and worship God as the One and only All-Powerful God; and

(b) observe the 613 mitzvos (precepts) of the Torah, as well as the extensions of these laws devised by the Sages.

On a national level, all Jews were to create a community of God as a model of righteousness for other nations to emulate. This would mean more than just a collection of good individuals. It would establish an entire culture devoted to God.

The most important task for the Jewish nation to fulfill is stated in the Torah: "Now, therefore, if you will obey My voice and keep My covenant, then you will be to Me a select portion above all nations, for the earth is Mine. And you shall be unto Me a kingdom of leaders and a holy nation." God tells us that in order for the Jews to be the Chosen People they must first be a holy nation.

The term "holy" as used in the Torah is really made up of two related themes which comprise the true meaning of the Torah. First, holy means to be separate, removed and distinct. In order for Yisrael to be holy, it must be a nation set apart from the others with its own unique way of life. This unique lifestyle must be all-pervasive, encompassing every aspect of life. The second theme of holiness is dedication to Hashem which leads to perfection. Only by devoting ourselves to Hashem's Torah and adhering to its mitzvos, can we accomplish this mission.

The Jews are like royal princes whose behavior reflects on the King and who therefore must act with greater caution. Today, too, when an advisor or special assistant to the president errs, it is greatly magnified by the public and the press. It brings disgrace both to that advisor and the president whom he is supposed to serve. Similarly, Jews who do not live up to the standards set by the Torah and who behave irresponsibly cause a lessening of God's esteem in the eyes of mankind. The mitzvos are special commitments and commandments, given only to the Jewish people. Other nations are not required to uphold them. Among other mitzvos, the Jews were told to abstain from working on Shabbos and from eating non-kosher foods. They were expected to maintain a higher level of moral purity.

ETHICS II

Honoring One's Father and Mother

The fifth of the Ten Commandments states: "Honor your father and mother, that your days may be prolonged upon the land which the Lord your God gives you."[3]

The Ten Commandments are divided into two groups. The first five commandments comprise laws of relationships between man and God, while the last five apply to laws of relationships between man and his fellowman. This dichotomy is clear-cut in all respects but one. The law to honor one's father and mother is included in the first grouping, which deals with man-to-God relationships, rather than those of man-to-man. The answer is that whoever honors his parents honors God, because he indicates a willingness to accept authority and to carry on the Jewish tradition. On the other hand, those who reject their parents' authority will tend to deny God's authority and will not continue the chain of tradition. Therefore, honoring one's parents becomes a law pertaining to one's relationship with God. As the Sages teach, whenever a person honors his parents, it is as if he has brought down the Divine Presence to him and honors God Himself.

We see that even an evil person like Esav earned great merit for the exemplary respect he showed his father. Though Rivkah recognized Ya'akov's superiority over Esav, Yitzchak lacked this insight. He was misled by Esav's practice of *kibbud av*, honoring his father, and as a result he did not discern Esav's true character. He thought that Esav was just as scrupulous in observing all mitzvos as he was in showing respect to his parents. This shows the power of *kibbud av*, for it could make Yitzchak believe that even one as degenerate as Esav was an honorable person.

If Esav, for all his wickedness, still was careful to honor his parents, then how can we claim to be good Jews if we fail to do the same?

To appreciate the lengths to which one should go in order to practice *kibbud av v'em* (honoring one's father and mother), one should remember the story of Dama, a non-Jew. Dama's father had a precious diamond which he kept under his pillow for safekeeping. One day, while his father was asleep, some businessmen came to Dama's house and asked to buy the diamond. Dama replied that he could not obtain the diamond, for to do so he would have to wake his father and he did not want to do this. The men offered greater and greater sums of money, but Dama still refused to disturb his father. Finally, in desperation, the men left and Dama lost his chance to make a fortune. Yet, for his devotion to his father, Dama received a just reward. Within his herd was born a *parah adumah*, a totally red cow, needed by Jews for purification purposes in the time of the *Beis Ha-Mikdash*. Such a red cow was extremely rare and very valuable. Dama was able to sell it at a very high price.[4]

If Esav and Dama could show such concern for their parents, certainly so should we.

Many stories are related about how our Sages honored their parents.

One day, Rabbi Abbahu asked his son, Rabbi Avimi, for some water to drink. Rabbi Avimi brought the water, but his father had fallen asleep. He stood next to his father with the water in his hand the entire time, until the latter awoke.

A man once came to Rabbi Chaim Soloveitchik of Brisk with the following question: His father had become ill in a distant city and he felt obligated to take a trip to visit him. However, since the law of *kibbud av v'em* (honoring one's parents) does not require a person to spend his own money to honor his father, and the train trip would cost him money, was he still obligated to go?

Rav Chaim's sharp reply was, "True, you aren't obligated to spend your own money on a train. Walk!"

When Rabbi Leib of Kelm was a young man he once came home very late at night from the yeshivah where he had been studying. His parents were already sleeping and he didn't have a key with him. In order not to awaken them, he remained in the street all night despite the extreme cold.

❧ Key People, Places and Things

AM KADOSH: a Holy Nation.

AM SEGULAH: a Chosen Nation.

ASERES HA-DIBROS: the Ten Commandments.

KIBBUD AV V'EM: honoring one's father and mother.

LAG BA-OMER: the thirty-third day of the *omer*, which is celebrated as a special day.

MATAN TORAH: the Giving of the Torah.

SEFIRAS HA-OMER: the counting of the forty-nine days between Pesach and Shavuos.

NOTES

1. *Talmud Yoma,* 76.
2. *Rashi, Shemos* 17:8.
3. *Shemos* 20:12.
4. *Talmud Kiddushin,* 36.

CHAPTER 7

The Giving of the Torah
(2448/1313 B.C.E.)

❦ HISTORY

THE GIVING OF THE TEN COMMANDMENTS

After the three days of preparation for *Mattan Torah* (the Giving of the Torah), on the sixth of *Sivan* thunder and lightning erupted and a dense cloud descended on Mount Sinai. The call of the trumpet was heard and Moshe brought the people to the foot of the mountain. Hashem summoned Moshe to its summit and told him to warn the Jews not to ascend the mountain.

Thereafter, the supreme moment in the history of the world occurred. The voice of God Himself was heard by every man, woman, and child throughout the world as He declared to the Jews the foundation of religious and moral conduct for all time:

1. I am the Lord your God Who delivered you from the land of Egypt....
2. You shall have no other gods before Me....
3. You shall not take the name of the Lord your God in vain....
4. Remember the Sabbath day to keep it holy....
5. Honor your father and your mother....
6. You shall not murder.
7. You shall not commit adultery.
8. You shall not steal.
9. You shall not bear false witness against your neighbor.
10. You shall not covet your neighbor's house....

The people were so awed and frightened by all they had witnessed that they withdrew from the mountain and pleaded with Moshe to speak to them in God's stead. Hashem allowed Moshe to do so.

Moshe then returned to the mountain and received a series of laws from God dealing with important aspects of Divine worship and the prohibition of idolatry.

LESSON I

The Giving of the Torah and the Establishment of the Jewish Nation

It was the exodus from Egypt and the accompanying miracles that make Judaism unique among all other religions. Other faiths began with a single individual who claimed to have a special message and gradually amassed a following. His followers then spread the word and gathered converts, until a new religion was born. Virtually every world religion follows this pattern with the exception of Judaism. God gathered an entire nation, three million strong, to the foot of Mount Sinai, and proclaimed His message. Every man, woman and child heard God's voice proclaiming the Ten Commandments. A permanent bond was thus forged between God and the Children of Yisrael. This unique event remained deeply imprinted in the soul of Yisrael, and, throughout history, it was something that was not to be forgotten. It marked the beginning of the Jewish nation, of God's Chosen People. We are therefore commanded to remember the Giving of the Torah at Sinai.

Although we have always been numerically insignificant, a very small nation, we have compiled a record of achievements and a rich history while surviving all attempts to assimilate and destroy us. We are successful because Hashem selected us to be His Chosen Nation. We are carefully nurtured by God to blossom as His select creation — provided we act properly.

A king once owned a beautiful, carefully tended orchard which he leased to a tenant farmer. After a while, he decided to visit the old orchard. He was shocked when he saw that the orchard had not been properly cared for and that it was no longer a thing of beauty.

"Destroy everything!" the outraged monarch decreed.

Then, as his men were setting out to work, the king came upon a single rose. It was a fragile thing, but its fragrance wafted through the air, and its beauty brightened the earth. The king was overwhelmed. His anger disappeared.

"Stop!" he now ordered. "I don't want the garden razed after all. If it can produce so beautiful a flower, it should be preserved."

Just as the whole garden was saved for the sake of that one flower, so, too, for the sake of the Chosen Nation, the whole universe will be saved.

The expression "Chosen People" is not intended to be used as an indication of superiority or eliteness, but rather implies a sense of responsibility to God and to mankind.[1]

LESSON II

The Torah and What It Consists Of

The Torah is Hashem's legacy to the Jews and to the world. The word "Torah" is derived from the Hebrew root meaning "to teach." The Torah is replete with God's teachings of justice and morality. It is the comprehensive blueprint for a proper Jewish society.[2]

The Torah was transmitted to the Jewish people at Mount Sinai, an act that signified the birth of Yisrael as a nation with a purpose. The Torah is therefore, in a sense, the constitution of the Jewish people. But it is a constitution devised by God rather than by man.

The Torah consists of two complementary parts: the *Torah she-b'Kesav* (Written Torah) and the *Torah she-b'Al Peh* (Oral Torah). The written Torah consists of the Five Books of the Pentateuch: Genesis (*Bereshis*), Exodus (*Shemos*), Leviticus (*Vayikra*), Numbers (*Bemidbar*), and Deuteronomy (*Devarim*). These show the development of the Nation, from the Creation of the world through the death of Moshe, when the Jews were about to enter the Holy Land. They also contain the codes and beliefs that are basic to Judaism. The events of the Five Books of the Torah are followed up in the books known as the Prophets (*Nevi'im*) and Writings (*Kesuvim*), describing the Jews' history from the leadership of Yehoshua to the building of the Second Temple. These books also contain the concepts that are fundamental to Jewish theology. The three sections of the Written Torah — *Torah, Nevi'im, Kesuvim* — are together referred to as the *Tanach*.

❦ HISTORY

THE TORAH'S TRUTH

The single most momentous and important historical event in the long history of the Jews was the Divine revelation at Mount Sinai. God Himself spoke to the entire nation of Yisrael and established firmly the Jews' complete faith and trust in Moshe. The great spiritual uplifting produced by the direct hearing of God's words deeply instilled in the soul of Yisrael an absolute trust in God and His Torah.

Also, certain facts and predictions that were written and later substantiated are a testimony to the eternal truth of the Torah. Would a mere man have the audacity to state that only three species of animal — camel, hare, and *shafan* — chew their cud but do not have split hooves, and that only a pig has split hooves and does not chew its cud? Wouldn't he have been afraid that some species of which he was not aware could also possess those traits? Only God could know this.

How could the Torah comfortably predict that if the Jews would not keep the Commandments, their Sanctuary would be destroyed and they would be dispersed throughout the world? What if it didn't come true? The fact that the Torah made these predictions indicates that only Hashem could have been the force behind it.

As for the claim that Moshe composed the Torah by himself — would the Torah present Moshe as an individual with faults and a physical deformity? If this were so, would he have originated laws without any obvious reasons? Would he have chosen Yehoshua rather than his own sons to succeed him as leader? Why would he have denied his fellow tribesmen, the *Leviyim* (Levites), a permanent portion of the Holy Land?

If Moshe wrote the Torah, why would the Torah declare and reiterate that he was sternly rebuked by God and punished and prohibited from entering the land of Kena'an, despite all his prayers and pleadings? Why would it write that Aharon, his brother, was sharply censured by God because of the episode of the Golden Calf? Why would the Torah recall the episodes of the Golden Calf, the complainers, the spies, the rebellion of Korach, the incident with the daughters of Mo'av — all of which cast a bad light upon the Jewish people?

This is a testimony to the authenticity of the Torah and its truthfulness. It proves that none of the criticisms which emanated from God were concealed or altered.

LESSON III

The Importance of the Torah

The Torah is the foundation of Judaism; without it, Judaism cannot and does not exist. Jews consider the Torah an all-inclusive "Blueprint for Life." It offers practical advice on establishing a humane society. Nothing is beyond the scope of the Torah. A *mishnah* in *Pirkei Avos*[3] summarizes the Torah's value: "Delve in it again and again, for everything is in it." The Torah is God's wisdom revealed to man. Without it, the Jews would have floundered, as yet another lost nomadic tribe in the Middle East. With it, the Jews can act as God's people.

The centrality of the Torah in a Jew's life can be better understood by compar-

ing it to a newly invented intricate computer. The inventor would undoubtedly provide precise operating instructions for such a complex and expensive machine. The customer would not be able to use the machine without thoroughly studying the instructions.

Life is infinitely more complex than any computer. Would it make sense to say that there is no instruction book? Clearly, if something manmade requires directions for the user, then life, which is given by God, certainly requires instructions for its usage. The Torah is the "instruction book" for this world.

ETHICS I

The Torah's Ethical Teachings

The Torah is God's wisdom revealed to man. The first Five Books of the Torah contain inspirational episodes, and ex-

plain the origins of the Jewish nation. They depict role models for Jews in the persons of Avraham, Yitzchak, Ya'akov,

Moshe, Pinchas, and the Matriarchs — Sarah, Rivkah, Rachel and Leah — and other righteous individuals. The Torah provides us with practical advice on establishing a world with ethical teachings.

The Torah is neither a history book nor a chronicle of some ancient heritage. Rather, it is a blueprint for behavior between man and his fellowman, man and the universe, man and his Maker. This absorption of the Torah's dynamics attunes the individual to a keen awareness of self, others, the universe, and, of course, God. By living and thinking by the principles of the Torah, one can develop into a special individual who radiates goodness through his speech and conduct. One therefore finds numerous accounts of how Torah-inspired personalities have inspired others for the good. This was accomplished not through pressure or proselytizing, but merely by examples set by their daily activities and behavior. Their lifestyle, even more than their teachings, became the most profound statement of the ideology and religion by which they lived.

A classic example is the Chafetz Chaim, the leading Jewish sage of the early twentieth century. For a short time he was the proprietor of a small grocery store which his wife managed. All their customers were greatly impressed with their honesty and the high quality of the merchandise. Anything that was even partially spoiled was immediately removed from stock. All the weights and measures were accurate, and prices were set according to strict Torah law. Because of his integrity, the residents of Radin flocked to his store. Instead of being pleased with this success, however, the Chafetz Chaim was worried that he might be taking away business from others, and he kept the store closed in the afternoon.

The Chafetz Chaim once had to testify in a Polish court as a character witness on behalf of a student who was falsely accused of a crime. After the Chafetz Chaim testified that his student's integrity was beyond reproach, the student's lawyer told the judge, "I would like to give the court a glimpse of the greatness of this rabbi. A thief once stole something from him, and he pursued him shouting, 'It's yours! I forgive you!' in order that the thief should not be guilty of sinning because of him."

The judge was skeptical, and asked the lawyer, "Do you really believe that story?"

"True, I did not personally witness it," replied the lawyer. "But, your honor, people do not relate such stories about you and me."

Another story is told of a certain young man who was questioning whether it was worthwhile for him to continue learning Torah. It was suggested that he consult the great sage, the Chafetz Chaim. He agreed to base his final decision on his encounter with the Chafetz Chaim.

When the young man entered the Chafetz Chaim's house, he saw him tearfully pacing, reciting Psalms. Inquiring about the source of the Chafetz Chaim's distress, he was told that a stranger whose relative was ill had come to ask the Chafetz Chaim to pray for his recovery.

Overwhelmed by this manifestation of love for a fellow Jew who was a complete stranger, the young man realized that only the study of Torah can cultivate such powerful compassion, and he be-came a disciple of the Chafetz Chaim.

Shavuos

Shavuos (Feast of Weeks) is celebrated on the sixth day of *Sivan*. This Festival is observed to commemorate the giving of the Torah on Mount Sinai seven weeks after Pesach, and to remind us of the first fruit offerings that were brought to the Temple as a thanksgiving offering of the early harvest. It is therefore also called *Chag Ha-Bikkurim* (holiday of the first fruits).

During this Festival, both the synagogue and the home are decorated with green branches as a symbol of the harvest season and to remind us of the greenery surrounding Mount Sinai when we received the Torah.

Shavuos is thus the culmination of the Festival of Pesach. The freedom the Jews had gained on Pesach would have been meaningless if it were not fashioned and guarded by the Torah, which they received on Shavuos.

THE LAWS AND CUSTOMS OF SHAVUOS:

There is a custom to remain awake the first night of Shavuos and study the Torah, to commemorate the receiving of the Torah, which the Jews awaited so eagerly.

There are special additions to the prayers on this holiday. They include saying *Akdamus*, which praises God, and reading the Book of Ruth. The reason we read the Book of Ruth on Shavuos is that Ruth gave up royalty, honor and wealth to become an observant Jewess. She then had a major impact on Jewish history because she was the ancestor of the royal House of David. Because she showed dedication, self-sacrifice and determination to be part of God's Chosen Nation, her reward was having a permanent influence on the lives of the Jewish people.

Moshe was astonished to hear of the special honor accorded a *ger* (convert), that he is grouped together with the *leviyim* when mentioned in the Torah. Hashem answered Moshe, "How much did I toil for the Israelites? I took them out of Egypt and lit their path through the wilderness. I brought them manna and fed them quails. I provided them with water and surrounded them with Clouds of Glory. Then they accepted My Torah. In contrast, this *ger* came to Me of his own free will and accepted the commandments of the Torah, without having benefited from any miracles. Should he not be considered at least the equal of a *levi?"*

❦ HISTORY

THE ORAL AND THE WRITTEN TORAH

The second part of the Torah is the Oral Torah, called *Torah she-b'Al Peh*. It consists of the teachings and interpretations which were communicated orally to Moshe as a supplement and explanation of the Written

Torah. However, unlike the *Torah she-b'Kesav* (the Written Torah), which was by definition always in written form, the Oral Torah was originally transmitted orally from one generation to another in an unbroken chain of continuity, until it was finally written down. This unbroken chain of tradition is called *mesorah*. The oral transfer from generation to generation was done so that the Jews would devote more time to examining the Torah carefully with others. It ensured their learning the law from an expert who could explain it in the proper way.

It was only when the Oral Torah was in danger of being forgotten, because of adverse conditions, that Rabbi Yehudah Ha-Nasi began to arrange it in written form. His endeavors became the six orders of the Mishnah, which were completed around 3948 (188 C.E.). Explanations of, and commentaries on, the Mishnah were compiled by succeeding rabbis, and are known as the Gemara. The combined text of the Mishnah and Gemara is often termed the Talmud. There are two editions of the Talmud: the *Talmud Bavli* (Babylonian Talmud), compiled by Rav Ashi in Babylonia, and the *Talmud Yerushalmi* (Jerusalem Talmud), compiled by Rabbi Yochanan in Eretz Yisrael. Those who have delved into the study of Talmud know that it is an unparalleled composite of practical law, philosophical discussion, logical arguments, and moralistic stories. It is no wonder that the Talmud has intrigued scholars for centuries, and has remained the mainstay of the Jewish people.

The Talmud states that Hashem concluded His covenant with Yisrael for the sake of the Oral Law. The Written Torah without the interpretations furnished by the Oral Law is often unintelligible. The commandments in the Torah are often briefly worded in very general terms. The Oral tradition supplies the details necessary for proper observance. For example, the Written Torah states that one must wear *tefillin* on the arm and on the forehead. However, what the *tefillin* are supposed to contain and look like are not stated. It is the Oral Law which furnishes the information about *tefillin* and tells us what it actually means. It is the Oral tradition which assists us in arriving at the true meaning of God's laws. Thus, the key to understanding the Torah is the Oral tradition handed down from the time of Moshe and embodied in the Talmud and Midrash.

LESSON IV

Torah Is Eternal

Just as God is eternal, so, too, is His Torah. This is a basic foundation of our faith — to believe in the eternal authority of the Torah. It is written in the Torah,

"Things that are revealed belong to us and to our children forever."[4]

Just as Hashem Himself does not change, so the Torah, which is His eternal testimony to Yisrael, cannot be changed.

For over 3,000 years the Torah has been kept by the Jewish people because it embraces the depths and heights of human nature. The principles of the Torah occasionally may be quite different from values found in contemporary society, or they may appear to be irrelevant to our times. However, while contemporary values are of human origin and are transient, those of the Torah are Divine and eternal. It is taught that when King Shelomo, the greatest genius of all time, presumed that certain commandments did not apply to him, God said, "A thousand like Shelomo will pass away, but not a single dot of the Torah will be changed."

LESSON V

Everyone Is Required to Learn the Torah

The Talmud tells us that every Jew is required to learn the Torah. The Midrash *Eichah* teaches us, "If they tell you there is Torah among the nations, do not believe them," for as Moshe taught us concerning the Torah, "It is your distinct form of wisdom and understanding in the eyes of the nations."

The Talmud relates that every Jew, after his life in this world is ended, will be brought before the Heavenly Tribunal. There he will be asked, "Why did you neglect Torah study, which is the primary occupation of every Jew?"

The pauper will defend himself, saying, "What should I have done? I had to support my family. How would we have lived had I studied Torah?"

"Who was poorer, you or Hillel?" will be the reply. "Hillel earned next to nothing, a *trepika* (small coin) a day. Yet he spent half of it to pay the guard at the door of the *beis ha-midrash* (house of study) and thus gain entrance, while the remainder had to provide for the needs of his family. One day, when he had no money and was not admitted, he climbed up to the roof of the adjoining building to hear the words of Torah from the mouths of Shemayah and Avtalyon. It was a cold winter day and the snow began to fall. The next morning, which was on Shabbos, Shemayah and Avtalyon noticed that the *beis ha-midrash* was dark. Looking up to the roof, they saw the frozen figure of a man on the skylight. They took him down, washed him, put oil on him, and revived him by the fire. 'This man is truly worthy of having the Shabbos profaned for his sake!' they proclaimed.

"If Hillel could do it, why not you?"

When questioned about his lack of Torah learning, the well-to-do businessman will come forward and excuse himself, saying, "What could I do? I had to keep my business going. I was unable to study any more Torah than I actually did."

The reply to this will be, "Are you wealthier than Rabbi Eliezer ben Charsom was? Rabbi Eliezer owned a thousand villages and a thousand ships, but he never knew what they looked like. He did not want to take the time to inspect his various properties because he preferred to spend day and night studying Torah. His own servants did not know their master. When they once saw him pass by, they thought he was a laborer, and they forced him to go to work. When they realized who he was, they let him go. If he could do it, why not you?"

Someone who was a slave to his desires will be asked, "What stopped you from learning Torah?"

"What should I have done?" he will excuse himself. "I am handsome and was unable to control my passions. Life is full of pleasures! How could I pass them up to study Torah?"

"Your excuse is not acceptable," he will be told. "Are you more handsome than Yosef? Potifar's wife tempted him daily, changing her clothes three times a day, but nevertheless, he overcame his *yetzer ha-ra* (evil inclination). Why couldn't you take an example from Yosef?"[5]

ETHICS II

Justice and Honesty

Right after enumerating the Ten Commandments, the Torah lists the basic body of civil laws, or *mishpatim*, which is founded on the principles of justice and honesty. *Mishpatim* and the Ten Commandments are juxtaposed to teach us that they are both essential parts of being a Jew. Whereas the Ten Commandments provide the foundation of all laws, they are especially designed to strengthen the Jewish society, of which justice and honesty are critical elements.

To be a good Jew, one must follow the civil laws that protect the moral fiber of man and society. They help regulate relationships between men, encouraging truthfulness, sincerity and kindness, while condemning immorality and deceit. They emphasize that it is not enough to follow laws that pertain to man and God, but it is also necessary to observe those laws between man and his fellowman.

There are Jews who claim to be observant but do not follow these laws. We must realize that some people who call themselves observant nevertheless act improperly. This indicates the existence of problems with the person rather than with the Torah itself. These people are not living up to the high Torah ideals, but are rather falling prey to the impulses of pride, greed, envy and hate. There is no excuse for such behavior. Those who present themselves to the world as religious Jews have a special obligation to create a positive image of themselves and be considerate of others. They must go out of their way to perform acts of kindness and to avoid corruption and greed. If they succumb, then they will be used as an excuse for those who downplay religion. This is tantamount to a *chillul Hashem* (profanation of God's Holy Name).[6]

A person who exemplified the appropriate level of honesty was Rabbi Pinchas ben Ya'ir, who lived in ancient Yisrael. He was extremely careful to be honest in dealing with his fellowmen. It happened once that two poor men, who came to seek a livelihood in that region, stopped at his house and left a small amount of barley seed in his care. They left, and failed to reclaim the seeds. A long period of time elapsed and still they failed to show up. In their absence, Rabbi Pinchas planted, sowed and reaped the barley year after year and stored all the proceeds in the barn.

Seven years later, the two men happened to pass by Rabbi Pinchas' home, and they suddenly remembered the seeds they had left there. "Please return the seeds to us, if you still happen to have them," they told Rabbi Pinchas. Instead of giving them a few seeds, Rabbi Pinchas led them to the barn and opened the doors. Noting their surprise, he told them, "It is all yours. Now go and bring donkeys and camels and take away your treasure."[7]

Rabbi Pinchas ben Ya'ir could easily have given the men a few seeds and kept the barley all for himself. However, Rabbi Pinchas wanted to be scrupulously honest in his dealings.

In the years before World War II and prior to his coming to America, the late revered Rav Ya'akov Kamenetsky was rabbi of a small Jewish community in eastern Europe. One of his congregants once came to ask him what to do about the following situation. A clerk in the post office had obviously made a mathematical error in the Jew's favor. Should he return the money to the clerk or just forget about it?

Rav Ya'akov told him that he must return it immediately. He had made it clear to his congregation on several occasions that absolute honesty was necessary when dealing with one's fellowman — Jew or gentile.

The man returned to the post office and pointed out the error to the clerk. The latter, who prided himself on his mathematical ability, at first could not believe that he had made a mistake. Then he could not believe that a Jew was honest enough to bring it to his attention. The clerk decided that he would deliberately make similar errors with more of the post office's Jewish clients. Each time, the Jew would return the money to the clerk and point out his error.

During World War II, when the Poles, Ukrainians, Lithuanians, and others joined forces with the Nazis in the extermination of their Jewish neighbors, that post office clerk was the only one in his town who helped save Jewish lives!

❦ Key People, Places and Things

GEMARA: explanation and commentaries on the Mishnah (together they comprise the Talmud), compiled by the rabbis in Babylonia and Eretz Yisrael.

GER: a convert. Among the great converts to Judaism were Ruth (ancestress of King David), and Unkelos, who wrote a well-known Aramaic translation of the Torah.

KESUVIM: Hagiographia, the third division of the Bible including the works of King David, King Shelomo, etc.

LELAMED TORAH: to teach Torah.

LILMOD TORAH: to learn Torah.

MEGILLAS RUTH: the Book of Ruth, the holy book (from *Kesuvim*) read on Shavuos that describes the life of the convert, Ruth, the ancestress of King David.

MESORAH: the unbroken chain of Oral Law from Moshe *Rabbenu* until today.

MIDDOS: (positive) character traits.

MIDRASH: a collection of non-literal interpretations and homiletic teachings of the Sages.

MISHNAH: a portion of the Oral Law, written and compiled by Rabbi Yehudah Ha-Nasi, and consisting of six orders.

MISHPAT: justice.

NEVI'IM: the Books of the Prophets, the second division of the Bible.

SEFER: a religious book.

SHAVUOS: the Festival that celebrates the Giving of the Torah at Mount Sinai. First fruits were brought to Yerushalayim for Shavuos, one of the three pilgrimage Festivals.

SHELOSHES YEMAI HAGBALAH: the three days of preparation prior to Shavuos.

TALMID CHACHAM: a Torah scholar.

TANACH: the Hebrew acronym for the three divisions of the Bible: *Torah, Nevi'im,* and *Kesuvim.*

TORAH: the Written and the Oral Law, the instruction and guidance book of the Jewish People. The word "Torah" is often used to denote just the Five Books of Moshe, the first division of the Bible.

TORAH SHE-B'AL PEH: the Oral Torah.

TORAH SHE-B'KESAV: the Written Torah.

NOTES

1. *Shir Ha-Shirim Rabbah*, 2.

2. *Bereshis Rabbah*, 1:1.

3. *Pirkei Avos*, 5:22.

4. *Devarim* 29:38.

5. *Talmud Yoma*, 35b.

6. Rambam, *Mishneh Torah, Yesodei Ha-Torah*, 5:11.

7. *Talmud Bava Metzia*, 28b.

CHAPTER 8

The Special Obligations of the Jews;
the Sin of the Golden Calf; the Mishkan; Shabbos
(2448 – 2449/1313 B.C.E – 1312 B.C.E.)

❧ HISTORY

THE GOLDEN CALF (2448/1313 B.C.E.)

Moshe had been on Mount Sinai for forty days and forty nights, and the people, fearing that he would never return, clamored for a visible object which they could venerate. They persuaded Aharon to fashion a molten image of a golden calf out of their golden jewelry. They brought burnt offerings to this idol, around which they sang and danced. God's anger was aroused by this idolatry and He sent Moshe down from the mountain, informing him of Yisrael's sin and declaring that He would destroy this treacherous nation. Moshe entreated the Almighty to be merciful and not give the Egyptians the opportunity to gloat over the Israelites' misfortune. He asked Hashem to be merciful also because of His eternal covenant with the Patriarchs. On hearing this plea, Hashem granted the people a new lease on life.

Moshe descended from the mountain on the seventeenth day of the Hebrew month of *Tammuz*, bringing with him the two stone Tablets of the Law, engraved by God. He then heard the cries of revelry, witnessed the disgraceful behavior of the people, and threw the Tablets to the ground. He proceeded to destroy the Golden Calf by throwing it into a fire, after which he ground the residue into powder. He threw the powder into a stream and made the people drink it. He reproached Aharon for his activities in making the calf. Aharon replied that he had been forced to carry out the people's demands. Moshe called upon all his supporters to rally around him, and the entire tribe of Levi and a small group from other tribes responded immediately. At his command, the *leviyim* went through the camp, slaying about three thousand people.

Moshe's love and compassion for his people led him to again implore God to forgive them, for if they were destroyed he had no desire to live. The reply he received was that only those who had willfully sinned would be punished, but, in view of Moshe's intercession on their behalf, the people would be led to the Promised Land by God's messenger. On learning of God's disapproval of their actions, the Israelites mourned and removed their ornaments as a sign of grief.

The Importance of Avoiding Negative Influences

The Jews were chosen by God and thus became a special nation. Being chosen, however, is a responsibility as well as a privilege. Yisrael has the mission of proclaiming God's teachings to the world as well as bearing witness to God's existence.

Because of Yisrael's unique place in God's plan, the people must constantly be corrected whenever they stray from the true path. Still, when God punishes Yisrael, He only does so as a father who punishes his children. Despite all these sufferings, God promised that Yisrael will always continue to exist to fulfill His purpose. Although Yisrael has been persecuted and degraded throughout history, the nation will survive.

A Jew must always be careful of outside negative influences that have a tendency to cause him to stray from proper behavior. Throughout Jewish history, the Jewish nation as a whole, as well as individuals, have sometimes been negatively influenced by their surroundings.

One prime example was the detrimental influence of the Egyptians who sup-posedly had converted to Judaism when they left Egypt along with the Jews. They adopted Judaism not out of any basic belief in God, but because they believed the Jews were the greatest power at that moment. Consequently, when Moshe did not return on schedule from Mount Sinai, they were the first to publicly abandon faith in God and Moshe. The Jews now seemed leaderless and lost. It was these questionable converts who became the prime instigators for adopting a new man-made god. Their plan had a devastating effect, for they influenced many Jews to subscribe to their ideas. They convinced the people to construct a Golden Calf to be used as an intermediary between them and God. When Moshe came down and witnessed the disgraceful behavior of the people dancing and cavorting around the Golden Calf, he broke the tablets of the Ten Commandments that he had been carrying. The false Egyptian converts influenced and contaminated the righteous *Bnei Yisrael* with their sinful proclivities.

The Reward for Those Who Sacrifice for God

When the Jews were about to make the Golden Calf, Chur (the son of Moshe's sister, Miryam), rose and did all in his power to prevent the angry mob from carrying out its plans. He lectured them severely, warning them that their act was sacrilegious and that they would later regret it. He put his life in danger, doing everything possible to bring them to their senses. Chur's opposition only aroused the Jews' fury, and the people compounded their sin by killing him.

Chur had clearly demonstrated his loyalty to God. And what did he merit for this act? His grandson became the chief craftsman of the *Mishkan* (Tabernacle). In fact, when the Torah speaks of his grandson, Betzalel, it not only mentions his father, Uri, but also mentions his lineage, listing his grandfather as well. The reason for this is clear. It was because of his grandfather, who gave up his life, that Betzalel merited being chosen by God as the master craftsman of the *Mishkan*.

Another loyal Jew who was willing to sacrifice his most prized possession, and even his life, for the sake of God and Judaism, was the great Rabbi Yitzchak. He was the owner of a uniquely beautiful gem. His jewel won widespread fame, and even the ruler learned of its existence. He promptly sent his emissaries to Rabbi Yitzchak and instructed them to purchase the gem for an enormous sum of money.

When these messengers made their offer, Rabbi Yitzchak was overwhelmed. He saw himself using his new-found wealth for the performance of countless mitzvos, and he felt extremely grateful to Hashem. Suddenly, though, a look of apprehension replaced his smile.

"What does the ruler want to do with this gem?" he asked.

"He wants to use it as the eye for his idol," was the reply.

Rabbi Yitzchak was aghast. "Never will I give you the gem for that purpose!" he exclaimed, and he asked the messengers to leave.

The ruler's agents plotted to obtain the gem. A message was sent to Rabbi Yitzchak informing him that there was a Jewish family being held captive on a boat in a nearby harbor. They would be released, but only if Rabbi Yitzchak appeared and redeemed them with his gem.

Rabbi Yitzchak did not hesitate for a moment. He grabbed the gem and rushed to the boat, whose whereabouts had been pinpointed in the message. The moment he boarded, though, he was met by the ruler's agents.

"There is no Jewish family here," they told him. "This was all just a trick to bring you aboard with your gem. Either you give us the stone or we will kill you." Disregarding the fortune that he was holding and the consequences of such an act, Rabbi Yitzchak threw the precious gem into the water. The ruler's agents were aghast. Rabbi Yitzchak's principles obviously meant more to him than the most precious gem in the world.

The Almighty repaid him very well. A son was born to Rabbi Yitzchak and his wife, whose knowledge was more valuable than all the jewels in the world. He became known as Rashi (the acronym for Rabbi Shelomo Yitzchaki), the great Sage who wrote the most widely used commentary on the Torah. Jews all over the world, young and old, learn Torah with Rashi's commentary.

❦ HISTORY

THE MISHKAN (TABERNACLE) (2449)(1312 B.C.E.)

Hashem commanded Moshe to build a *Mishkan* (Tabernacle), to be constructed according to a Divine blueprint, which would symbolize His Presence among the people. The Tabernacle was a portable sanctuary which traveled with the Jews through the wilderness.

Betzalel, of the tribe of Yehudah, and Oholiav, of the tribe of Dan, were chosen by Hashem to apply their skill in craftsmanship by supervising the work of the construction of the Sanctuary.

Under God's command, a census of the Jewish men was taken. Each man was required to contribute a coin of one-half shekel to be used for the Tabernacle. The coins were then counted and the total indicated how many men had been numbered.

ETHICS I

Avoiding Hypocrisy

The holiest structure around which Jewish life revolved, prior to the building of the Temple, was the *Mishkan*, which contained the Holy Ark. The Ark was constructed with a layer of gold on both the outside and inside. This arrangement provides a lesson for every individual. Just as the Ark was golden from both within and without, so, too, should every person be righteous both inwardly and outwardly. Instead of behaving one way in the glare of public life and another way in private, one should remain virtuous at all times. He should at all times practice what he preaches. If his actions are consistent with his words, then others will realize that he is sincere. On the other hand, if one behaves appropriately in public only, and then acts immorally or unjustly behind closed doors, he is branded as an untrustworthy hypocrite. One who deceives others deceives himself as well.

The great Torah sage known as the Chafetz Chaim was renowned for never assuming a false facade. Whoever saw the Chafetz Chaim knew that he was seeing his true self. His character was perfect, and he had no faults to hide.

One day, the Chafetz Chaim visited a town he had never before entered. He lodged at an inn and had a lengthy conversation with the innkeeper. After over an hour of talk, the innkeeper finally asked, "Could you tell me your identity?"

The Chafetz Chaim was reluctant to reveal this, for he did not want the innkeeper to go to any extra bother to serve him. He hesitated, but before he could come up with any reply, the innkeeper said, "Wait — you must be the Chafetz Chaim or another righteous sage. I have never before seen you, but from what I have heard, it must be, for we have talked for a very long time and you have not yet said even a hint of a bad word about anyone."

This, then, characterizes a Torah sage

— one who can be easily identified by his great deeds and character. It was the Chafetz Chaim who drove home the concept of brotherhood by closing his store early so that other businessmen in the area could also prosper. If someone overpaid him, he would go to extraordinary lengths to find the individual and return the money to that person.

These are the characteristics of our leaders, and it is hoped that we will be wise enough to learn from their examples.

Although we must do everything possible to avoid behaving hypocritically, we should not use that as a crutch to keep us from doing positive and worthwhile things. For instance, an excuse that some parents give for not sending their child to a Hebrew school is that since they are not religious at home, they feel it would be hypocritical for them to send their children to yeshivah while they themselves are totally non-observant.

Hypocrisy means not acting in accordance with firmly held beliefs. But it is not hypocritical for a person who has religious doubts to try to observe as much as he can in any specific area of Jewish faith. By keeping the teachings of our traditions, even at times when one has doubts, we retain the possibility for a wholehearted return to God.

The parent who introduces traditional observance to satisfy the needs of his child is anything but a hypocrite. Rather, he is sincere in trying to provide his child with Jewish experiences and direction. One never knows — perhaps the experience will move the parents to adopt more positive feelings about their faith and its way of life.

LESSON III

Serving God with Sincerity and Consistency

In the Tabernacle, where the Jews brought their sacrifices to God, two separate flames burned — the *ner tamid* (the perpetual light), and the *esh tamid* (perpetual flame). The fact that both flames burned continuously is significant. This tells us that we, too, must continuously act in accordance with God's wishes and we must be consistent in our observance of Judaism. This means that we cannot be pious just on Yom Kippur or on the day of a yahrtzeit (anniversary of someone's death), but we must be holy every day of the year. We cannot make religion a matter of convenience. Our religious observance must glow at all times, as did the flames in the Tabernacle.

The Dubno Maggid related a parable showing the foolishness of those who appear in synagogue only during the High Holy Days.

A storekeeper arrived for work one day to find his warehouse had burned to the ground and all his possessions had been destroyed. He was penniless, and worse, he now had a large debt, for all his merchandise had been bought on credit. What could he do?

Near despair, he went to the manufacturer and told him his tale of woe. The manufacturer's pity was aroused, and he agreed to not only wipe the debt off the books, but also to give the storekeeper additional goods on credit. That way, the storekeeper would be able to go back into business.

Word spread about the manufacturer's generosity. Soon, another man arrived at the manufacturer's door and began pleading for money. "How dare you?" said the outraged manufacturer. "You don't deserve a penny, so leave immediately!"

"But you gave the storekeeper all that credit," replied the man. "Why did you help him, but refuse to help me?"

"How can you possibly compare yourself to that storekeeper?" exclaimed the manufacturer. "I've done thousands of dollars of business with him for years! I know him and I can trust him; he's always paid me back before. Therefore, when something tragic happened to him, I extended him some credit. But in your case, I don't know you at all. If I lend you some money, how do I know that you'll ever pay me back?"

"This," taught the Dubno Maggid, "is the plight of a Jew who is not consistent in his observance of Judaism, as opposed to one who is constantly faithful. The person who has a 'good credit rating' with God through his regular attendance at synagogue and observance of commandments will be given 'credit' during times of need. But the person who is a stranger to the Almighty and does not perform His commandments regularly will not automatically receive the same response when he requests it."

However, constant service must not be marked by tired, careless efforts. For example, we must not pray just because it is a habit, and stumble and mumble our way through it. Rather, we should remember Whom we are addressing and say each word carefully. We should not fulfill the commandments as a routine, but rather with devotion and inspiration.

The following story, related by the Chafetz Chaim, illustrates the fallacy of reciting our prayers mechanically and by rote. When we pray, we should really mean every word we say.

"All employees report to the manager's office!"

The call went out over the factory's public address system, and soon all the workers were assembled before the manager. This procedure had been going on each day for several weeks, ever since the company owner had left the country on an important business trip. He had always personally directed the factory's operations, but now he had appointed a manager to oversee the work of his employees and to assure that everything functioned smoothly during his absence.

Now all of these employees listened, bored, as this manager read aloud the instructions left behind by the boss. He carefully pronounced each word just as the owner had ordered and did a masterful job of delivering the instructions.

When the boss returned, he was shocked to see the condition of his factory. Machines needed repairs and workers stood around idle. He angrily called in the manager and asked him for an explanation.

"Did you follow the instructions I left behind with you?"

"Why, of course," the manager defended himself. "I read them to all of the workers every day while you were gone."

"Now I know why there is such a mess!" cried the boss. "You only read these instructions, but you didn't bother to see that they were implemented. The lazy workers took advantage of your foolishness and almost ruined my entire business. Do you think that I left these instructions behind only for reading? I gave them to you so that you would know how to run the factory in my absence. Reading them has not achieved this goal."

The behavior of the poor manager is similar to that exhibited by people who study Torah and pray daily only out of force of habit. They recite the words, but they consider them as reading material, not as a plan of action. The Torah and the *tefillos* are, like the instructions left by the owner, a guide for practical action. If we do not realize this, and we do not actually practice what we say, then our words have no meaning or purpose at all.

MITZVAH

Shabbos

The sanctity of the Shabbos is stressed again in the account of the preparation of the *Mishkan*, for the Torah states that the Shabbos may not be violated even for so sacred a cause as the building of the House of Hashem. Even before the *Bnei Yisrael* received the Ten Commandments at Mount Sinai, they were bidden to refrain from collecting and baking the manna on the day to which Moshe referred as "a solemn rest, a holy Shabbos unto Hashem." The Shabbos is a memorial not only of the Creation of the world but also of the exodus from Egypt.

THE IMPORTANCE OF SHABBOS

"Remember the Shabbos day to keep it holy. Six days shall you labor, and do all your work; but the seventh day is a Shabbos unto the Lord your God. On it you shall do no manner of work,...for in six days the Lord made heaven and earth, the sea and all that is in them, and hallowed it."[1]

"Speak also unto the Children of Yisrael, saying: Verily you shall keep My Sabbaths, for it is a sign between Me and you throughout your generations, that you may know that I am the Lord Who sanctifies you...."[2]

The Hebrew word "Shabbos" means to cease from work. But the Shabbos is not only a day of rest. It is also a unique day of holiness when man should cast aside material pursuits and devote himself to rejuvenating himself spiritually.

Our Sages tell us that whoever enjoys the Shabbos in the proper manner:

(a) will be saved from *shibud malchiyos* (domination by a foreign government);

(b) will be saved from the destruction of Gog and Magog; and

(c) will receive his reward in *Olam Ha-Ba* (the World to Come).[3]

Every storekeeper or shopowner places a sign over his store entrance that describes his business. Even if he leaves for a few weeks, the sign indicates that he is still in business. However, if the sign is removed, it is certain evidence that the store is closed.

So it is with the Shabbos. The Shabbos is a sign between the Creator and the Jews that He created heaven and earth in six days and rested on the seventh. The

Shabbos is also a sign for every individual Jew testifying to his Jewishness and the covenant between God and His people. Even if it should happen that a Jew violates some commandments, he still hasn't lost his Jewishness. The temporary absence of the storekeeper doesn't mean that the sign is taken down. As long as he observes the Shabbos, he is still "in business." But if a Jew intentionally desecrates the Shabbos, it is as if he takes down the sign atop his entrance and announces that he has abandoned his Jewish heritage, just like the storekeeper who has abandoned his store.

This is what our Sages meant when they said, "One who desecrates the Shabbos is considered as one who denies the entire Torah."

HOW TO PREPARE FOR SHABBOS

I. The Torah states, "Remember the Shabbos day to keep it holy." This includes remembering it during the entire week. The great Torah leader Shammai was known to save special foods for Shabbos, starting from the beginning of the week. Anytime he saw something appropriate, he set it aside *"l'kovod Shabbos"* (in honor of the Shabbos). Thereafter, if he found finer food, he would use the first item during the week and save the better one for Shabbos.

The Talmud relates that Rav Chiya bar Abba once asked a wealthy individual, "My son, how do you deserve such riches?"

He replied, "I used to be a butcher. Whenever I saw a particularly nice animal, I set it aside for Shabbos."

Rav Chiya then responded, "It is not without reason that you have become rich. Your merit is great."

2. A person should spend extra money to honor the Shabbos. If one does not have enough money to prepare for the Shabbos, he should borrow it and God will give him the means to repay the loan.[4]

3. Enough food should be prepared for three meals. It is preferable that each meal include fish.

4. One should do the housecleaning and Shabbos preparations on *Erev Shabbos* (Friday), making it obvious that they are being done in honor of the Shabbos. However, when Friday is very short, some of these Shabbos preparations should be done earlier.

5. One must make sure to wash himself, cut his nails, and if need be, cut his hair, in honor of the Shabbos.

6. Before the Shabbos candles are lit, the table should be set in preparation for the Shabbos. Even if there are no guests, the house should be neat, and the members of the household should be dressed for the occasion.

7. One should be especially careful not to have any quarrels before or during Shabbos.

THE LAWS OF LIGHTING THE SHABBOS CANDLES

I. The ritual of lighting the Shabbos candles is considered the duty of the woman of the house. Even if the husband wants to light the candles, the wife has priority. If for some reason the woman of the house is unable to light the candles, then the husband or another individual is required to light them.

2. At least two candles are lit in honor of the Shabbos, to symbolize the twofold command of Shabbos observance: "Remember (*zachor*) the Shabbos day to keep it holy" and "Observe (*shamor*) the

Shabbos to keep it holy."

3. The Shabbos candles help bring peace and harmony into the house. They are also a sign of blessing. That is why women often add a special prayer for their children when saying the blessing over lighting the Shabbos candles. They pray that their children should grow up to follow in the ways of Hashem.

4. If someone is away on vacation, he must light the candles where he is staying for Shabbos.

5. In some households, it is customary to light seven candles, or even ten. Others light a candle for each member of the household.

6. It is best to place the challahs on the table before lighting the Shabbos candles.

7. The candles are lit approximately twenty minutes before sunset. Once the sun has set, the candles can no longer be lit.

8. If for some reason the parents do not light the candles, then any one of the children should do so with a *berachah* (blessing).

9. A woman who is in a hospital which prohibits lighting candles may light an electric candelabra or any other bulb instead. One should consult a rabbi whether or not to make the blessing on such candles. In any event, the husband should light the candles at home with a blessing.

l0. If it is impossible for one to light the candles where he is eating, then he may do so in the room where he is sleeping.

ll. General procedure for lighting the Shabbos candles:

    (a) The woman lights the candles.

    (b) She extinguishes the match and discards it (her husband may do so afterwards).

    (c) She then covers her eyes, and

    (d) recites the following blessing: "*Baruch Atta Hashem, Elokeinu Melech ha-olam, asher kidshanu b'mitzvosav v'tzivanu l'hadlik ner shel Shabbos.*"

12. Once the woman has lit the candles and made the blessing, she has been "*mekabel Shabbos,*" (accepted the restrictions of Shabbos) and is no longer allowed to move the candles or matches. The husband, however, is still allowed to do work that is normally forbidden on Shabbos, as long as it is not yet the exact time for accepting the Shabbos, or until he is *mekabel Shabbos* (by saying the appropriate prayers in the Friday evening service).

The unique role of the Shabbos candles in Jewish life transcended even the tragedies of the the Nazi era. At the very outset of his book, *The Shabbos*, Dayan Grunfeld cites an eyewitness account of a remarkable incident which took place in a packed cattle car transporting Jewish victims from their homes to a Nazi concentration camp.

The train dragged on with its human freight. Pressed together like cattle in the crowded trucks, the unfortunate occupants were unable even to move. The atmosphere was stifling. As the Friday afternoon wore on, the Jews in the Nazi transport sank deeper and deeper into their misery.

Suddenly an old Jewish woman managed with great effort to move and open her bundle. Laboriously, she drew out two candlesticks and two challahs. She had just prepared them for Shabbos when she was dragged from her home that morning. They were the only things she had thought worthwhile taking with her. Soon the Shabbos candles lit up the faces of the tortured Jews and the song of "*Lechah Dodi*" transformed the scene. Shabbos, with its atmosphere of peace, had descended upon them all.

HOW TO CONDUCT THE SHABBOS

Upon returning from synagogue on Friday night, one sings "*Shalom Aleichem*" (a psalm welcoming the Shabbos), and recites the Kiddush on wine or grape juice as soon as possible. The Torah tells us to "Remember the Shabbos to keep it holy." One fulfills this commandment by reciting the Kiddush both at the nighttime meal and the day-time meal. Women and children are obligated to fulfill the positive precept of Kiddush, just as they are required to fulfill the negative precepts of Shabbos.

When making Kiddush on the wine, one should cover the challahs to remember the manna in the desert that was covered by a layer of dew both above and beneath. The Kiddush should be recited in the place where one eats.

One must have two whole challahs or matzos on the Shabbos table to remind us of the double portion of manna which fell on Friday in the desert. One person at the table (either the father or other head of the family) makes the blessing on the challahs and has in mind to fulfill the obligation of *lechem mishneh* (two loaves) for the others present.

Three meals are eaten during the Shabbos: One on Friday night; the second, Shabbos by day; and the third, known as *seudah shelishis*, eaten late in the afternoon — from at least 12:30 standard time, preferably after the afternoon service (*Minchah*) and begun no later than at twilight.

Just as we "remember" the Shabbos on its entrance, so we "remember" the Shabbos on its departure, with the special prayer and blessing known as *Havdalah*. It is recited after the evening prayer (*Ma'ariv*). One cannot start eating after dark until the recitation of *Havdalah*. If one cannot obtain wine for *Havdalah*, he may use beverages commonly used in this country, such as beer.

Before *Havdalah* is recited, the cup is completely filled with wine so that it overflows slightly. Besides a cup of wine, one must also have a *Havdalah* candle which has at least two wicks. If he does not have a *Havdalah* candle, he should hold two candles together so that the two wicks burn as one. If he cannot get two candles, he should at least use one candle.

A candle is lit in the *Havdalah* ceremony to remind us that it was after Shabbos that Adom, the first man, learned how to kindle a fire. Since the "additional Shabbos spirit" leaves us, we inhale the aroma of spices (*besamim*) to make up for the loss, and to add some fragrance to our lives for the coming week.

HOW TO REFRAIN FROM DESECRATING THE SHABBOS

By refraining from work on Shabbos, the Jew shows the importance and significance that Shabbos plays in his life. It enables us to devote one full day each week to our task of becoming a "kingdom of priests and a holy nation," thus beautifying our lives. It prevents our becoming enslaved to our work and our secular activities.[5] In this way we show that we are free men as we were when we were freed from the bondage of Egypt. The Shabbos is a memorial to this freedom. Most important, it proves our trust in the Almighty — that He will provide for us even without the possible material gain of working on Shabbos. The following story illustrates this concept.

A man was riding in his carriage down a long winding road one day. He passed an old man trudging along, groaning under the heavy load on his back.

"Can I offer you a lift?" asked the rider. The old man readily agreed and entered the coach. He took a seat, but did not remove the heavy package from his back. After he had observed the old man for a while, the rider could not contain his curiosity. He turned to the old man and asked, "Why don't you remove the package from your back and put it down?"

The old man shook his head. "You were nice enough to give me a lift. How can I have the nerve to impede your trip by placing such a heavy burden in your carriage?"

"Don't worry," responded the rider. "The carriage is bearing the weight of your burden anyway, whether you place it on your back or on the floor of the coach. You may as well put it on the floor, sit back and relax, and let the horses do the work."

Likewise, we must have enough faith in God to trust His ability to bear our burden, even on the Shabbos. After all, it is He who carries us through every other day of the week. Therefore, there is no need to worry that if one observes the Shabbos he will suffer a great loss. In the long run, he who keeps the Shabbos has

only to gain from his trust in the Almighty.

The Torah instructed the Jews to do all the work that was necessary to construct the *Mishkan*, only during the six days of the week. They were not permitted to do any of this activity on Shabbos. The type of labor actually performed in the *Mishkan* is called *melachah* and there are thirty-nine different *melachos*. The thirty-nine *melachos* cover a whole range of productive and creative human activity. Among the thirty-nine categories of work that are forbidden on Shabbos are: planting, cooking, baking, sewing, writing, erasing, building, demolishing, kindling a fire, extinguishing a fire, any activity that puts a final touch on an article, and carrying.

In addition to Shabbos, all of these laws apply to Yom Kippur, Rosh Hashanah, Sukkos, Pesach and Shavuos, with the following exceptions that are permitted on the Festivals (except Yom Kippur): cooking or baking food which is needed for the day, or carrying things that are needed for that day. Some examples are carrying a *lulav* to the synagogue, or wheeling a baby carriage. If *Yom Tov* falls on Shabbos, then the above exceptions do not apply.

If *Yom Tov* falls on *erev Shabbos*, and one wants to cook on *Yom Tov* for the Shabbos, one is permitted to do so, provided two conditions are met:

(a) The cooking should be sufficiently completed before Shabbos so that it should be edible on *Yom Tov*.

(b) Each household must set aside its own *eruv tavshilin*, which is a roll or matzah and a piece of cooked food such as an egg or fish. The two foods are then put aside to be eaten on Shabbos.

In the World to Come, a Jew will be asked: "Why did you open your shop on the Shabbos? Weren't you aware of the severity of the prohibition of desecrating the Shabbos? Every defiler of the Shabbos is considered to have denied the entire Torah itself. Is it worth it to defile the valuable vessel given to the Jews, for a few additional pennies of profit?" The man will certainly reply: "What can I do? The needs of a man are many and his sustenance is meager. I felt obligated to keep my business open."

To whom can he be compared? To the same fool who thought he could get more cups of water out of his jug by adding another spout. It didn't even occur to him that the new tap not only couldn't add any more water, but it would empty the jug even faster.

The Lord of our universe nourishes and sustains the entire world. He prepares our weekly food according to how we have pleased Him; for some: in abundance, for others: not. Our weekly income comes to us from six "faucets." Only a fool could think that he will receive more sustenance by opening additional ones. Therefore, how does the Jew who has desecrated the Shabbos benefit?

A farmer used to bring his grain to a certain Jewish dealer. They made an arrangement for recording the number of sacks sold. Each time a sack was weighed, the dealer would make a line on the wall. At the end, they would count up the lines and would know how many sacks the farmer had brought.

After a while, the farmer decided that this system was dangerous, since the dealer could erase one of the lines and cheat him out of a sack. He therefore suggested a different arrangement. For every sack weighed, the dealer would put a coin of small value in a plate. At the conclusion, they would count the coins to determine how many sacks must be paid for.

They started using this new system. But as the farmer saw the pile of coins growing, he could not resist the temptation. When he saw that the dealer wasn't looking, he sneaked a coin from the plate and quickly put it into his pocket.

Naturally, the dealer later paid him according to the number of the coins in the plate. By sneaking a few coins from the plate, the farmer had cheated himself out of a large sum of money.

So it is with anyone who tries to cheat the Shabbos. He is following the example of the "smart" farmer. We depend on the kindness of the Almighty to send us His blessing and He has commanded us in His Torah, "Six days shall you labor and do all of your work and the seventh day you shall rest." Our Sages have explained that the blessings for the entire week flow from the Shabbos. If one cheats the Shabbos and takes off hours from its beginning and its end, he is only cheating himself, for he is ultimately cutting down the influence of the Shabbos on his entire week.

❦ HISTORY

THE DESECRATION OF THE SHABBOS IN THE WILDERNESS

While in the wilderness, the Jews found a man violating the Shabbos. The man was held in custody until Hashem declared to Moshe that the man should be stoned to death by the congregation. They carried out the punishment as dictated by the Torah. The Torah does not mention who this individual was, so as not to embarrass him.

ETHICS II

The Importance of Saving a Life Even on Shabbos

It is important to bear in mind that all the restrictions and prohibitions of the Shabbos do not apply if there is a question of someone's life being in jeopardy. In that case, one must do everything possible to save a life. It is not only permissible, but one is actually obligated to do whatever is necessary to help the person.

Rabbi Hillel, the son-in-law of Rabbi Chaim of Volozhin, was seen carrying a burning lamp through the streets on Shabbos. When he returned without the lamp, people asked him why he had carried a lamp on Shabbos.

He replied, "In that house, there is a person who is dangerously ill. The light had gone out, and they were unable to take proper care of the sick person. The family sent a messenger to me, asking what could be done. I immediately took a lamp and brought it to their house on Shabbos, for it is a commandment to save the life of a dangerously ill person, even if it means desecrating the Shabbos."

❦ *Key People, Places and Things*

ARON: the Holy Ark.

AVODAH ZARAH: idol worship.

EGEL HA-ZAHAV: the Golden Calf.

EREV SHABBOS: Friday, when we prepare for Shabbos.

ERUV: a halachic arrangement by which carrying limits are established for the Shabbos.

HADLAKAS NEROS: candle-lighting; lighting at least two candles, marking the onset of the Shabbos.

HAVDALAH: the ceremony marking the close of the Shabbos, utilizing wine, spices and a candle.

KIDDUSH: the sanctification of the Shabbos, usually recited over wine.

LAMED-TES MELACHOS: the thirty-nine categories of labor prohibited on Shabbos.

LECHEM MISHNEH: the two loaves of challah or bread which begin the Shabbos meal.

MESIRAS NEFESH: self-sacrifice for the Almighty.

MISHKAN: the Tabernacle.

MIDBAR: desert; wilderness.

MUSAF: the added prayer service on Shabbos and Festivals.

SEUDAH SHELISHIS: the third Shabbos meal.

SHABBOS: the Sabbath, a holy day on which we cease to work; a Sabbath observer is known as a *shomer Shabbos.*

NOTES

1. *Shemos* 20:8-11.

2. *Shemos* 31:13-14.

3. *Talmud Shabbos,* 118.

4. *Mishnah Berurah, Aruch Chayim,* 242, quotes the *Yerushalmi.*

5. Rav Moshe Feinstein, *Iggros Moshe, Yoreh De'ah,* 3:71.

❧ *Introduction to Chapters 9 - 10*

Becoming God's Chosen Nation brought with it certain obligations and duties. However, this holy nation which had just received the Torah did not fully comprehend the responsibilities incumbent upon it. Moshe constantly reminded the Jews that their success depended upon their spiritual loyalty. Yet even in the desert, the warning was not properly understood. The men who had explored the Promised Land returned to report that it could not be conquered from its inhabitants. The very depth of their faith was being tested and they failed to rise to the challenge. They feared the physical prowess of the inhabitants of Kena'an and were unmindful that the will of God decided the fate of the Land. Thus, another forty years of wandering in the desert were necessary until a new generation — completely faithful to Hashem — was ready to enter the Holy Land.

During these forty years in the desert, Moshe and the Jews were beset by various problems: the rebellion of Korach (ignited by his jealousy), the death of Aharon's sons, the people's complaints regarding the lack of meat and water, Moshe striking the rock, the wicked Balak and Bilam, the immorality of the daughters of Mo'av and the manner in which Pinchas dealt with it. Despite these problems, God showered them with favor and Divine protection as shown through the miracles of the manna, the traveling well of water, and the pillars of clouds and fire.

It was during this period that the Jews were transformed from a group of oppressed people into a nation. We see a clear picture of the difficulties which confronted Moshe and the Jewish people, and how with the help of God they were able to overcome them. Finally, it was during the period of the forty years' wandering in the desert that the nation truly became a people of God. This generation was now deemed worthy of entering the Holy Land and building God's state.

CHAPTER 9

The Jews – A Nation of Faith
Korbanos; Kohen; Meraglim; High Holy Days
2449/1312 B.C.E.

❧ HISTORY

KORBANOS (SACRIFICES)

The Jews were instructed to bring *korbanos*, animal sacrifices, to Hashem. What is the purpose of these sacrifices? A clue to the answer comes from an examination of the word *korbanos*, which contains the same root as the word *karov*, meaning "near." A *korban*, then, is a means of approaching Hashem, supplicating for Divine forgiveness or demonstrating appreciation for Divine assistance, and thereby bringing one closer to Him. Thus, the *olah* (burnt offering) symbolized man's complete surrender to the will of God; the *shelamim* (peace offering) was intended as a demonstration of gratitude to God for His bounties; and the *challas* (sin offering) was symbolic of regret and sorrow at having strayed from the way of God.

LESSON I
The Privileges and Responsibilities of the Kohen

In an impressive ceremony conducted in the court of the Sanctuary, Aharon and his sons were installed by Moshe in their official positions as priests, while the Elders looked on. They dressed in distinctive garments when they conducted the sacrifices in the *Mishkan*.

Due to the importance of his function, the *kohen* had to maintain an especially high standard of purity and perfection. He was permitted to attend the funeral only of his nearest relatives, for contact with the dead defiled him and kept him from performing his holy duties. In addition, he could not marry a divorced woman. More rigid rules applied to the *Kohen Gadol*, who was not to attend the funeral of even his closest kin, and who could marry only a virgin. Certain physical defects disqualified the *kohen* from officiating in the *Mishkan*.

In return for his services, the *kohen* received portions of the sacrifices. He collected the *pidyon* (redemption money for firstborn sons, and firstborn sheep and goats) and received portions of the harvest, known as *terumah*. He also received *bikkurim*, challah, and other gifts. Even in our own time, the *kohen* has the honor of getting the first *aliyah* (being called up to the Torah).

PIDYON HA-BEN

On the thirty-first day, all firstborn male Jewish infants are required to be redeemed by their fathers from a *kohen*. This ritual is known as *pidyon ha-ben* (redemption of the firstborn).

1. The *pidyon ha-ben* is performed after thirty days have elapsed since the birth (the thirty-first day). It should not be delayed or postponed, unless that day is *Shabbos*. In that case, it is postponed until after *Havdalah*.

2. The *pidyon ha-ben* is accomplished by giving a *kohen* the equivalent of five shekels of silver. At the same time, the father declares that the coins are being given in exchange for his son.

3. Silver coins containing ninety-six grams of silver are most commonly used. Checks or dollar bills representing the correct value may not be used.

4. If the *kohen* chooses to do so, he may return the silver coins to the father or put it in trust for the child.

5. The father himself should perform the ceremony of redeeming his son and recite the blessing.

6. The *pidyon ha-ben* is not performed if either parent is a *kohen* or *levi*, if the oldest child is a girl, or if the boy was born through Caesarean section.

ETHICS I

Obligations of the Kohen to the Jewish People

The *kohen* blesses the congregation with the *Birkas Kohanim*, the Priestly Blessing. This procedure, in which the *kohanim* mount a platform to face the congregation in order to bless them, is also known as *duchen*ing.

The tribe of *Levi* was the only one that did not receive an allocation of land in Eretz Yisrael. Instead, they were dispersed throughout the Land in the forty-eight cities that were given to the tribe of *Levi*. The *leviyim* depended on the tithes given them by the people of Yisrael for their sustenance. In return, the *leviyim* provided spiritual guidance for the Jews.

One who considers the Torah's instructions regarding the *leviyim* might be puzzled. The *leviyim* were, after all, the jewel in the crown of Yisrael. They were the group whose loyalty prompted Hashem to appoint them as guardians of His Sanctuary. They were considered princes of the people, models of holiness. And yet, for all their high position, they were not granted their own territory in the Promised Land. Instead, they had to be sustained through the donations and offerings of the rest of the populace. Why was this so?

The matter can be explained through the following parable told by the Dubno Maggid.

A wealthy merchant set out on a lengthy journey and asked his sons to accompany him. To avoid unnecessary expenses along the way, he told his servants to remain at his home, expecting his sons to assist him in performing all necessary chores. However, soon after the trip began, it became evident that most of his sons were not able to prepare food properly. Only one of the sons had received training in the art of cooking and the others depended on him. The brothers feared, however, that he would not want to bother cooking large quantities for the whole family. Anticipating this possibility, the father had made sure to acquire only the largest cooking utensils. Using a very big pot, the son would be forced to prepare very large portions, so that if he cooked for his own benefit, he would be cooking for the others at the same time. If the son put in the pot food sufficient for only himself, it would quickly burn. He had no choice but to cook enough food for everyone.

The Dubno Maggid compared the *levi-yim* to the young man who was the only one in the family able to cook. The *levi-yim*, too, have an ability that the rest of Yisrael does not possess — namely, bringing down Hashem's blessings upon His people.

If every *levi* were busy caring for his own field, he would possibly yield to the temptation of praying only for himself. But all Jews are in need of God's blessings for their crops. The *levi*, whose welfare is dependent upon the prosperity of his brethren, will therefore be sure to pray with greater devotion to Hashem that He be generous with His bountiful blessings to the entire Jewish nation.

❦ HISTORY

THE TRAGIC DEATHS OF AHARON'S TWO SONS

Nadav and Avihu, Aharon's oldest sons, offered incense on an unconsecrated fire not taken from the altar. Such an offense by priests, who were to set an example for the rest of the assembly, was unpardonable. The two of them were therefore punished by being consumed "by fire which came from before the Lord," and they died instantly. Aharon was overwhelmed with grief at this tragedy. Moshe consoled him by saying that his sons attained a high spiritual level and had a special responsibility to maintain the high standard of sanctity demanded of them by Hashem. To prevent the remaining priests from becoming defiled by touching the dead bodies, Aharon's cousins Misha'el and Eltzafan (who were not priests), were told to bury the bodies. Aharon and his two remaining sons, Elazar and Isamar, were instructed not to exhibit any mourning, thereby demonstrating to the people their submission to God's will. The priests were also warned not to drink any liquor (as Nadav and Avihu had) before discharging their duties in the *Mishkan* or instructing the people.

Faith in God that He Will Supply Us with Our Needs

During the forty years that the Jews traveled through the desert after leaving Egypt, manna descended from the heavens every morning at the command of the Almighty. Every Jew was ordered to collect a set amount per person. If he tried to collect more than he was allowed, the extra manna miraculously disappeared when he was at home. If he set aside any of his manna for the next day, that manna began to rot and serve as a breeding place for worms. The reason for this was that the act of gathering extra food was a blatant indication of lack of trust in the Almighty's ability to provide food every day. It showed that the person did not believe God's word that the manna would reappear every day.

There is a Torah commandment that in the Land of Yisrael all farmers must allow their land to lie fallow during the year of *shemittah*, which occurs every seven years (the most recent being in the year 5754-1993). During the Sabbatical year, the produce, if any, does not belong to the landowner. The entire land and its products are to be considered under the ownership of Hashem. The reason for this is to acknowledge that all of our earthly possessions, our land and produce, are ultimately under God's rule. We should never let ourselves be deluded into thinking that we are in full control and complete ownership of anything. The Jew is promised that if he is deserving, his produce in the first six years will be sufficiently abundant to supply him for the seventh year as well. It is man's faith in God that will give him the peace of mind to know that his needs will be taken care of.

A student of Rabbi Yisrael Salanter once complained to him that he did not have enough funds to be able to live comfortably. The rabbi replied, "Have complete faith in God. If you do, then He will provide you with $1,000." The man left, reassured.

However, a month later, he was back. "I've been waiting quite a while for the money, and I haven't received anything yet," he protested.

"Have you maintained full faith in God, that He will give you the $1,000?" asked the rabbi. The man nodded. "Well," continued the rabbi, "I have $500 here. Would you take that instead of the $1,000?"

The man replied eagerly that he would.

The rabbi shook his head. "This shows that you do not have complete faith in God, for if you truly did, then you would not be willing to accept the $500 instead of the $1,000 promised."

Unfortunately, the Jews did not always have complete faith in God. This resulted in tragedies and severe punishment for the entire Jewish nation in the desert.

❧ HISTORY

THE JEWS' MURMURING AGAINST HASHEM

During their journey through the wilderness, the people began murmuring against Hashem's leadership. Hashem punished the people for their lack of faith and caused a fire to burn in their midst, prompting terror and destruction. The fire abated only after Moshe prayed to Hashem on the people's behalf.

However, the people had not learned their lesson. Urged by the uncommitted converts that had accompanied them out of Egypt, they complained again, this time about the lack of meat in the desert. Their murmurings led Moshe to feel that the burden of leading the people was too great for him to bear alone. Hashem responded by telling Moshe to assemble seventy Elders who would assist him in leading the people. The Elders were assembled and the spirit of prophecy rested upon them.

In response to the people's complaints about a lack of meat and the boring consistency of manna, Hashem caused the wind to blow an abundance of quails from across the sea. The people gathered the quails greedily, but when they began to eat their meat, many people fell dead.

THE TRAGIC CONSEQUENCES OF THE MERAGLIM

Despite all the miracles that Hashem had performed for the Israelites, occasionally the Jews still strayed from the path. They lacked total and absolute faith in Hashem and therefore complained twice in the desert about the lack of water. They stated that they would rather have died in Egypt than die from thirst in the desert.

The greatest sin, however, was their lack of complete faith in God's ability to bring them into the Promised Land.

The Israelites had reached Kadesh in the wilderness of Paran, close to entry into the Promised Land. Twelve representatives, one from each of the tribes, were sent by Moshe to explore the land of Kena'an and to report back on the condition of its populace, dwelling places, and soil. Yehoshua and Kalev were among those in this group of *meraglim* (spies).

After spying out the land for forty days, the *meraglim* returned to the Jews in the wilderness, bringing with them huge fruits as evidence of the land's fertility. However, ten of the spies claimed that it would be impossible for the Jews to conquer Kena'an. They declared that the cities were too strongly fortified and that the inhabitants were too powerful. Kalev and Yehoshua completely disassociated themselves from this pessimistic report and counseled that the people should march on to Kena'an. The people, however, sided with the majority report and lost heart. They broke into open rebellion and proposed the selection of a leader to lead them back to Egypt. They refused to listen to the renewed pleas of Kalev and Yehoshua and threatened to stone them.

The Jews lost their absolute faith in Hashem despite all the miracles He had performed for them, and wanted to return to Egypt rather than risk their lives. God saw in this attitude a weakness of commitment and a tendency to ingratitude. He expressed great anger and declared His intention to destroy the people and to form a new nation exclusively from Moshe's descendants. Moshe again interceded successfully on the Israelites' behalf. But while their destruction was avoided, the Jews were condemned to wander in the wilderness for forty years, one year for each day the spies had searched the land, until all men over the age of twenty (with the exception of Kalev and Yehoshua) had died. Then a new generation would enter the Promised Land to witness the fulfillment of God's promise.

The ten spies who had delivered the negative report died of a sudden plague. Some of the people belatedly realized their error and attempted to go by themselves to the Land of Yisrael. However, they ignored Moshe's warning that God was not with them, and were soundly defeated by the tribes of Amalek and Kena'an who lived in the area.

LESSON III

God's Severe Punishment

What was the punishment for those who sinned because of the spies? Not only were the spies themselves killed by a plague, but the people were condemned to wander in the wilderness for a full forty years. The date of this tragic error was Tishah B'Av (the ninth day of the Hebrew month of *Av*) which became a day of tragedy for Yisrael throughout all the generations. The destruction of both Holy Temples, the fall of the great city of Beitar, and the expulsion of the Jews from Spain occurred on this date, as did World War One, which uprooted most European Jewish communities.

To comprehend this, one must realize that until this point the Israelites had adopted the attitude of *"Na'aseh v'nishma"* ("We will do and we will listen" — their declaration made at Mount Sinai before receiving the Ten Commandments). This showed a total and unequivocal faith in the Almighty and His commandments. They had been willing to accept God's leadership without any doubts or questions. When the spies delivered their pessimistic report, however, the people's outlook changed. Despite the fact that God had guaranteed their protection, they began to question.

They lost their basic faith. Their unchallenging belief in God was gone and they no longer accepted His word without proof. It was for this loss of faith that they suffered, and it was this lack of trust that led to the later tragedies.

During times of crisis — and Jews have known many such times throughout their history — it has been their absolute faith in the Almighty that has filled the Jews with the will and ability to persevere. Without this faith, the Jews would have succumbed to oppression and despair long ago. If we lose faith in God's ability to aid us, then all is indeed lost.[1]

MITZVAH

The High Holy Days

The High Holy Days and Sukkos renew our faith in the Almighty. We look towards Hashem during the High Holy Days, we beg for forgiveness for any sins that we have done, and then we sit in the *sukkah* with the security of our faith in Hashem.

ROSH HASHANAH

The first day of the Hebrew month of *Tishrei* is the Judgment Day for all human beings, when all the deeds of the past year are scrutinized and measured. This day begins a period of soul-searching during which man can alter this judgment by sincere repentance.

We start blowing the shofar (ram's horn) a month before Rosh Hashanah. It is a time for introspection, for man to examine his past deeds and to try to improve himself. Special prayers, known as *Selichos*, asking for forgiveness, are recited in the days prior to Rosh Hashanah.

It was in the month of *Tishrei*, in the eighteenth century, that Reb Levi Yitzchak of Berditchev was standing at his window when a gentile cobbler passed by and asked him, "Have you anything to mend?"

Later the *tzaddik* sat himself down on the ground, and wept bitterly, crying, "Woe is me, and alas for my soul, for the Day of Judgment is almost here, and I have still not mended myself."

The Festival of Rosh Hashanah marks the beginning of the Jewish New Year and is observed on the first and second days of the month of *Tishrei*. On Rosh Hashanah we pray that every person will be inscribed in the Book of Life for the coming year. The actual meaning of Rosh Hashanah is "head of the year." According to the teachings of Judaism, it is the nerve center of the year. From it flow the decisions for the twelve months to come.

Amidst much prayer, the shofar is sounded to herald the first of the Ten Days of Penitence and to proclaim God as the Master of the universe. The shofar inspires us to pray for forgiveness and dedicate ourselves to Hashem.

Rav Sa'adyah Gaon, the great sage and leader of the Jews in pre-medieval times, explained why Hashem commanded us to blow the shofar on Rosh Hashanah. One reason is that Rosh Hashanah commemorates the Creation of the world. Just as kings have trumpets and horns blown on the anniversary of their coronation, so, too, we blow the shofar on Rosh Hashanah to commemorate and accept the kingship of the Creator.

Another reason is to remind us of the Jews' acceptance of the Torah on Mount Sinai. At that time, the sound of the shofar was heard. We blow the shofar in order to show that we desire the Torah just as our fathers did when they said at Mount Sinai, "We will do and we will listen."[2]

Since the purpose of the shofar is to inspire us to adopt humility and repentance, it is not elaborately decorated. In fact, if decorations or ornaments pierce the sides of the horn completely, it is unusable. Perhaps this can serve as a reminder to us of the importance of simplicity and humility.

On Rosh Hashanah, certain symbolic customs are followed to indicate our prayers and hopes for a good year.

1. We dip a piece of apple into honey and pray that it be God's will to "renew for us a good and sweet year." For the same reason, we eat sweet foods and avoid bitter ones.

2. We eat pomegranates, which have a lot of seeds, to symbolize our hope that God will multiply our merits.

3. We do not eat nuts, because the numerical value of the Hebrew word for nut is the same as the numerical value of the Hebrew word for sin.

4. We recite a special prayer, Tashlich, near a body of water, preferably one containing fish. Just as fish are hidden from the eye, are envied by no one, and are wished evil by no one, similarly we pray that no evil envious eye will ever affect the Jewish nation. We want to be hidden from the attentions and the evil intentions of wicked people. Fish are known to multiply very rapidly. We pray

to Hashem that the Jewish nation will grow and multiply as well.

In ancient times, a king's coronation ceremony took place at a body of water. Thus on Rosh Hashanah, when we proclaim God as our King, we recite this plea for mercy at the water's edge.

Furthermore, Tashlich recalls the willingness of both Avraham and Yitzchak to follow God's commandment, even when it meant losing their very lives. When Avraham was traveling to fulfill the commandment of God to sacrifice his son Yitzchak, the two were faced with a large body of water, impeding them from fulfilling their mission. They started going into the water, and miraculously overcame this obstacle.[3] We commemorate this bravery in the service of God, by saying this prayer on Rosh Hashanah near a body of water.

YOM KIPPUR (THE DAY OF ATONEMENT)

Yom Kippur, the tenth day of Tishrei, is the holiest day of the entire year. It is the last of the Ten Days of Penitence, when the Book of Life is finally sealed. Beginning with the Kol Nidrei service just before sunset, all Jews, young and old, assemble in the synagogue to ask Hashem forgiveness of their sins, and fast until after the next nightfall.

Yom Kippur is set aside as a fast day for the purpose of repenting and rectifying our misdemeanors towards our fellowmen and our Creator. Man asks forgiveness for his shortcomings from Hashem and resolves to live nobly, exemplifying the ideals of his faith.

On the day before Yom Kippur it is best to eat a full meal in order to have strength to fast the next day. But one should not overindulge to the extent that it might make him uncomfortable or sick.

Besides abstaining from food and drink on Yom Kippur, there are additional prohibitions: washing, wearing leather shoes, and having marital relations is not permitted (allowing for certain exceptions).

The morning prayers on the High Holy Days begin with the word, "*Ha-Melech*" (the King).

There is a story told about a rabbi who was officiating as a cantor for his congregation. When he reached the word "*Ha-Melech*" he burst into bitter crying. Later, he gave the following reason for his emotional outburst.

"When I came to the word '*Ha-Melech*,' I was reminded of this story told in the Talmud:

"During the time when the Jews lived in Yisrael under the domination of the Roman Empire, the great Sage, Rabbi Yochanan ben Zakkai, appeared before the Roman general, Vespasian, to ask for certain privileges for the Jewish populace. He referred to him as 'king.'

"Vespasian, who was still only general of the army and was about to receive the news of his having been made emperor, replied, 'If you call me "king" why didn't you come to me before now?'"[4]

Concluding his story, the rabbi explained, "Today, when I cried out the word '*Ha-Melech*,' I imagined that I was being asked in heaven, 'Why didn't you come before? Why did you wait so long before you repented before the Ruler of the universe?'"

ETHICS II

Bein Adam l'Chavero (Dealing Properly with One's Fellowman)

Another important aspect of *teshuvah* deals with interpersonal relationships. Although Yom Kippur atones for sins committed against God alone, sins committed against people are not forgiven until the sinner has asked forgiveness from his fellowman.

One important aspect in improving our attitudes towards others is giving charity. The giving of *tzedakah* (charity) to the needy on the day before Yom Kippur, during Minchah (the afternoon service), helps set the foundation for peace between Jews and their Father in heaven.

Showing compassion towards others is especially important at this time of year. The following story illustrates the compassion of a righteous Jew.

On the eve of Yom Kippur, the saintly Reb Levi Yitzchak of Berditchev was proceeding to shul before *Kol Nidrei*, when he heard an infant crying. He entered the house and found a baby alone in his cradle. His parents had gone to shul and left him without anyone to care for him.

Reb Levi Yitzchak soothed the child and began rocking him. After *Kol Nidrei* was over, the parents returned home to find this great man rocking their baby's cradle.

How great is the compassion that the pious feel for their fellow Jews! On Yom Kippur night, when everyone hurried to the *Kol Nidrei* service, this pious man felt that easing the anguish of a Jewish child was more important than his praying with the congregation.

MITZVAH

Sukkos (the Feast of Tabernacles)

The *sukkah* should be built in the proper dimensions: not less than 38 inches, nor more than 35 feet, in height. If the *sukkah* is smaller than 27 x 27 inches, it is too small and not kosher. Although any materials can be used for the walls, so long as they can withstand normal winds, the top, known as the *sechach*, must be of plant origin that is detached from the ground. Branches, bamboo, poles, or narrow wooden slats less than 2 inches wide are usually used. Edible foods should not be used. It is best for an adult male to eat in the *sukkah* at all times during the week of Sukkos. More than an olive-sized piece of cake or bread must be eaten in the *sukkah*.

Even though the Jews went out of Egypt in the spring and that is when they started to utilize their *sukkos*, God did not command us to build *sukkos* in that season. Since the weather is warm, it might seem that they are being built for our own comfort. Hashem therefore commanded us to make a *sukkah* in the Hebrew month of *Tishrei*, in the cooler fall weather, to ensure that we are building and utilizing the *sukkah* for the sake of God's commandment.[5]

The Festival of Sukkos is the third pilgrimage festival and the Torah associates it with rejoicing. It is the time when the farmer rejoices after he has gathered in his produce from the autumn harvest. His granaries are overflowing and he is full of thanks for his good fortune. Thus the Festival is also known as *Chag Ha-Asif*, the ingathering of the harvest.

In addition, we are also taught by our Sages that living in a *sukkah* serves as a reminder that this world is but a temporary one. Therefore, our goal in life should not be to possess and cherish worldly goods, but rather to serve Hashem. In addition, leaving our homes to dwell in a hut serves to remind us of those less fortunate than we and that we should be more charitable toward others.

Rabbi Levi Yitzchak of Berditchev used to invite all his neighbors, including those of lower social strata, to eat with him in his *sukkah*.

Once he was asked why he went out of his way to invite poor people. He replied with good humor, "In the future, in the World to Come, when all the righteous people will be invited to the great *sukkah* that will be created out of the skin of the Leviathan, I, Levi Yitzchak, will also wish to enter. No doubt, someone stationed at the entrance will stop me and demand angrily why I, a nobody among great personalities, have the nerve to force my way into the *sukkah*.

"I will answer, 'Please do not be angry with me. In my own *sukkah*, I also spent the Sukkos holiday with very ordinary people and I was not at all ashamed of them.'"

THE FOUR SPECIES

An important observance which is part of the Sukkos festival is the mitzvah of holding the Four Species. It is a Biblical commandment on Sukkos to hold in one's hand the *Arba'ah Minim* (Four Species): an *esrog* (citron), a *lulav* (palm branch), three *hadassim* (myrtle branches), and two *aravos* (willow branches). These are taken on all seven days of Sukkos except on Shabbos. If one does not have all the *minim* (species) he should elevate whatever he has available. However, he has not completely fulfilled the mitzvah and therefore cannot recite the special blessing.

When buying a *lulav* and *esrog*, one must exercise great care. There are many things that may invalidate them, and one who is not familiar with the laws should have his *Arba'ah Minim* checked by a rabbi.

In order to recite the blessing, one takes the *lulav*, to which the *hadassim* and *aravos* are bound, in his right hand, and the *esrog* in his left. Left-handed people hold the *lulav* in their left hand and the *esrog* in their right. Before the blessing is recited, the *esrog* is held upside down (with its *pitom* [opposite end from the stem] downward). After the blessing, he turns the *esrog* upright. Special prayers are recited throughout Sukkos.

Hallel and *Hoshannah* prayers are recited on all seven days of Sukkos. According to the Sephardic custom, the *Hoshanah* prayers are said after *Hallel*. According to the Ashkenazic custom, they are said after the *Musaf Shemoneh Esreh*.

The *lulav* is shaken in all six directions during *Hallel* when *Hodu La-Shem* and *Ana Hashem Hoshi'a Na* are said. There are various customs concerning the exact order of the directions in which to wave the *lulav*. During the *Hoshannah* prayers, the men carry their *Arba'ah Minim* in a procession that goes counterclockwise around the *bimah* (pulpit).

Although our religion is laden with meaningful practices which extend far beyond symbolism, nevertheless, there are mitzvos which can be interpreted to have certain specific significance, such as the Four Species.

The *esrog*, which is edible and emits a pleasant fragrance, is symbolic of those people who do good deeds and are learned in Torah. The *lulav*, which comes from a date tree that bears fruit, is compared to those who are learned in Torah but lacking in good deeds. The *hadass*, which has a pleasant fragrance but grows on a bush that bears no fruit, is compared to those who do good deeds but are ignorant of Torah. The *aravah*, which has neither taste nor aroma, represents the Jew who, unfortunately, has neither good deeds nor the knowledge of Torah to his credit.[6]

The Torah tells us to gather these Four Species, which represent four types of Jews, and hold them together. This symbolizes the importance of Jewish unity, as it is written in the prayers of Rosh Hashanah, "And they (Yisrael) shall all form a single bond to do Your will with a perfect heart."

ADDITIONAL LAWS OF SUKKOS

The first two days of Sukkos in the Diaspora are considered *Yom Tov* days. They have all of the prohibitions of Shabbos except for cooking and carrying. The next five days are *Chol Ha-Mo'ed*, when work is permitted. However, if one can arrange his vacation then, it is best to do so. Except for specific exceptions, it is not permissible to take a haircut or wash clothes during the five days of *Chol Ha-Mo'ed*. One is allowed to wash clothing for babies when necessary, because they need a constant change of clothing. The fifth day of *Chol Ha-Mo'ed* is called Hoshannah Rabbah. At the conclusion of the special *Yom Tov* prayers, we strike the floor with a bundle of five *aravos* (willow branches) at least five times.

The eighth day of Sukkos is Shemini Atzeres, and the following day is Simchas Torah. Both are considered full *Yom Tov* days. (In Eretz Yisrael, they are both celebrated on the eighth day.)

NOTES

1. Rav Chayim Volozhin, *Nefesh Ha-Chayim.*

2. *Shemos* 27:4.

3. *Midrash Tanchuma, Vayera.*

4. *Talmud Gittin,* 56.

5. Tur, *Shulchan Aruch,* 625.

6. *Vayikra Rabbah,* 30:12.

❦ Key People, Places and Things

ARBA'AH MINIM: the Four Species, which the Bible commands us to hold on Sukkos: an *esrog* (citron), a *lulav* (palm branch), 3 *hadassim* (myrtle branches), and 2 *aravos* (willow branches).

ASERES YEMEI HA-TESHUVAH: the Ten Days of Penitence, from Rosh Hashanah through Yom Kippur, designated for repentance and introspection.

KOHEN: a member of the priestly family who are descendants of Aharon. The *kohanim* performed the service in the *Beis Ha-Mikdash.*

KOHEN GADOL: the High Priest.

KORBAN (-OS): the sacrifice(s) offered in the Temple, a means of bringing a person closer to the Almighty.

MERAGLIM: the twelve spies who were sent to spy out the land of Kena'an. With the exception of Kalev and Yehoshua, they returned with a negative report about the land.

"NA'ASEH V'NISHMA": the Jews' commitment at Mount Sinai, stating, "We will do and we will listen."

ROSH HASHANAH: The Jewish New Year, a day of judgment and introspection.

SHEMINI ATZERES: the eighth day of Sukkos.

SHEMITTAH: the Sabbatical year (every seventh year), when the land in Eretz Yisrael must be left fallow.

SHOFAR: the ram's horn that is blown on Rosh Hashanah.

SIMCHAS TORAH: the last day of the Sukkos Festival, when we rejoice with the Torah. It coincides with Shemini Atzeres, the eighth day, in Eretz Yisrael. Elsewhere it is a separate Yom Tov — the ninth day.

SUKKOS: a joyous Festival lasting for seven days, when we dwell in a *sukkah* (a small hut).

TA'ANIS: a fast.

TASHLICH: a special prayer recited during the Ten Days of Penitence near a body of water, preferably one containing fish.

TISHREI: The Hebrew month corresponding to September/October, which contains the High Holy Days and Sukkos.

YOM KIPPUR: the Day of Atonement.

CHAPTER 10

The Jewish Nation Must Remain Holy
Korach's Rebellion; Balak and Bilam; Pinchas' Zealousness
(2449 – 2488/1312 B.C.E. – 1273 B.C.E.)

❧ HISTORY

THE REBELLION OF KORACH AND HIS FOLLOWERS

Korach was a prominent and very wealthy individual from the tribe of Levi. As a first cousin to Moshe and Aharon, he felt that he was not being given his due share of leadership. He was envious of the fact that Moshe was the leader of the Jewish nation and his brother, Aharon, was the high priest. When he was passed over for the position of prince (*nasi*) of the tribe of Levi, he could contain himself no longer. He assembled Dasan and Aviram, two agitators who felt that because they were from the tribe of Reuven, the eldest of Ya'akov's sons, they should also be leaders.

Korach, heading a group of *leviyim*, and Dasan and Aviram, leading a group from the tribe of Reuven, instigated a revolt against Moshe and Aharon. Included in this rebellion were two hundred and fifty prominent members of the assembly.

Moshe asked Korach and his followers to appear the next day. After warning the populace to stay clear of Korach and his assembly, Moshe announced the method with which God would indicate His selection of their leaders. If the rebels would die of natural causes, Moshe would be proven wrong, but if they would be swallowed alive by the earth, then Moshe's leadership would be confirmed.

No sooner had Moshe spoken than Korach and his fellow rebels, as well as all their possessions, were swallowed alive by the earth. The remainder of the people fled in terror.

Those who had survived began to murmur against Moshe, holding him responsible for the deaths of Korach and his followers. They were in turn punished through a plague, which took the lives of an additional 14,700 people. It was only when Aharon walked among the people with a pan of incense, as instructed by Moshe, that the plague subsided.

The rebellion and dispute that Korach led against Moshe and Aharon was begun purely because of jealousy and ego. He and his followers tried to make their motives seem sincere by sounding democratic and stating that everybody in the Jewish nation was holy and pure, but their real reason was to strengthen their own positions. They appealed to the populace by adopting a deceptively attractive argument: "What right do Moshe and Aharon have to act as the sole leaders of the Jews? Aren't all Jews holy? Let us have leaders who are chosen democratically."

Their protests were made for personal gain at the expense of Jewish unity. They were destructive rather than constructive and meant to benefit themselves rather than God's law.

There are other examples in history of jealousy which caused major disputes and civil war. During the period of the Judges, Avimelech, son of Gidon, was not content to be just a leader, but he killed sixty-nine of his seventy brothers, to ascertain that he would have no competition or threat to his leadership. Eventually he, too, was killed.

ETHICS I

The Pursuit of Peace

Aharon, the brother of Moshe, has been accorded a special place of affection in the history of the Jews. When he was alive, he was exceedingly popular. When he passed away, he was deeply mourned by all. Aharon was renowned as a peacemaker, one who loved and pursued peace. He was deeply concerned about the well-being of his fellow Jews and tried to improve their ways, not through harshness but friendship.

The Torah makes a point of stating that when Aharon died, all of the congregation of Yisrael wept for him for thirty days. This was because Aharon considered it his personal mission to settle all quarrels within the congregation and do his utmost to bring peace among them.

He went out of his way to see that husbands and wives who had quarreled were reunited. Whenever Aharon heard that two people were involved in a quarrel, he would go to one of them and tell him that he had recently met his friend,

who had stated, "This quarrel was my fault and I bitterly regret it." Aharon would then go to the second person and tell him the same story. When the two would meet again, they would hug each other and be reconciled. Thus, the nation wept when Aharon died, because they remembered his compassion and love for them.[1]

Moshe was also willing to relinquish his pride and honor in pursuit of peace. When Korach led a rebellion against him, Moshe himself went to search for the rebels to try to placate them. He did not rely on his high office and wait for them to come meekly to him. Instead, he took the initiative in the interests of peace. He did not worry about forfeiting his personal honor at this time.

Men should not let their pride become an obstacle to peace. If they do, then they are like the farmer who went every day to the barn to get milk, but returned with an empty pail.

"Why don't you ever bring back any milk?" his wife asked.

"The only way for me to get milk," answered the farmer, "is to bend down and milk the cow, and I would rather die than lose my pride and bend down to a cow."

Great Sages strove to emulate Aharon's trait of seeking peace. The great *Tanna*, Rabbi Meir, demonstrated this characteristic by the way he settled a dispute between a husband and wife.

The wife was a devoted follower of Rabbi Meir and frequently came to the *beis midrash* to hear his Torah discussions. One day, the lecture ran longer than usual and the woman arrived home late. Her husband was already home, tired and very hungry after a long day's work in the fields. When he realized why his supper was not yet prepared, he was furious with his wife. He told her that he would not admit her into the house until she would first spit in the eye of the revered Rabbi Meir. The woman was understandably upset but could do nothing about it, since she certainly could not spit in Rabbi Meir's face. She ended up wandering the streets.

People became aware of her unfortunate situation and word reached the ears of Rabbi Meir who summoned the poor woman to his *beis midrash*. He told her that he thought he had cataracts on his eyes and that if she were to spit in his eyes it would improve his condition. It was believed that a substance in the saliva improved cataracts. The woman at first refused, but when Rabbi Meir persisted she did as he bade her. Having fulfilled her husband's demand to spit in the face of Rabbi Meir, she was now able to return to her home. Their *shalom bayis* (family peace) was saved.

Rabbi Meir's students were very angry at that woman's husband and would have liked to see him punished for the indignity he had caused to their revered rabbi and teacher. Rabbi Meir, however, did not feel that he had suffered any indignity. There was absolutely no question of his personal honor involved, where *shalom bayis* between husband and wife was at stake. Rabbi Meir's honor was in no way diminished.

If both Aharon and Rabbi Meir were willing to go to such great lengths to bring about peace, we, too, must struggle to achieve the same results!

In the same vein, a rabbi once used his wisdom to secure true peace. Two Jews came before him and requested that he resolve their dispute. It seemed that they had both purchased burial plots in the same area, and each one wanted the better-landscaped spot.

After listening to the claims of each, and pondering for a moment, the rabbi announced: "Both of you have valid claims. Therefore, I have decided that the nicer spot should go to the one who dies first."

There was a long silence and from that moment on, there was no more argument about the burial plot!

❦ HISTORY

BALAK, BILAM, AND THE PLOT AGAINST THE JEWS

King Balak of Mo'av wished to hire Bilam, a noted sorcerer and wicked prophet of the gentiles, to destroy the Jewish nation by cursing them. Bilam hesitated since he had been warned by Hashem not to go with Balak's emissaries. Balak sent a second delegation offering greater rewards if Bilam agreed to cooperate. Bilam was finally given permission by Hashem to go to Balak, but only on the condition that he spoke as directed by Hashem. During the journey to Balak, Bilam's donkey saw an angel bearing a sword obstructing the path and so it turned aside. The impatient Bilam struck the animal several times in an attempt to make it proceed. Suddenly the donkey began to speak and protested this undeserved cruelty. Bilam finally saw the angel himself and was told that he was at fault for wanting to accept Balak's offer. Bilam offered to return home, but was told to continue on his trip and speak exactly as Hashem ordered him.

In response to Balak's request that he curse the Jewish nation, Bilam responded, "How can I curse the ones that Hashem has not cursed? Behold, it is a people that lives apart and is not included among other nations." Despite Balak's urgings, Bilam once again disappointed Balak by declaring that Hashem would not break His promise of blessing Yisrael and that no magic could prevail against them. In despair, Balak asked Bilam to desist from either cursing or blessing the Israelites. However, before departing, Bilam foretold the sovereignty of Yisrael and the doom of Mo'av, Edom, Amalek and other enemies of the Israelites.

Since God did not allow Bilam to curse the Jews, Bilam devised another plan. He suggested to Balak that he could cause the destruction of the Jews through other means. Enticing the Jews to commit the terrible sin of immorality with the Mo'avite women would be sure to cause God to be angry at His nation. Balak and Bilam carried out their infamous plan, which indeed aroused the wrath of the Almighty against the Jewish nation. As punishment for their participation in this grievous sin, 24,000 Israelites perished in a plague. If not for the zealousness of Pinchas, even more lives would have been lost.

Pinchas, the grandson of Aharon and son of Elazar the *Kohen Gadol* (High Priest), witnessed a flagrant act of immorality between Zimri, prince of the tribe of Shimon, and Kozbi, a Midyanite woman. Zealously defending the laws of God, he executed the evildoers. As a reward for his zeal in defending the honor of God, the priesthood was conferred on Pinchas and he was promised that it would be retained forever by his descendants.

LESSON I

Transmitting Jewish Values to the Family

There is an important blessing in the Torah which stresses the importance of the family, the foundation of Judaism. "How goodly are your tents, O Ya'akov, and your dwelling places, O Yisrael!" This was the blessing that came forth from Bilam's lips when he saw the camp of the Jews. He realized that the Jewish family is the mainstay of Jewish life. It is the family that provides the individual with love and a sense of worth. It is the family that passes down God's traditions from generation to generation. It is the family that makes the individual feel part of a larger group, which is the Jewish nation.

Judaism sees the family unit as the cornerstone of the Jewish people, the basic structure protecting its existence. A strong religious family helps all its members weather the tempests of life. A stable home guarantees the transmission of Jewish tradition.

An integral part of the observance of the holiday of Pesach is recounting to our children the story of the exodus from Egypt. The unusual foods and customs at the Seder table are meant to prompt questions from the children. Jews must be especially careful to satisfy the curiosity of their children in the ways of the Torah. They are essential links in the chain that keeps our Jewish tradition strong and growing.

Parents who raise their children prop-erly are true heroes and their work can never be sufficiently praised. Sometimes in raising a child, it is necessary to discipline him, as when we read at the Pesach Seder of the wicked son who asks, "What is all this to you?" This question shows that he considers himself separate from the Jewish nation. That is why we strongly rebuke him, saying, "If you had been in Egypt at the time of the redemption, you and those like you would not have been saved. You would have remained in Egypt and died there." (This is actually what happened to the wicked Israelites who didn't want to leave. They perished during the plague of darkness.)

King David, although loyal and faithful to God, did not admonish and punish his sons when necessary. The result was that his son Avshalom rebelled against him. This led to a civil war, with the loss of many lives, including that of Avshalom. Later on, another son, Adoniyahu, also rebelled and unsuccessfully attempted to assume the throne.[2]

Every parent is obligated to train his children in the observance of the commandments in accordance with each child's age and capacity, as it is written, "Chanoch la-na'ar al-pi darko" ("Educate the child according to his way").[3] From the time Jewish children begin to talk and possess minimal understanding, their parents teach them short verses from the Torah that are crucial to a Jew's life. The verses of: "*Torah tzivah lanu Moshe, morashah kehillas Ya'akov*" ("Moshe commanded the [laws of the] Torah to us; it is an inheritance to the community [nation] of Ya'akov") and "*Shema Yisrael Hashem Elokeinu, Hashem Echad*" ("Hear O Yisrael, the Lord our God, the Lord is One,") are the first things that Jewish parents should teach their young ones.

A parent is required to teach his children Torah and to ensure that they receive formal instruction in Jewish religious studies. This is in fulfillment of the Biblical precept, "And you shall teach them [these words of the Torah] to your children..."[4] The family should regularly attend the synagogue. A child, however, should not be brought to synagogue until he is old enough to control his behavior.

The Jewish family's best opportunity for being together is at the Shabbos table. The meal is enhanced with the singing of special Shabbos songs (*zemiros*) and discussion of stories with Jewish themes. To waste these very impressionable early years solely on stories and songs that have no lasting value is irresponsible and foolish.

LESSON II

Pinchas' Zealousness Helped Save the Jewish Nation

The Torah relates that after Pinchas killed Zimri, Hashem told Moshe to greet him with the covenant of peace and to inform the people that Pinchas' act brought forgiveness for them. Pinchas' reaction might have appeared to betray a cruel and harsh nature. It could easily have been interpreted as having been motivated by a tendency towards violence or personal hatred. Therefore, Hashem informed the Jews that Pinchas was motivated in his act solely by great love for the Almighty and devotion to the Jews.

There might be those who scorn Pinchas' actions as being too "hard-line" and inflexible. They would rather advocate caution and compromise and would have tried to find possible excuses for Zimri and Kozbi. Going further, they might have tried to moderate the very law that the Jewish nation is holy and must be separate from the other nations. Pinchas risked his life to uphold the law, which saved the Jews from a catastrophe.

Pinchas possessed two qualities essential for his mission: zeal in protecting Hashem's commandments and a great love for his fellow Jews. It was for this reason that Pinchas' reward was not in the form of mere earthly possessions, but rather a permanent heritage for all his descendants, a reward that has lasted to this very day. It is to such rewards that the individual Jew must aspire by exhibiting his zeal and faith in Hashem to extraordinary degrees.

Until now, only Aharon and his two surviving sons were *kohanim*. (Their descendants would be *kohanim* as well.) After Pinchas' great zeal on behalf of the Almighty, however, he and his descendants were also designated to be priests forever after. His brave and courageous action prevented future tragic punishment of the Jews.

❦ HISTORY

THE CONQUEST OF MIDYAN

The Jews were ordered to prepare for an offensive war against the Midyanites, who had been primarily responsible for their degradation. The attack on the Midyanites was made by 12,000 Israelite warriors, 1,000 men from each tribe. They were accompanied by Pinchas, who took with him the holy vessels and trumpets for sounding during the battle. During the war, every male Midyanite was slain, including the five kings of Midyan, as well as Bilam. The victors took the women, children, cattle, and other possessions of the Midyanites with them as spoils of war. Moshe, however, reprimanded them for keeping alive the older women, who had been the cause of the plague on the Jews, and who were ordered to be immediately executed.

Because of the wickedness of Midyan's plan for enticing the Jews, there is a positive precept in the Torah to oppress the Midyanites. On the other hand, there is a prohibition against oppressing the Egyptians even though they tried to physically destroy the Jews. The reason for the more severe approach with regard to Midyan is that they did more than try to destroy us physically. They attempted to destroy us spiritually as well. The physical destruction of a human deprives him of life in this world. However, spiritual destruction results in his losing his eternal life in the World to Come.

The Midyanites realized that the strength of the Jews lies in their spiritual power, in being a holy nation that occupies a special status before God. Because of this special status, the Jewish people are considered a priestly kingdom and merit Hashem's special protection.

MITZVAH

Kashrus

"Sanctify yourself and be holy for I am holy."[5]

"You shall be holy unto Me, for I the Lord am holy and I have set you apart from other people to be Mine."[6]

This is the rationale of the laws of *kashrus. Kashrus* is the Hebrew word that refers to the Jewish dietary laws. It is related to the word kosher, which means fit, proper, or in accordance with the religious law. Any food that satisfies the requirements of Jewish law is fit for eating — it is kosher.

Those who criticize the observance of *kashrus* on the grounds that it tends to separate us from other people and faiths, fail to understand the very purpose of the laws of *kashrus*. The barriers that are automatically erected by the laws of *kashrus* are indeed intentional. They prevent assimilation and intermarriage which are the plagues of the Jewish nation. We find the connection between separation and *kashrus* explicitly stated in the Torah. "I am the Lord your God Who have set you apart from the nations. You shall therefore separate between the clean beast and the unclean and between the unclean fowl and the clean..."[7] The breakdown in *kashrus* observance has been a strong contributing factor to the increase of intermarriage and assimilation. *Kashrus* by itself does not make a Jewish home or provide the holiness which is its primary purpose; however, any attempt to build a Jewish home without *kashrus* is like erecting a building without a foundation.

Kosher food refers to ritually acceptable food in accordance with Jewish law. The dietary practice has transformed the process of eating from a purely animal act to one in which spirituality plays a part. The signs which differentiate kosher animals from non-kosher ones are stated explicitly in the Torah. Kosher animals have cloven hoofs and chew their cud. All birds of prey are forbidden. All birds that have the characteristic of picking food out of the air without waiting for the food to reach the ground are prohibited. All fish that have fins and scales are kosher. Insects, creeping things, and the like are abominations and are prohibited as food. Animal and fowl which have died without ritual slaughter are forbidden.

Animals utilized for food are slaughtered according to strict Jewish law (Halachah) under expert supervision. The soaking and salting of meat are for the purpose of eliminating as much blood as possible.

While it is certainly true that the Torah is concerned about people's health and well-being, this is not the only rationale for *kashrus*. The Torah is also concerned with our spiritual well-being and inner purity. Therefore, when the Torah tells us to avoid certain foods, it thereby provides for our spiritual cleanliness. Foods which are inherently unclean and disgusting, such as the meat of animals that died of disease, or the products of insects and pigs, are not kosher. Those who eat them have little regard for their own spiritual purity. Similarly, foods of naturally vicious animals, such as birds of prey and beasts of the forest, are prohibited, while products of domesticated animals, like the chicken and the cow, are allowed. We are, in a way, influenced by what we eat.

We must be very careful of the food that we allow to enter our bodies. One must make sure that the foodstuffs one buys do not contain any non-kosher ingredients. One should ascertain that the meat was properly prepared. This is something that cannot be taken for granted.

It is prohibited for a Jew to:

(a) cook, roast, bake, or fry dairy and meat together,

(b) eat milk and meat together,

(c) or derive any benefit or pleasure from their mixture. (One cannot sell it or give it as a present.) Chicken and other fowl have the same law as meat, but eggs are considered *pareve* and may be eaten with either meat or dairy.

Dishes, pots or any kind of utensils that are used for milk or milk products should not be used for meat, and vice versa. Therefore, every Jewish household must have two sets of tableware, dishes, pots and pans, kitchenware, soaps, steel wool, dish brushes, dishpans, sink grates, and dishwasher racks. If something is confused or a mistake was made, a rabbi should be consulted immediately.

If one has eaten meat, he must wait approximately six hours before eating dairy. Jews of German descent have the custom of waiting only three hours. If one has just eaten a milk meal or a dairy snack like a milk-chocolate bar or ice cream, and would like to eat meat, he should wash his hands, and rinse out his mouth to remove any traces of the milk, before proceeding to eat meat. One must wait six hours after eating Swiss cheese or any aged cheeses before eating meat.

"Keeping a kosher home" is unfortunately no longer identical with "observing kashrus." Eating like a Jew at home and like a gentile outside the home leads to the ridiculous situation where some Jews are more particular about what goes onto their household dishes than what goes into their stomachs.

The laws of kashrus are included in the category of chukkim (statutes). These are statutes specified by the Torah for which there are no readily apparent reasons. Yet we must observe these laws for they are the stated will of Hashem. This point was made by a rabbi who was once stopped by a fellow Jew as he was hurrying through the streets.

"Excuse me, Rabbi," said the other man, "but since you are a learned individual, perhaps you could explain to me why we are prohibited to eat pork. There seems to be no reason for this prohibition."

"I would really like to discuss this with you at length," replied the rabbi, "but I'm on my way to the pharmacy to buy some medicine and I must get it right away."

"But why are you making this long trip yourself?" asked the man. "Why didn't you send a messenger to buy the medicine?"

"Because I also want to ask the pharmacist about the effectiveness of the medicine."

"I'm sorry, but I don't understand," said the man. "Why must you ask the pharmacist about the medicine? Isn't the advice of a doctor good enough?"

"Ah!" exclaimed the rabbi. "Do you hear what you have just said? You want me to accept the word of the doctor unquestioningly. Then why do you not accept God's laws as they are? If Hashem has ordered us not to eat pork, then He must feel that this is beneficial for us. The laws of kashrus, whether we understand them or not, are like medicine that must be taken for one's benefit. The duty of a rabbi is merely to explain how to follow the laws of the Torah correctly, just as it is the job of the pharmacist to explain how to use the doctor's prescription correctly."

❧ HISTORY

THE DEATH OF MIRYAM (2488/1273 B.C.E.)

For thirty-eight years, the Israelites roamed through the wilderness, during which time all of the older generation between the ages of twenty and sixty died. Yehoshua and Kalev were exceptions; they entered the Land of Yisrael. At the beginning of the fortieth year from the exodus, the remainder of the populace returned to a place called Kadesh. It was there that Miryam, the sister of Moshe and Aharon, died. At her passing, the well of water that had miraculously accompanied the Israelites in the desert ceased to exist.

LESSON III

The Jewish Woman's Contribution to Jewish History

Besides the Matriarchs (Sarah, Rivkah, Rachel, and Leah), whom we discussed earlier, there are other great Jewish women who contributed to the growth and survival of the Jewish nation. During the bleakest time of Egyptian slavery, it was the righteous Jewish women who gave their husbands the needed moral support and encouragement. In fact, the Talmud states that it was due to the merit of the righteous women of Egypt that the Jewish people were finally redeemed from slavery.[8]

The ruthless regimen of work and agony inflicted by their Egyptian slave-masters drove the men to such a state of despair that they felt utterly spent, and there was danger that the Jewish people would, God forbid, cease to exist. It was the valiant Jewish women of that era who inspired their husbands with faith and courage. They breathed into them their own indomitable spirit to live so that even under these seemingly hopeless conditions they continued their normal family lives in order that the Israelites should thrive and multiply. They had complete faith in God, believing fully that it is within His power to sustain and feed all and that He could and would save the Children of Yisrael. In this way, the women hastened the redemption.

When the oppression of slavery descended upon the Jews of Egypt, and Paroh decreed that all male Jewish children be thrown into the Nile River, many husbands separated from their wives, and refused to father any additional children. Among these was Amram, the father of Miryam and Aharon. It was Miryam who persuaded her father to change his mind and return to his wife. As a result of her influence, Moshe was born.

It was also due to Miryam's greatness that the Jews were given a well of water that miraculously traveled along with them during their sojourn in the desert. Miryam is ranked among the seven female prophetesses.[9] She was also the one to lead the women in singing *shirah* (songs of praise to the Almighty) after Hashem split the Red Sea for the Jews.

Another prominent Jewish woman who was a judge, a leader, and also a prophetess, was Devorah. She inspired and successfully led the Jews against their oppressors. They were victorious because of her leadership. She then sang songs of praise to the Almighty in gratitude for His saving the Jews from their enemies.

Ya'el is another woman of distinction. She is mentioned in the Bible because of the heroism she showed in killing the enemy general, Sisera.

Ruth, whose love for Judaism caused her to abandon her royal background and become a convert to Judaism, merited being the ancestress of the dynasty of King David.

In the time of the Maccabees, when Judaism was threatened by the Greeks and Hellenists, the heroism of Channah and her seven sons stands out as an inspiration to all Jews to resist all attempts to destroy our religion. Another heroine from this period was Yehudis. She risked her life to save the Jews by killing a Greek general.

"A good wife, who can find? Far above rubies is her worth; the heart of her husband trusts in her... Her children rise up and call her blessed."[10]

"He who finds a wife, finds good."[11]

"Home is the wife. I never call my wife, 'wife'. I call her 'home' (bayis) for she makes my home."[12]

"Love your wife as you love yourself and honor her more than yourself."[13]

"Be careful to honor your wife, for blessing enters the house because of her."[14]

We must remember that because of physical and perhaps psychological differences, men and women can often best serve God in different ways. Because the woman is so necessary in managing the household, it is she who is assigned some of the mitzvos associated with the home, such as the mitzvah of lighting the Shabbos candles and taking off a portion of the dough (taking challah).

On the other hand, man is given many of the commandments relating to public life, such as prayer in the synagogue, rabbinical officiation, and testifying in public court. The fact that a man's mitzvos appear to be more in the spotlight does not make him superior to a woman. Remember that according to Jewish law, the decision on whether or not a child is Jewish is based on the religious identity of the mother, not the father. The mother therefore plays a pivotal role in the development of the Jewish family. Jewish mothers have proven to be the key element in the survival of the family, despite a history filled with pogroms, expulsions, and oppression.

The Torah nowhere implies that women are in any way inferior to men. In fact, we have seen that Jewish women have reached the highest level of prophecy. There is no reason to believe that a woman could not perform the same tasks as men. Nor is there any reason why women who perform the exact same jobs should not receive equal pay. However, one should bear in mind that a woman should not sacrifice her family for the sake of a profession. It is certainly permissible for a woman to work outside her home, and even be involved in a career; however, the Torah outlook is that one should strive to find satisfaction and fulfillment in one's Divinely ordained role and not pursue outside interests to the detriment or exclusion of the main task in life for which there is no substitute. Judaism severely condemns the exploitation of women as sex objects, or the stereotyping of women as a group rather than as individuals.

The Torah certainly recognizes the central role played by women in passing on Jewish values and customs. It especially appreciates the capabilities of women in raising Jewish children. Therefore, women are exempted from certain mitzvos to allow them sufficient time for their vitally important activities. This does not mean, however, that women are second-class Jewish citizens. On the contrary, they are essential partners in the maintenance of the Jewish nation.

Some point to the daily blessing, "Blessed be You, O God...Who did not make me a woman," as evidence that Judaism considers women inferior. This is not true. Rather, the blessing refers to the fact that men are obligated to perform more mitzvos than are women, and therefore thank God for this extra opportunity. The Torah did not want to compel women to go to the synagogue or *beis ha-midrash* to pray and learn at length each day. If this were required of them, who would care for the children, and who would supervise the house? (Another possible reason for women's exclusion from these mitzvos is that women are generally secluded from the negative influences of society, and are on a higher spiritual level, having a greater role in the Godly act of creation through giving birth. Men, having more association with the outside world, are more likely to come into contact with negative influences, and therefore need the reminder of these mitzvos to keep them constantly aware of God's supremacy.) Since she is absolved from these mitzvos, the woman has more time to attend to important matters in the home.

ETHICS II

Guarding One's Tongue from Evil Gossip

Miryam was a very righteous person, but she was once punished with a leprosy-like condition for speaking about her brother Moshe in a bad light. She did not have bad intentions, but it was wrong nonetheless, since it was gossip.

Speaking evil of another is considered a most heinous act. It does more harm than physically assaulting the person. It is true that one who has just been hurt physically feels a very definite pain, but usually that pain subsides in a short while. On the other hand, a disparaging remark can linger and haunt the victim for years. Someone who makes the stray comment that a prospective job applicant looks untrustworthy can cost him not only one job, but other jobs as well. Word spreads very easily, especially if it's a bit of juicy gossip.

Speaking evil can be compared to opening a bag of feathers. Even if one later wanted to gather them all back together, one could not, because they would have already been spread far and wide by the wind.

The Chafetz Chaim, the great sage who lived from 1839-1933, was legendary in avoiding and stopping evil gossip. He wrote books and essays devoted to this topic.

The Chafetz Chaim once paid a visit to a prospective supporter of his academy. When he arrived, the man, a wealthy businessman, was in the midst of preparing a telegram to his business partner. He rose to greet the Chafetz Chaim and engaged him in conversation. Soon it became apparent to the Chafetz Chaim that the discussion was leading to talk about a certain individual and that *lashon ha-ra* (evil gossip) might ensue.

The Chafetz Chaim suddenly arose and glanced at the telegram on the man's desk. "It looks as if you have carefully thought out every single word here," he commented, "for you've rewritten this several times."

"I certainly have," said the man. "Every unnecessary word here will cost me extra money."

The Chafetz Chaim marveled at this. "If only everyone would be as careful as this when choosing what to say!" he noted. "Don't people know that every unnecessary word they speak will cost them dearly in the World to Come?"

The Chafetz Chaim was once traveling in a wagon with horse dealers. During the trip, his traveling companions were discussing topics relating to horses and cattle. In the middle of their conversation, one of the travelers began to speak against another dealer.

The Chafetz Chaim reprimanded them for speaking and listening to *lashon ha-ra*, and asked them to continue discussing animals rather than people. When he saw, however, that the dealers refused to pay attention to what he told them, he asked the wagon driver to stop, and got off in the middle of the road.

Speaking *lashon ha-ra* is really a serious offense. Note that the punishment mentioned in the Torah for the sin of speaking *lashon ha-ra* is affliction with a disease called *tzara'as*. For instance, it was with *tzara'as* that Miryam was stricken after speaking to her brother, Aharon, concerning their brother, Moshe.

Those who speak evil about others believe that they are gaining status for themselves by belittling others and causing them to become isolated. That is why the one who speaks evil of another is afflicted with *tzara'as* and must be isolated. This is the same condition that he inflicted upon the person he spoke about. Now that he knows what it is like himself, he will be more careful in the future.

The great *Tanna* Rabbi Yannai once observed a peddler striding through town and chanting, "Who wants to buy the elixir of life?" Rabbi Yannai approached the peddler and asked him to reveal his secret potion for a lengthy existence. The peddler refused, but Rabbi Yannai persisted. Finally, the peddler responded, "You do not need any special potions. The key to a long, happy life is contained in your holy books, which state, 'Who is the man who desires life... Guard your tongue from evil....'"[15]

Rabbi Yannai turned to his companions and said, "I did not fully understand the meaning of this verse until the peddler clarified it. He brought it to my attention that avoiding *lashon ha-ra* is in itself a remedy for the torments of life." If one refrains from speaking ill of others, and if one keeps away from animosity and arguments, then he has a better chance of living a calmer, more peaceful, and, therefore, longer life.

❧ HISTORY

THE END OF MOSHE'S LEADERSHIP

After the death of Miryam and the disappearance of the well, the people began to complain against Moshe and Aharon due to the lack of water. Hashem told Moshe and Aharon to speak to a specific rock and command it to give forth water. However, Moshe was so angered by the people's disrespect that he impatiently struck the rock instead of just speaking to it. Because they had not followed Hashem's instructions and did not honor Him before the people, Moshe and Aharon were told that they would not be allowed to enter the Holy Land. Aharon died shortly after and Moshe installed Aharon's son Elazar as the next *Kohen Gadol.*

Moshe then began his final discourse to the people. He appealed to them to remember Hashem their God, Who took them out of slavery in Egypt, watched over them during the years of wandering in the wilderness, and Who would continue to protect them in the future.

Towards the end of the discourse, Moshe warned the nation that if they observed God's commandments, they would receive numerous blessings. These would include prosperity from the fields and within their cities, abundant livestock, the subjugation of enemies, and supremacy over nations. But the alternative would lead to disaster: disease, famine, and death would result. The Land of Yisrael would be overrun by a cruel nation. The Jews would be scattered throughout the world and they would once again become slaves.

The life of the great leader was nearing its end. Moshe ascended the mountain of Nevo, where he was shown Eretz Yisrael. At the age of one hundred and twenty, Moshe went to his everlasting rest. The Almighty Himself took care of the burial of His most devoted servant, Moshe. Thus, no one knows the exact location of Moshe's burial site.

The Torah concludes with the statement, "There has not arisen a prophet in Yisrael like Moshe, whom the Lord knew face to face."

❧ Key People, Places and Things

BALAK: the king of Midyan, who hired Bilam to curse the Jews.

BILAM: the gentile prophet who was hired to curse the Jews but was thwarted by Hashem, and ended up blessing them.

DASAN AND AVIRAM: agitators from the tribe of Reuven who joined Korach's rebellion.

FLEISHIK: (Y.) containing meat or meat products.

KORACH: the leader of a rebellion against Moshe and Aharon.

KOSHER: food that is halachically permissible for a Jew to eat.

LASHON HA-RA: evil gossip.

MILCHIK: (Y.) containing milk or milk products.

PAREVE: food that is neither dairy nor meat and may be eaten with either one.

SHEMIRAS HA-LASHON: guarding one's tongue.

TREIF: non-kosher.

NOTES

1. *Otzros D'Rabbi Nasan, Ohev Shalom,* 12:3.
2. *Shemos Rabbah,* 15:1.
3. *Mishlei* 22:6.
4. *Devarim* 11:10.
5. *Vayikra* 11:44.
6. *Vayikra* 20:26.
7. *Vayikra* 20:24-25.
8. *Talmud Sotah,* 116.
9. *Talmud Megillah,* 14.
10. *Mishlei* 31:10.
11. *Mishlei* 18:22.
12. *Talmud Yoma,* 2; *Talmud Shabbos,* 118b.
13. *Talmud Yevamos,* 62b.
14. *Talmud Bava Metzia,* 59.
15. *Midrash Rabbah,* 16:2; *see also Talmud Avodah Zarah,* 19b.

❧ Introduction to Chapter 11

This chapter tells of the conquest and settlement of the Promised Land. As the successor to Moshe, Yehoshua led the Jewish people through seven years of conquering Eretz Yisrael. During that time, he defeated many nations. The spectacular victories of the Jews were highlighted by revealed miracles performed by God, including the fall of the walls of Yericho and the sun at Givon standing still. The initial setback at Ai, due to the transgression of Achan and the Jews' subsequent victory there, proved God's involvement in these events.

The conquest of Eretz Yisrael and the expulsion of its inhabitants were commanded by God. As stated in *Parashas Shemos,* "They (the enemy nations) shall not dwell in your land lest they cause you to sin against Me" (23:33). "If you will not drive out the inhabitants of the land before you, those whom you leave shall be pricks in your eyes, and thorns in your sides ...and it shall be that which I intended to do to them, I shall do to you" (*Bemidbar* 33:55-56). Bnei Yisrael were commanded to drive out the Kena'anites and were forbidden to live alongside of these heathen and degenerate nations, for they would have exerted a negative influence on the Jews.

We must remember that when we speak of the conquest of Eretz Yisrael, we are not stressing the military prowess of Yehoshua and the Jews, but rather (as Yehoshua himself emphasized) the Divine help given to the Jews to achieve its conquest. Since the conquest came about because of Hashem's direct intervention in assisting the Jews, their continued existence in the Land is contingent upon their obeying and fulfilling God's wishes. That is why the Book of Joshua begins with the words: "This book of the Torah shall not leave your mouth; you shall meditate therein day and night, in order that you may observe to do all that is written in it, for then will you succeed in all your ways and then will you prosper" (1:8). It concludes with Yehoshua's own plea for *Bnei Yisrael* to enter a covenant with the Almighty. Of their own free will, they committed themselves to worship only Hashem and to follow His commandments.

CHAPTER 11

Yehoshua and the Conquest of Yisrael
(2488-2516/1273 B.C.E. - 1245 B.C.E.)

❧ HISTORY

YEHOSHUA, NEW LEADER OF THE JEWISH PEOPLE (2488/1273 B.C.E.)

After the death of Moshe, the greatest leader the Jewish people have ever known, God spoke to Yehoshua, telling him that it was time to lead the Jewish nation across the Jordan River to the Land that Hashem promised them. Yehoshua was chosen to assume the leadership of the Jews because of his exemplary devotion to Moshe. This made him worthy of filling his master's position. Like Moshe, he had the two basic qualities required of a leader of the Jewish people. He was personally humble in spirit, but to the public he showed a stern and courageous stance on behalf of God and His people. It was Yehoshua who did not agree with the spies, sent by Moshe, who spoke ill of Eretz Yisrael. He publicly contradicted the spies and tried to encourage the people to follow God's commandment of conquering Yisrael.

LESSON I

True Leadership

Moshe is considered the greatest leader the Jewish people ever had. He is one of the very few leaders referred to as the Servant of God. This attribute is the highest praise that can be given to a human being. It testifies to that individual's total devotion to his Master. Moshe's extreme devotion to God was in no way motivated by personal aspirations for glory. For instance, we find that after the Israelites made the Golden Calf and God wanted to destroy them and start a new nation from Moshe's descendants, Moshe pleaded with the Almighty not to destroy the Jews. Then he went further and requested that if God were to destroy the Jews, then he, too, should be erased from God's Book.

Maimonides lists in his Thirteen Principles of Faith for a Jew, that it is incumbent upon a Jew to recognize the unsurpassed stature of Moshe. As the Torah states, "There has not arisen a prophet in Yisrael like Moshe, whom the Lord knew face to face."

With regard to Moshe, the Torah states, "No man knows his burial place." Our Sages explain that this means that Moshe is not enshrined in an ordinary tomb, but rather he is within the heart of every single Jew.

The great leader who succeeded

Moshe was his own disciple, Yehoshua. Yehoshua served Moshe with total devotion, from morning to night. He was a reflection of Moshe's own greatness. He showed great personal courage and integrity even before becoming leader of the Jewish nation. Yehoshua was one of the twelve spies sent by Moshe to scout out the land of Kena'an. Upon their return, he refused to go along with the negative and despairing report given by ten of the spies. Rather, he sought to counter their disheartening words. He was rewarded by being chosen by Hashem to lead the Jewish people into the Land of Yisrael.

God assured Yehoshua that his authority would remain unchallenged. Just as He had supported Moshe, so, too, would He support his successor. God encouraged him to be strong and courageous and to observe carefully all the laws that Moshe had handed down to the nation. God guaranteed Yehoshua that if the Jews would remain faithful, they would merit His constant protection.

A leader of the Jewish people must have total belief in God and, through personal example, should inspire others to feel likewise. He must be one whom others will respect and model themselves after. He should possess the personal attributes of sincerity and concern for others and should not consider himself superior to his fellowmen. Yet he should also be firm and unwavering in his devotion to God. If God's supremacy or commandments are challenged, he should react with vigor against those who are rebelling against His laws. In this sense, a Jewish leader must be strong and dynamic, rather than weak and vacillating.

ETHICS I

Rachav Risked Her Life To Protect Others

Yehoshua immediately put into effect all that God had told him, and ordered his officers to prepare for the journey. Yehoshua sent two spies, Kalev and Pinchas, to explore the land of Kena'an, especially the fortified city of Yericho. This was to be the first city conquered in Kena'an. Upon reaching Yericho, the two went to the house of a woman named Rachav. Soldiers of the king came to seize them, but Rachav, who had risked her life to hide the two men on her roof, responded, "Yes, the men were here, but I do not know where they came from. When it grew dark, they left, and I don't know where they went. If you chase after them immediately, you will overtake them."

While the soldiers set off in pursuit of the spies, Rachav returned to the roof to assure the two men of their safety. She told them that after having heard of all the miracles that God had performed in taking the Jews out of Egypt, she realized that He would also fulfill His promise to give the Land to the Jews. Her people were consequently disheartened and discouraged.

She asked the two men to swear to her that, upon their return, they would deal kindly with her and her family and spare their lives. The men replied that so long as she did not betray them, they would indeed save her and her family when God gave Yericho into their hands. Rachav then lowered them by rope from a window and warned them to go to the hills and remain hidden there for three days until the search parties disbanded.

"When we return to Yericho," they instructed her in turn, "tie this scarlet string in your window. Gather your parents and entire family into your house. If any of them leave, they will be responsible for their own deaths and we shall be guiltless. If, however, you reveal to anyone all that we have said to you, we will no longer be bound by the oath which you have made us take."

The two men followed Rachav's instructions. They stayed in the hills for three days and then returned to Yehoshua with a full report of what had transpired. They summarized the success of their mission by stating, "God has given the entire Land into our hands and the people are overcome with fear of us."

The name Rachav means "wide," meaning that her merits were plentiful. She was willing to risk her life for the sake of helping the two *meraglim* (spies), Pinchas and Kalev. After she recognized the greatness of Hashem, she converted to Judaism. Ultimately, Yehoshua married Rachav. By her willingness to risk her own life in order to save theirs, Rachav merited having great descendants, among whom were prophets and priests. Those who are willing to risk their lives to save others, merit special rewards among the Jewish nation.

LESSON II

No Matter How Low One Has Fallen Spiritually, One Can Still Repent

Who was Rachav? Scripture refers to her as a *zonah*. According to some commentaries, this (*zonah*) means someone of the lowest moral standards. This descriptive title was given to her up until the time that she hid the spies. Rachav was a member of the lowest element of society, yet she was able to repent and reach such a high level that she was worthy of eventually becoming the wife of Yehoshua. They were the progenitors of great people in Jewish history.

Rachav became the symbol of repentance. Her descendants, such as Yirmeyahu, later called upon *Bnei Yisrael* to do *teshuvah* and pointed out the example of their ancestress, Rachav. On occasion, a person can think that he has already committed so many terrible sins, has sunk to such depths, that there is no hope of salvation for him. One can then point to Rachav as an example of one who went from the depths of sin to the heights of *teshuvah*. There is always hope for the repentant, the *ba'al teshuvah*.

In our daily prayers we request Hashem's help in removing the evil inclination from inside us. What does this mean? It means that even after the evil inclination has accomplished its goal of causing one to sin, it proceeds further to convince the poor sinner that it is too late for him to do anything to remedy the situation. The person then feels hopelessly engulfed in sin and that *teshuvah* will no longer help him. That is why we pray that the Almighty should remove the evil inclination from inside us, so that even after we have sinned we should be able to return and repent.

❦ HISTORY

GOD'S MIRACLE AT THE CROSSING OF THE JORDAN RIVER

Yehoshua and the nation prepared to cross the Jordan River. Hashem spoke to Yehoshua and told him that his greatness would increase in the eyes of the nation when they behold the coming miracle. The people would then come to realize that God was with him, just as He had been with Moshe.

God told Yehoshua to instruct the priests to remain standing at the edge of the Jordan River with the Holy Ark, while the rest of the nation was crossing over. As soon as the bearers of the Ark reached the Jordan River and their feet touched the edge of the water, the flowing waters came to a halt, and stood as a wall. When all the people had finished crossing over on dry ground, the bearers of the Ark advanced to the front of the people. Then the waters of the Jordan resumed their natural course and flowed as before.

After the whole nation saw this great miracle, they realized that God was indeed among them and that He would drive out their enemies from the Land.

Yehoshua commanded that a person from each tribe take one stone from the Jordan River and set it up at Gilgal as a monument. These stones were to be a testimony to future generations of God's great miracle shown to the Jews.

When all the kingdoms in the land of Kena'an heard of the miracles God had performed on the Jews' behalf, their hearts melted and they had no spirit to fight.

LESSON III

The Commandment to Conquer Eretz Yisrael

Until the splitting of the Jordan River, the Children of Yisrael were unsure as to whether or not it was proper for them to capture the land of other nations who were dwelling in Eretz Yisrael at that time. The splitting of the Jordan River was a clear sign to the *Bnei Yisrael* that it was not they who were capturing the land, but rather Hashem Himself, Who was going before them. The Jordan split out of respect for the Master of the uni-verse, and it is He Who has the right to take land from the hands of one and give it to another.

There are people who ask, By what right did the Israelites conquer the land of Kena'an from the nations who had lived there for so many years? Even to-day, there are people who ask what right the Jews had to settle and colonize Eretz Yisrael in seeming disregard of the Arabs and "Palestinians" who now live there.

These questions are best answered with a parable of the Dubno Maggid.

A wealthy merchant who owned a beautiful home decided to travel abroad and settle elsewhere for a while. He did not want to sell his ancestral home, but neither did he want it to decay while he was away. He solved this problem by turning over his home to a reputable young man who would have full use of the home and the surrounding land while he was away, but on condition that whenever the owner would return, he must not be denied any request in connection with the house. He must be treated with respect, as befitting a landlord. Legal documents were drawn up in the presence of a lawyer, listing all the numerous rights of the tenant, and also his obligations to the real landlord of the house.

After an absence of many years, the landlord returned to his home. He didn't really want to bother the young man who was living there. In fact, he was willing to allow him to continue to live there so long as he did not disturb the landlord and abided by the conditions set forth by the latter.

Despite the landlord's good intentions, the tenant's response was, "You are a stranger here. You have no rights to this house. It is mine and I am free to do as I please."

"Stranger? Who is the stranger in this house?" asked the landlord. "You seem to forget our agreement. This is my house! I built it, raised my family here, and was kind enough to allow you to live here, rent-free, so long as you cared for the property and followed my rules."

The young man saw that he couldn't persuade the old man to leave willingly, and so he took the case to court. At first the judge was inclined to rule in favor of the tenant. However, when the old landlord showed him the conditions of the original deed of transfer, he agreed that the law was on the side of the old man. Turning to the young man, the judge said, "Had you lived up to your part of the agreement and allowed him to live peacefully with you in the house, following his conditions as landlord, you may be sure that you would not have been thrown out of your home. Instead, you violated the one condition under which he ceded the property to you. You were insolent and refused to abide by the conditions set forth by the owner."

The same is true with regard to Eretz Yisrael. Hashem promised the Land to Avraham and to his children forever after. When the *Bnei Yisrael* returned to the Land, they were like the old landlord returning to his ancestral home. Just as the landlord had set conditions for the tenant to be able to continue living in the house, so, too, had Yehoshua and the Jews set certain conditions if the Kena'anites wished to remain unharmed in the Land. These conditions were set forth in written proclamations sent by Yehoshua to the Seven Nations inhabiting Eretz Yisrael before the Jews crossed the Jordan River.

Had the Seven Nations been willing to accept these conditions (among which was the demand that they abolish all idol worship), then the Israelites would have made a covenant of peace with the inhabitants of the Land. Since the Seven Nations refused to accept the terms, the Jews had no choice but to destroy or drive them from the Land, in keeping   with the command of Hashem.[1]

MITZVAH

Bris Milah (Circumcision)

At this time, God commanded Yehoshua to circumcise all Jewish males. The earlier generation that had been circumcised in Egypt had all died and did not enter the Land of Yisrael. This generation had been born in the desert and due to the circumstances, it was medically unwise to circumcise the babies at the proper time. However, now that they were about to enter the Land, they were commanded to be circumcised.

"God said to Avraham: 'And as for you, you shall keep My covenant, you and your seed after you, throughout their generations. This is My covenant which you shall keep, between Me and you and your seed after you: every male among you shall be circumcised.'"

Circumcision is the way in which the Jew expresses his wholehearted faith in God.

1. It is a positive commandment for the father to circumcise his son when he is eight days old. Since most fathers are not experienced in this operation, a person trained in this procedure, called a *mohel*, does it for him. The *mohel* should be a righteous person, skilled, and familiar with all the laws pertaining to circumcision. A circumcision should not be performed by a non-Jew or a non-religious Jew.

2. The circumcision must be performed in the daytime, after sunrise.

3. The *mohel* has special instruments, specifically designed for the circumcision.

4. A couple, known as the *kvater* and *kvaterin*, bring the child into the room where the circumcision will take place. He is then given to the *sandek*, the one who holds the child during the *bris*.

5. At every *bris milah*, a special seat is designated for the Prophet Eliyahu.

6. The father of the child designates the *mohel* as his representative to fulfill the commandment. The *mohel* then recites a special blessing before the circumcision. The father recites a blessing immediately after the *mohel*, who then completes the entire procedure of *bris milah*. The guests then call out in Hebrew, "Just as this child has entered the Covenant (of God), so too should he enter a life of Torah, marriage, and good deeds."

7. The blessing of "*Borei peri hagafen*" is recited over wine, followed by a special blessing. The child is then given a Jewish name and a few drops of wine are placed in the baby's mouth.

8. It is best to have a *minyan* (ten adult Jewish males) present at the circumcision. Then there is a festive meal, known as a *se'udah*, in which everyone should participate.

9. The infant cannot be circumcised unless he is healthy. If there is any problem, the circumcision is delayed until the doctors and the *mohel* determine that the baby is ready.

10. Even if the eighth day happens to fall on Shabbos, the circumcision is performed. However, all preparations should be made before Shabbos.

11. A male child is given his name at

the *bris milah*. (A female child is given a name when her father is called to the Torah in shul, shortly after her birth.)

A person must never forget that his *bris milah* is a symbol and a reminder that he is spiritually different from others. He must not be influenced by others who permit themselves to do whatever their hearts desire. Since *bris milah* is a mitzvah and not merely a health practice, it must be performed by someone who is a competent *mohel*. He must be well acquainted with both the necessary medical techniques and the various religious laws required in the performance of this great mitzvah. Since God's people are different spiritually, He wanted them to be different physically also.[2]

During the period of Roman persecution of the Jews in Yisrael, there existed harsh decrees against the Jews, one of which prohibited the *bris milah*. Those who performed a *bris* on their children were threatened with death. Nevertheless, Rabbi Shimon ben Gamliel, the *Nasi* of the Jewish community in Yisrael, went ahead with the performance of this commandment when a son was born to him.

The Emperor soon heard rumors that Rabbi Shimon had disobeyed the law, and summoned him for a trial. He told him to bring along his son, so that he could ascertain whether the baby had indeed undergone a *bris*. On their way to the trial, Rabbi Shimon and his wife stopped at an inn and befriended a Roman noble aristocratic family who was lodging there. The wife of the aristocrat had also just given birth to a child, and when she heard of Rabbi Shimon's plight, she offered to temporarily ex-

change her son for his. Consequently, when ordered to present his baby before the Emperor, Rabbi Shimon was able to display an obviously uncircumcised son, and the charges against him were dismissed. On the way back home, Rabbi Shimon and his wife once again exchanged babies with the Roman noblewoman at the inn.[3]

Rabbi Shimon's son grew up to become the great Sage, Rabbi Yehudah *Ha-Nasi* (Judah the Prince). The son of the Roman noblewoman grew up to be Antoninus, Emperor of Rome. He maintained a close friendship with Rabbi Yehudah *Ha-Nasi* and was a benevolent ruler with regard to the Jews.

Even in our times, there are millions of Jews living in Russia who are discouraged from fulfilling the mitzvah of circumcision. When these Jews, however, are fortunate enough to emigrate from Russia, the mitzvah of *bris milah* is one of the first things they undertake.

An Israeli soldier, wounded in battle at the Suez Canal and hospitalized in Be'er Sheva, asked the surgeon taking care of him to circumcise him. The soldier, who had emigrated to Israel with his parents from Russia, had not been circumcised. He had been drafted shortly after his arrival, and with one thing and another, he had not arranged to be circumcised. When, however, he found himself wounded and hospitalized, he asked the attending surgeon to circumcise him. The latter — an Orthodox Jew and a qualified *mohel* — refused, however, because he felt the soldier was still recuperating and too weak to undergo even minor surgery such as circumcision.

When the Yom Kippur War began, that

soldier was called up with his reserve tank unit, which helped contain the advance in the Suez Canal region. He was wounded and, when he regained consciousness, found himself at the hospital in Be'er Sheva. He immediately called upon Dr. Abramovits, the same surgeon who had attended him before. The soldier remembered the doctor from his previous hospital stay, and asked that he perform his circumcision. This time, the doctor could not refuse his request. After the soldier recuperated from his wounds, the *bris milah* was performed.

When he returned from the operating room, he was surprised by his fellow patients, who had prepared a small party for him in honor of the occasion. "Now I have a clear conscience and I shall leave the hospital as a complete Jew," he declared. Dr. Abramovits was overheard saying to himself: "I wish I had to perform only this kind of operation!"

❦ HISTORY

THE MIRACLE OF THE FALL OF YERICHO

The walls of Yericho were heavily fortified against the impending attack by the Jews. Through Yehoshua, God commanded the people to march around the city while the seven priests blew seven shofars. They circled the city in this manner for six days.

On the seventh day, they circled the city seven times and the seven priests blew the shofar. Yehoshua then commanded them to shout and the walls of Yericho collapsed. Thereupon the Jews stormed the city and captured it.

ACHAN AND THE CONSECRATED TREASURE OF YERICHO

The people were forbidden to take anything from the spoils of Yericho or to rebuild the city. Anyone who dared to transgress this edict and rebuild the city would suffer a terrible curse: the death of all his sons. His oldest sons would die at the time the foundation would be laid; his youngest would die when he would rebuild the gates. Just as one is not allowed to use and enjoy the first fruits of a tree, similarly, the Jews were commanded to consecrate to God the spoils of Yericho, the first city in Kena'an to be captured.

Despite these warnings, a Jew named Achan transgressed God's commandment not to take from the spoils of Yericho. God punished the entire nation by causing them to lose a battle and flee from the small city of Ai. Yehoshua tore his clothing in mourning and cried out to Hashem over the defeat that they had suffered. He was seriously concerned about the dire consequences it would have once the other nations heard of it. God responded that the defeat was a punishment for disobeying His commandment by taking from the spoils of Yericho.

The reason why the Jews suffered a serious defeat and were dealt with so harshly, was because despite all the miracles that Hashem had performed on their behalf, someone still had the audacity to transgress His commandment regarding the spoils of Yericho.

In order to find the transgressor, Yehoshua ordered all the people to pass before the Holy Ark, tribe by tribe, then family by family. There were indications that the guilty one was from the tribe of Yehudah and this was narrowed down to the family of Achan. He confessed to having taken some garments, gold, and silver, and hiding them in his tent. Achan and all of his possessions were taken to the Valley of Achu where he was stoned. His possessions were burned and then covered with stones.

God told Yehoshua that he should no longer fear the people of Ai. Yehoshua set an ambush using 30,000 people hiding in the woods, waiting to attack the city. Since they were confident following their last victory, the men of Ai went out to fight the Jews and left their city defenseless. Yehoshua then gave the signal for those waiting in ambush to attack and burn the city of Ai. Once the people of Ai saw their city burning, panic spread. They could no longer return to their city and found themselves caught in the trap between the 30,000 ambushers and Yehoshua's army.

The inhabitants of Ai were defeated and their king was hanged. Yehoshua then allowed the Jews to take from the spoils of the conquered city, as commanded by God. Following this victory, the Jews assembled before Yehoshua and he read the Torah to them. The Jews realized that without God's assistance they would lose. However, with the help of the Almighty they were able to conquer without suffering any casualties.

THE PLEDGE TO GIVON

After hearing what had happened to Yericho and Ai, the remaining kings of Kena'an united to fight against the Jews. However, the inhabitants of Givon decided to use a different approach to save themselves. A few of their men dressed themselves in very worn garments and took along dry and moldy foods to give the impression that they had been traveling for a long time from a very distant place.

The Givonites came to Yehoshua, requesting that he sign a peace treaty with them. Had Yehoshua known that they were really from a nearby area, he would not have agreed to this. Since all the nations of Kena'an had been approached by the Jews to make peace and had refused, they were all to be destroyed, including Givon. However, since Yehoshua and the Elders had signed a treaty with them, they could do them no harm, even after they discovered that the Givonites were in reality their neighbors. Once Yehoshua and the Jews had given their word, it would have been a disgrace for them to break the treaty, even though it had been achieved through trickery.

The Givonites were assigned to be water carriers and woodcutters for the nation of Yisrael. This was meant to ensure that they would remain in an inferior position and would not be allowed to intermarry with the people of Yisrael.

THE MIRACLE OF THE SUN IN THE BATTLE AGAINST THE KENA'ANITES

When Adoni-Tzedek, king of Yerushalayim, heard that such a great city as Givon had concluded a peace treaty with the Jews, he united with four other kings to attack Givon. The latter quickly appealed to Yehoshua for assistance. God told Yehoshua not to fear the Emorite kings.

Yehoshua carried out a surprise attack, causing the enemy to flee in panic. As they were fleeing, God caused huge hailstones to fall from the heavens. More of the enemy were killed by the falling stones than were killed by the sword.

The sun was beginning to set and Yehoshua prayed to God for more time to conclude the battle. Hashem caused the sun to remain in the sky for another full day. Never before had such a miracle occurred. The five kings were found hiding in the caves of Makkedah. All five were hanged. The Jews continued their battle to destroy the remaining towns.

Kena'anite kings, located east and west of the Emorites, allied themselves against the Jews. A huge force, with countless horses and chariots arrayed themselves for battle against the Jewish nation. Before the battle, God told Yehoshua to have no fears, for He would be with him and give the enemy into the hand of the Israelites.

Yehoshua carried out every detail of God's command concerning the battles against the Kena'anites. As a result, the enemy was decimated. The strong cities, however, were not destroyed by the Jews, except for Chatzor, which Yehoshua ordered to be burned.

Yehoshua warred for a long time against the kings of Kena'an. Not a single city sought to make peace with the Jews, except for the Givonites. After all these battles, the Jews rested, victorious, just as Hashem had promised.

In all, thirty-one kings and their territories were conquered by the Jews under the leadership of Yehoshua.

THE DIVISION OF THE LAND (2495/1266 B.C.E.)

Yehoshua was already old and there was land yet to be conquered. Some pockets of resistance still remained, but these were left to the individual tribes to deal with.

God spoke to Yehoshua, telling him to divide the inheritances according to lots. Nine tribes, plus half of the tribe of Menashe, received territories on the western side of the Jordan River. The only tribe not to receive an inheritance in the land was the tribe of Levi.

The tribe of Reuven was the first to receive its inheritance, followed by Gad and half of Menashe. Their land was given to them by Moshe from the territory captured from Sichon and Og. This territory is located on the eastern side of the Jordan River. It was conquered by the Jews while Moshe was still alive. Sichon and Og were giants and the strongest kings of their time. Their defeat at the hands of Moshe was truly miraculous.

While Yehoshua was in the process of dividing up the Land, Kalev came to him, accompanied by members of the tribe of Yehudah. Kalev reminded Yehoshua of the promise Moshe had made to him following his return from Kena'an along with the other spies. Unlike the ten spies whose report had caused the Jews to fear entering the Land of Yisrael, Kalev and Yehoshua had spoken most favorably about the Land. Moshe had then promised Kalev that he would inherit the city of Chevron, the burial place of the Patriarchs, where he had gone to pray earlier. (Chevron was previously known as Kiryas Arba [the city of Arba]. Arba was the greatest of the giants who lived in that land.)

Although Chevron was still in the possession of Kena'anites and despite his advanced age of eighty-five years, Kalev was confident in receiving God's assistance and in his own ability to conquer this territory. Kalev drove out the three sons of the giant Anak, the son of Arba: Sheshai, Achiman and Talmai. He then went up to capture the city of Devir, formerly known as Kiryas Sefer. The only city that the tribe of

Yehudah was not able to capture at this time was Yerushalayim, which was inhabited by the Yevusites.

Despite the fact that Yehoshua was the great leader who led the nation in the conquest of the Land, he himself requested but a small town whose land was not fit for cultivation, and whose fruits were inferior to those of other territories. Like Moshe before him, he did not ask for personal wealth and did not transfer his leadership to his son.

God gave the Jews the entire Land that He had sworn would be an inheritance to their forefathers. He delivered them from the hands of their enemies and allowed them to live in peace.

ETHICS II
Controlling One's Anger

The tribe of Shimon did not get a separate portion entirely unto itself, but rather received one in the midst of Yehudah's territory. This was in fulfillment of Ya'akov's prophecy to his son, Shimon; "I will divide them in Ya'akov, and disperse them in Yisrael."[4]

Thus was Ya'akov's prophecy concerning Shimon and Levi fulfilled. Levi was scattered in the cities of refuge (*arei miklat*) while Shimon received no direct allotment, but dwelled among the people of Yehudah. The two brothers, Shimon and Levi, had shown an overabundance of fury in their punishment of the people of Shechem. The Almighty found a way to dilute their wrathfulness by dispersion among their brothers. The *leviyim* were teachers, scholars and the recipients of charity in the form of tithes. This served to humble them. Shimon's situation was similar. Their vocation as teachers trained them in self-control and humbled them.

Our Rabbis taught: "Who is mighty? He who conquers his own passion." As it says in *Mishlei* (Proverbs), "He who is slow to anger is better than the mighty,

and he who rules his own spirit is better than one who conquers a city."[6]

When one becomes angry, even God is lightly esteemed in his eyes.[7]

The positive *middah* (character trait) of self-control is apparent in the following story:

The followers of a great chassidic rebbe, Rav Mordechai of Neschitz, knew how very much their rebbe wanted a *tallis katan* (tzitzis) from Eretz Yisrael. Travel was not as quick and easy in those days as it is today, but the loyal chassidim managed, after considerable time, to obtain a *tallis katan* for their rebbe. It was not completed, however, and was given to one of the chassidim to finish sewing.

The chassid had to cut out a hole in the middle, but due to some error in the way in which he had folded the material, he cut out two holes instead of one. The chassid was filled with agony and remorse at what he had just done, albeit accidentally. With great fear and trepidation, he gave the *tallis katan* to his rebbe and explained what had happened.

To his amazement the Rebbe replied calmly, "Why are you so worried? It needed two holes anyway; one for my head and the other to test me to see whether I would become angry."

❧ HISTORY

THE TRIBES ON THE EASTERN SIDE OF THE JORDAN

Yehoshua told the tribes of Reuven, Gad, and half of Menashe, who had come to help the other tribes conquer Yisrael, that they could return to their homes and families on the other side of the Jordan. He cautioned them to remain loyal to God and His Torah, and not to deviate from the mitzvos in any manner.

When these tribes returned home, they built an altar to God as a monument to the great miracles that had been performed for them. When the rest of the tribes heard about this, they mistakenly thought that this altar was erected for the purpose of bringing sacrifices to God. This would have been considered a grave sin, as there was already a *Mishkan* (Tabernacle) constructed at Shiloh and outside sacrifice was prohibited. The tribes assembled to fight against the two-and-a-half tribes. When the latter explained that the altar was only intended as a monument to God, the tribes withdrew. The tribes of Reuven, Gad and half of Menashe feared that the Jordan River would serve as a barrier, alienating them from the rest of the Jewish nation. They were concerned that with the passage of time, the tribes residing on the western side of the Jordan would tell the children of those tribes living on the eastern side that they had no part in the God of Yisrael. It was for this reason that they built the altar — to bear testimony for generations to come that their service was only to God. They considered the altar a witness signifying that they would never rebel against the Almighty.

After years of battle and conquests, God allowed the Jews to rest from their wars and to live in peace. Yehoshua was very old when he called together all of Yisrael, including the Elders, Judges and officers. He reminded them of all that had Hashem had done for them, including all the miracles and battles that He had fought for them. Yehoshua warned the Jews not to be influenced by the unconquered nations that still remained in their midst. He warned of terrible consequences if they were to follow the false gods of their neighbors. This would arouse God's wrath against His own people. Just as He had fulfilled all the blessings and promises that He had made to the Jews, so, too, would He keep His word concerning the evil He would bring to punish the Jews for transgressing the covenant.

❧ Key People, Places and Things

ACHAN: the individual who stole from the consecrated spoils of Yericho. This transgression resulted in all of Yisrael being punished and losing the first battle of Ai.

BRIS MILAH: the covenant of circumcision.

GIVON: the nation that tricked the Jews into making a peace treaty.

KALEV: one of the two spies chosen by Yehoshua to go to Yericho. He proved himself worthy of this honor, because he and Yehoshua had been the only spies, from the original twelve sent by Moshe, not to give a negative report about the land. He and his family merited the inheritance of the city of Chevron, burial site of the Patriarchs.

KVATER: (Y.) the man who brings in the baby for the *bris milah* and hands him to the *sandak*.

MOHEL: the specially trained person who performs the circumcision.

PINCHAS: one of the two spies sent by Yehoshua to Yericho; he was worthy of that responsibility because he had shown great courage and strength in the defense of God's honor. Later, he became the High Priest.

RACHAV: the woman who hid the two spies and saved their lives. She recognized God's greatness and became a full convert to Judaism. Ultimately, she married Yehoshua.

REUVEN, GAD AND HALF OF MENASHE: these tribes received their shares of the Land of Yisrael on the eastern side of the Jordan but still assisted the other tribes in the battle for the rest of Eretz Yisrael.

SANDEK: The person given the honor of holding the baby during the circumcision.

THE MIRACLE OF THE CROSSING OF THE JORDAN RIVER: God showed that He still protected the Jews, by splitting the waters of the Jordan and allowing the Jews to cross on dry land. A memorial for future generations was established there.

THE MIRACLE OF THE FALL OF YERICHO: the walls of the heavily fortified city collapsed, allowing the Jews to conquer Yericho. The people were forbidden to take anything from the spoils or to rebuild the city.

YEHOSHUA: Joshua, the great leader who succeeded Moshe *Rabbenu* and led the Jews in the conquest and division of the land of Kena'an.

ZEKENIM: the Elders of Yisrael who assumed the leadership of *Klal Yisrael* immediately after the death of Yehoshua, and who served until the era of the Judges.

NOTES

1. *Talmud Yerushalmi, Shevi'is, perek* 7.

2. *Sefer Ha-Chinnuch, mitzvah* 3.

3. *Tosafos, Talmud Avodah Zarah,* 10b.

4. *Bereshis* 49:7.

5. *Mishlei* 16:32.

6. *Pirkei Avos,* 4:1.

7. *Talmud Nedarim,* 22b.

❦ Introduction to Chapters 12-13

This chapter describes the period of the Judges, which begins with the death of Yehoshua and extends to the era of Eli, the last of the Judges.

During the era of the Judges there was no king. The people were basically capable of governing themselves and received their spiritual guidance from the judges. This period lasted roughly 350 years and was a unique era in Jewish history. Although on the surface it would seem that this was a turbulent time, close examination reveals otherwise. Most of the period passed peacefully without any strife. Even when the Jews sinned, they were quick to repent. There were only two tragic episodes about which the Prophet stated, "In those days there was no king in Yisrael. Every man did what was just in his eyes."

The Judges did not establish dynasties, and their positions were not automatically passed on to their sons. No one seized power over the nation through force or violent means, except for Avimelech, the son of Gidon, who was punished soon thereafter. These great Judges realized that their own power was insignificant and that they were merely serving as messengers of the Almighty.

As Yehoshua had predicted, the remaining heathen nations in the Land of Yisrael continually posed problems for the Jewish conquerors. Isolated from one another by Kena'anite areas, many of the Jewish settlements came to concentrate on their local concerns and were sometimes even influenced by the immoral styles of behavior which they saw among the Kena'anites whom they had been charged to eradicate.

But Providence did not allow them to fall victim to these dangers. Recurrent attempts by the Kena'anites to recover their former dominions forcefully reminded the Jewish tribes of their need for national unity and their undivided loyalty to God.

The history of Judges conveys to the Jewish nation a clear message. They are constantly under Divine guidance. When the Jews sin, the enemy rises and subjugates them. Conversely, when *Bnei Yisrael* obey the law, they are able to succeed in their endeavors.

CHAPTER 12

Shoftim (Judges) (Part I)
From the Death of Yehoshua to the Death of Yiftach
(2516 – 2785/1245 B.C.E. – 976 B.C.E.)

❦ HISTORY

AFTER THE DEATH OF YEHOSHUA (2516/1245 B.C.E.)

After the death of Yehoshua at the age of 110, God indicated that the tribe of Yehudah should be the first to lead the battle against the remaining Kena'anites. The tribe of Yehudah made an agreement with its closest neighbor, the tribe of Shimon, so that the latter would help them secure their territory. In return, Yehudah would then assist Shimon in the conquest of their own territory which was spread out all over the country.

Yehudah and Shimon were successful in their conquests, for God gave the land into their hands. They also captured Adoni-Bezek, the leader of Bezek, and cut off his thumbs and large toes. He realized that this was punishment for his having done the same thing to seventy kings who scrounged for food under his table.

The tribe of Yehudah was led by the courageous, pious and learned Osniel ben Kenaz who had married the daughter of Kalev.

Almost all of the tribes (except for Yehudah) were guilty of not having driven out all of the Kena'anites from their territories, as commanded by God.

LESSON I

True Leadership Requires Self-Sacrifice

Why did Yehudah deserve to be the leader of the tribes at this time? Why did he merit that among his descendants would be the royal house of King David, including the Messiah?

This was because the members of the tribe of Yehudah always showed courage and the qualities of leadership. This was best exemplified by the heroism of Nach-shon ben Aminadav, who was Nasi of the tribe of Yehudah. When Bnei Yisrael came to the Red Sea with the Egyptians in hot pursuit after them, it was Nachshon ben Aminadav who was the first to jump into the sea, prompting others to follow suit. Then Hashem caused the waters of the Red Sea to split.

The Midrash relates that after Nachshon leaped into the towering waves of the Red Sea, he was followed by the tribe of Binyamin. When the tribe of Yehudah saw this, they became jealous that Binyamin had preceded them.

When Hashem saw how eager both tribes were to glorify His name and to show such *mesiras nefesh* (self-sacrifice), He decided to reward both of them. Thus, the *Beis Ha-Mikdash* was built within the territory allotted to Binyamin. Also, Sha'ul, the first king of Yisrael, came from the tribe of Binyamin. Yehudah was rewarded with *malchus* (kingship). Starting from King David, all the kings of Yisrael, until the Messiah (except for a brief period during the time of the Hasmonean dynasty) have and will come from the tribe of Yehudah.

The competition between the two tribes can best be illustrated through a *mashal* (parable) about two sons. The younger son had been instructed to wake his father as soon as the sun rose.

At sunrise, the younger son went to wake his father, but the older one barred the way and sought to stop him. "Father must only be awakened at seven o'clock." He felt his father could sleep longer and still be on schedule.

"But he commanded me to wake him at sunrise," insisted the younger son. The commotion of the two brothers awoke the father who said, "I know that you both acted for my sake, and I will reward both of you."

❦ HISTORY

SUCCESSORS TO YEHOSHUA

The Jews served God all the years that Yehoshua was alive. They continued to do so during the days of the Elders who succeeded him. The unbroken chain of learned tradition begun by Moshe and continued by Yehoshua was now carried on by the Elders. Their rule lasted for seventeen years (2516-2533).

A messenger [angel] from God came to speak to the Israelites to remind them that it was the Almighty Who had taken them out of Egypt and brought them to the Land that He had promised to their forefathers. God promised never to break the covenant He had made with their forefathers. At the same time, He reminded the Jews not to make any covenants with the other inhabitants of the Land, but rather to destroy their altars so as to prevent them from becoming a stumbling block in the future.

After a generation passed, all of the Elders of Yisrael had died. A new generation arose, one that did not know of God's great deeds on behalf of His people, and they worshiped the idols of their heathen neighbors. This aroused God's anger, and He gave them into the hands of their enemies.

ETHICS I

Paying Respect to the Deceased

The commentaries explain that the Elders' years were cut short because they failed to eulogize Yehoshua properly. In fact, the Midrash says that the earth quaked because they did not pay proper respect to their great leader. That is why Yehoshua was buried on Mount Ga'ash. The word *ga'ash* means to erupt. Because the Jews failed to properly eulogize Yehoshua in a manner befitting the stature of such a great individual, Hashem caused the mountain to erupt on the day of his burial.

Rav Chiya bar Abba said in the name of Rabbi Yochanan: "If someone does not give the proper *hesped* (eulogy) upon the passing of a *talmid chacham* (scholar), his days will not be lengthened." This punishment is *middah k'neged middah* (measure for measure). Properly eulogizing and mourning the passing of a *gadol* (great person) is an indication of the great value placed on that person's life. When people fail to eulogize him, they are, in effect, stating that the *gadol*'s life did not have any exceptional value before Hashem. For that reason, they are worthy of punishment and their lives are shortened.[1]

The Midrash relates that when Rabbi Shimon, the son of Rabbi Akiva, passed away, the huge multitudes that attended the *levayah* (funeral) brought comfort and solace to the bereaved father. Rabbi Akiva mounted a bench in the cemetery and declared, "My brother Jews, hear me! Not that I am a scholar — there are greater scholars present than I am. Not that I am wealthy, for there are many men who are wealthier than I. I know that your reward is great, for you troubled yourselves to come for the glory of the Torah and for the sake of a mitzvah." The multitudes attending a funeral are proof of the greatness of the deceased.[2]

❦ HISTORY

THE BEGINNING OF THE RULE OF THE JUDGES

In order to bring the Jews back onto the righteous path, God provided Judges to lead them. However, after a while, the Jews did not obey the Judges either. They especially strayed from the path following the death of each Judge. Due to their abandoning their covenant with the Almighty, God became angry. Hashem said that He would not drive out the remaining nations that had not been conquered in the days of Yehoshua. Instead, He would allow them to remain as an obstacle, to test the loyalty of the Jews.

The Israelites angered the Almighty by serving the gods of their neighbors and by intermarrying with them. God punished them by causing them to become subservient for eight years to Kushan

Rishasayim, the king of Aram Naharayim. The Jews cried to God to save them from their oppressors. Help came from Osniel ben Kenaz, Kalev's younger stepbrother, whom God enabled to successfully lead the battles against their enemies. Thereafter, the Land was quiet for forty years, (2533-2573/1228 B.C.E.-1188 B.C.E.) until the death of Osniel, the first Judge.

LESSON II

The Importance of Driving out the Kena'anites from the Land of Yisrael

The Torah is replete with warnings from Hashem to beware of the influence of the Kena'anites and other peoples residing in the Land of Yisrael. "They should not dwell in your Land lest they cause you to sin against Me."[3] "You must destroy them: the Hittite, the Emorite, the Canaanite... as the Lord your God commanded you, in order that they should not teach you to do according to all their abominations."[4]

One may ask why Hashem had to constantly warn the Jews about the need to destroy or drive out the nations so that they should not remain as obstacles. Why couldn't the Jews be allowed to live peacefully alongside the former inhabitants of the Land? To understand the answer to this question, one must understand the type of nations that were involved. The depravity of the Kena'anite, the abominations they performed ("Even their sons and daughters they burn in fire to their gods,"[5]) and the murders they committed made them unique in their

wickedness. The Jews could not be allowed to live alongside such degenerate nations without expecting their evil influence to rub off on them as well.

God's command to drive out these seven nations was significant because they were residing in the Holy Land, which exacts a different level of accountability. Evil practices that might go unpunished for a while elsewhere are punished immediately by Hashem when committed in the Holy Land.

The reluctance and subsequent negligence on the part of the Jews to destroy the evil nations demonstrated further that this plan to destroy the Kena'anites was not conceived by the people of Yisrael but was imposed upon them by God, very much against their own pacifistic inclinations. The result of this reluctance to follow Hashem's command was that the children of the original Jewish settlers were eventually subjugated by those Kena'anite nations who had been allowed to remain in the Land.

❦ HISTORY

EHUD'S RULE (2573-2653/1188 B.C.E.-1108 B.C.E.)

Following the death of Osniel (2573/1188 B.C.E.), the Jews returned to their former ways by following the culture of their neighbors. God punished them by causing them to become subservient to Eglon, king of Mo'av, for eighteen years.

Once again, the Jews cried out from the depths of their misery and suffering, asking God for His forgiveness. A new Judge by the name of Ehud ben Gera arose to help his people. He was left-handed, with a shriveled right hand. Under the pretense of bringing a gift to the king of Mo'av, Ehud presented himself before Eglon while carrying a concealed double-edged sword on the right side of his clothing. He escorted the messengers that were carrying the tribute to Eglon and then told the king that he had to relay a secret message to him. Eglon dismissed all who were present in his chamber.

When Ehud told Eglon that he had brought a message from God, Eglon arose from his seat. Because of the respect Eglon showed by rising to hear the word of God, he merited having Ruth as his descendant. From Ruth, in turn, came David *Ha-Melech*, the progenitor of the Royal House of David. However, because of Eglon's extreme cruelty to the Jews, another of his descendants was Orpah, the ancestress of Golyas.

Ehud thrust his sword into Eglon. The latter was so heavy that the fat of his stomach closed over and concealed the short weapon that Ehud had used. Ehud locked the door to the king's chambers and fled. The servants, seeing the locked door, assumed their king was attending to his personal needs. It was not until much later that they discovered their king was dead. By then, Ehud had escaped and had returned with an army to attack Mo'av. He assured his followers that God would give Mo'av into their hands.

Thereafter, peace reigned in the Land for eighty years (2573-2653/118? B.C.E.-1108 B.C.E.).

After Ehud, Shamgar ben Anas was the Judge who led the Jews. He was known for having killed six hundred Pelishtites (Philistines) with an ox goad. He judged for only one year (2654/1107 B.C.E.).

THE PROPHETESS DEVORAH (2654-2694/1107 B.C.E.-1067 B.C.E.)

The Jews continued to anger the Almighty and were subjugated by Yavin, king of Kena'an. His chief of the army, Sisera, commanded 900 iron chariots and oppressed the Jews for twenty years.

At this time, there lived a prophetess by the name of Devorah, who was also a Judge. Devorah was worthy of becoming a prophetess and leader of the Jewish people because of her acts of devotion to Hashem. She made thick wicks for her husband, Lapidos, to bring to the Tabernacle. Since she was concerned with increasing the Light of God, He caused her light to shine over Yisrael.

Devorah lived in Mount Efrayim, where she judged the people while sitting under a palm tree. The Prophetess Devorah chose to sit under a palm tree when conducting public affairs because the palm symbolized the wholehearted piety of her beloved people. Another reason for her conducting judgment in the open field was to assure that there would not be any questions of immodesty or impropriety.

Devorah sent for Barak ben Avino'am and told him that God wanted him to take 10,000 people from the tribes of Naftali and Zevulun and lead the fight against Sisera's army. Barak, however, did not wish to go unless Devorah went with them. She agreed, but told him that his greatness would be overshadowed by her presence. Barak did not mind and still insisted upon her presence.

Sisera attacked them with his 900 chariots, but the Jews were victorious and destroyed his entire army. No one but Sisera remained alive. He fled on foot and arrived at the tent of Ya'el, the wife of Chever the Kenite. He felt secure there, because the Kenites were his allies.

Ya'el assured him that all would be well. When he asked for a drink of water, she gave him milk, which made him drowsy. After he fell asleep, she drove a tent spike into his temple. When Barak and his army arrived at her tent, Ya'el showed them Sisera's body. They were then able to wipe out the remainder of Yavin's nation, finally killing Yavin himself.

Devorah sang a song of praise to the Almighty for all the miracles that He had done for His people. The Land remained at peace for the next forty years.

Following the death of Devorah, the people returned to their evil ways. God gave them into the hands of Midyan for seven years. Midyan oppressed the Jews by destroying their crops after they had been sown, leaving the Jews without enough food to eat. One of the severest punishments that a person can incur is to work hard to earn his food, yet be denied the chance to enjoy it. Once again, the Jews cried to Hashem to rescue them from their oppressors.

MITZVAH

Honoring One's Parents

An angel of God was sent to remind the Jews of all that the Almighty had done for them. The nations whom they had neglected to conquer or chase out of the Land were now the cause of their misery. This angel appeared to Gidon and told him that God would be with him. He appeared while Gidon was beating out wheat in the winepress. Gidon was honoring his father by doing this work in his stead, for if the enemy were to appear suddenly, his elderly father would be free to flee. Because Gidon fulfilled the commandment of honoring his father, God found him worthy to save Yisrael.

The Torah states that one must be very careful about honoring one's father and mother. The reward for honoring one's parents is given both in this world and in the World to Come. We see that Gidon's actions on behalf of his father helped cause him to be chosen as a judge and leader of the Jews.

One should serve his parents cheerfully. If one can perform a task for his parents and thus make their lives more pleasant, as in the case of Gidon, he is thereby honoring them.

Our Sages teach us, "One may feed his father fine foods and incur terrible sins, while another makes his father grind millstones and merits great rewards." A man used to serve his father fine fattened chickens. When his father once asked him, "My son, where are these from?", the son angrily replied, "Eat, you old fogey! Eat and be quiet." Although he fed his father fine foods, he incurred terrible punishment for his action.

At the same time, there was a king who summoned and drafted the millers of the land to come work for him. One young man took pity on his elderly father and said to him, "Father, it is better that you go where I am currently working and grind in my place, while I go to work for the king. If the king's work involves humiliation, then I shall be humiliated and not you; if it involves lashes or suffering, I shall suffer them and not you!" That man made his father grind at millstones yet he merited Paradise![6]

Even if one's parents become senile, physically handicapped, or mentally disturbed, one is not allowed to treat them rudely or disrespectfully.[7]

The Talmud relates the story of the gentile named Dama whose mother had emotional problems. She had fits of anger when she yelled and spat at him for no apparent reason. Though Dama was greatly embarrassed by her actions, he did not speak to her harshly. She was, after all, his mother, and despite all the hardships she caused him, he treated her royally.[8]

It is a grave sin for someone to curse his parents or hurt them in any way. One is not allowed to openly contradict one's parents. If a child cannot afford to support his needy parents, he must still show them the proper respect and do everything possible to ease their burden. One is obligated to respect one's parents even after their death. That is one of the reasons why one says Kaddish after a parent's death, and why one should conduct oneself in a proper Jewish way. These actions will bring honor and respect to one's parents.[9]

❦ HISTORY

GIDON (2694-2734/1067 B.C.E.-1027 B.C.E.)

Gidon asked the angel whether, after all the miracles that God had done for the Jews, He had now forsaken them.

God responded through the angel and said that Gidon was given the power to lead the Jews against the Midyanites. Gidon hesitated. How could he, the youngest in his father's house, which was the poorest in Menashe, lead the nation? God responded that He would be with him and that he had no need to worry. Gidon, however, still requested signs that this was truly an angel of God telling him to go to battle against the Midyanites. The angel provided the signs immediately. God continued to reassure Gidon that peace would be with him and Gidon, in thanksgiving, built an altar to Hashem.

God commanded Gidon to destroy the altar of the idol, *ba'al*, and the *asherah* (a tree utilized for idol worship). By fulfilling this command, Gidon was actually putting his life in jeopardy. Because he was ready and willing to sacrifice his life while sanctifying God's Holy Name, he was found worthy to lead the Jews to victory over their enemies.

Gidon did exactly as he was commanded by God, but did it in the still of night. When the people discovered their *ba'al* and *asherah* had been destroyed, and that the person responsible was Gidon, they went to his father, Yo'ash, demanding he hand over his son for punishment. Yo'ash responded that if the *ba'al* was really a god, it should be able to take care of itself. The people did not have to avenge it. On that day, Gidon was called Yeruba'al, because he had fought against *ba'al* by destroying its altar. He had the courage to eradicate the evil from among his people.

Gidon gathered the Jews to fight against Midyan and Amalek. Again he requested signs from God that he would be victorious. God again fulfilled his request and performed a miracle in front of his eyes.

Yeruba'al (Gidon) and his army camped in Ein Harod in preparation for battle. But Hashem told him that since he had too many people with him, the coming victory would not be interpreted as a miracle from God. He was, therefore, ordered to send back many of the 32,000 who were with him. First, he sent home all those who were fearful. Ten thousand people remained, and that was still too many. God then told Gidon to have his followers drink from a stream. Those who knelt down to drink were to be sent home, while those who lapped up the water with their hands were allowed to remain. After this, only 300 men were left with Gidon.

God insisted that the war be waged with very few people, so that it would be obvious to all that the victory had come from God and was in no way due to a large army. He wanted to reassure the people that God had not forsaken them; that when they repent, God would rescue them from any predicament.

God told Gidon that if he would hear what the enemy were saying among themselves, he would gain strength. At night, Gidon proceeded with a servant to the edge of the enemy's camp. There he heard one person saying to the other that he had a dream in which he saw a roasted cake of barley tumble into the camp of Midyan. The barley cake hit a tent which tumbled over, again and again. The person said to his friend that this was a sign of Gidon's impending victory. When Gidon heard this, he returned to his camp and told his men that God would give the enemy into their hands.

LESSON III

Reward for Those Who Bless God, No Matter What the Circumstances Are

Why did the revelation of the coming conquest of Midyan come through the medium of a roasted cake of barley? Barley bread represents the poorest quality of bread. That was what *Bnei Yisrael* subsisted on at that time, due to their extreme poverty under the yoke of Midyan. Yet, despite their poverty and suffering, they still blessed Hashem by bringing the offering of the *omer* (which consisted of barley).

Hashem reciprocated here, *middah k'neged middah* (measure for measure). Though there was really very little reason for Jews of that time to deserve Hashem's salvation, He nevertheless did save them because they had thanked Him for the poor barley bread upon which they subsisted.

A man once asked the Maggid of Mezritch, "How is it possible to fulfill the injunction of our Sages, 'A man is obliged to utter a blessing on hearing evil tidings just as he does on hearing good tidings'?"

"I think you should go and look for my disciple, Reb Zusya of Hanipoli," advised the rabbi. "He will be able to answer your question."

Throughout his life, Reb Zusya had lived in utter poverty. When he was told the purpose of the man's visit, he was puzzled and replied, "I am most surprised that our rabbi should have sent you with this question to me, of all people. A question like this should surely be put to a man who at some time in his life has experienced something bad. I'm afraid that I can't be of any help to you since nothing evil has ever befallen me, even for a moment. Thank God, I have had only good things happening to me from the day I was born. So how could I know anything about evil?"

The man had received his answer. This obligation to bless God upon hearing evil tidings just as one does upon hearing good tidings was now clear. A person's entire life can be a blessed and happy one if he devotes his energies to noble and productive causes, and if he focuses on the good moments of his life. Whatever reverses he might experience are taken in stride since they are part of God's master plan. By facing life in this way, a person will be able to bless God even when he hears evil tidings.

❦ HISTORY

GIDON'S VICTORY

Gidon divided his men into three groups. Each man held a shofar in one hand and a pitcher containing a torch in the other. When Gidon blew his shofar, the others would shout, "*l'Hashem u'l'Gidon*" (to God and to Gidon). They would then blow their shofars and smash the pitchers. The men did as they were commanded, causing total confusion in the enemy camp. The Midyanites fled in disarray. Then Gidon sent messengers to Mount Efrayim, saying that they could capture the land up to the waters near Beis Barah and the Jordan River. The men of Efrayim also captured and killed two princes of Midyan.

The people of Efrayim were angry with Gidon for not being called earlier to join in the fight against Midyan. They felt that they had been ignored by Gidon, and consequently were looking for a pretext to fight. His response was conciliatory. He praised their accomplishments as being greater than his since they had captured two strong princes of Midyan. Gidon's efforts to appease the men of Efrayim at the expense of his own honor prevented much bloodshed among the tribes. The people of Mount Efrayim were satisfied with his answer.

The people of Yisrael wanted Gidon and his sons to rule over them, but he refused to comply. All he asked from them was that the golden nose rings which had been taken as spoils should be given to him. Gidon then recast them into an *efod* (belt) as a reminder of the great victory against their enemy. However, this *efod* turned out to be a snare for the Jews in future generations. This was true even though Gidon's intention in making the *efod* was not for it to be used in idol worship, but rather for it to commemorate his participation in the miracle that God had performed.

AVIMELECH AND HIS GREEDY PURSUIT OF POWER (2734-2737/1027 B.C.E.-1024 B.C.E.)

The land was quiet for forty years. Gidon had seventy sons from his many wives. Another son by the name of Avimelech was born to his concubine in Shechem. Gidon died after having lived a long life. Following his death, the Jews once again strayed from the path of God. Gidon's having too many wives and concubines, which the Torah warned against, cost him dearly. It led to his having a son, Avimelech, who had a great thirst for supreme power.

Avimelech spoke to the people of Shechem saying, "Would it not be better to have one person rule over you, rather than seventy people? Remember, I am your flesh and blood." They agreed, and gave him seventy pieces of silver. Avimelech used the seventy pieces of silver to hire men to kill his seventy brothers. All were killed except Yosam who was hiding at the time. The people of Shechem then declared Avimelech to be their king. Avimelech was never considered one of the Judges of Yisrael, but was rather a usurper who gained power by violence. This marks the sole instance in the period of the Judges that someone did so. The harmful influence of the heathen nations was evident in his behavior. Avimelech followed the gentile practice of killing all his brothers in order to seize power.

Addressing himself to the people of Shechem, Yosam declared that had the people of Shechem dealt justly with the family of Gidon who had saved them from the hands of Midyan, there would have been reason for rejoicing. Since, however, they had not done so, a fire would consume them and Avimelech as well.

Yosam fled to Be'er, and Avimelech ruled over Shechem for three years. Then Hashem caused dissension between Avimelech and the people of Shechem. It led to a civil war in which many people were killed. When Avimelech arrived at the fortifications of Shechem to burn them down, a woman threw a millstone down on his head. As he lay dying, he requested that someone stab him with a sword, lest it be said that Avimelech had been killed by a woman.

LESSON IV

God's Punishment Is Measure for Measure

The curse of Yosam came true. God repaid the wickedness of the people of Shechem who had suffered greatly at the hands of Avimelech. He, in turn, was killed by the people of Shechem.

From the above occurrences, we see how God's punishment is "measure for measure." The people who thought there would be more peace and harmony by following one leader, namely Avime-lech, were punished with dissension, strife, and civil war. Avimelech, who had killed his sixty-nine brothers upon one stone, in the end suffered the indignity of being killed by a woman with a stone.

All through history, we see how the Almighty punishes according to the dictum of *middah k'neged middah* (measure for measure), for it precludes the possibility of chance. Some examples of this are the following: The Egyptian decree to drown Jewish baby boys resulted in their own punishment by drowning at the time of the splitting of the Red Sea. Haman prepared a gallows for Mordechai and in the end was hung on the very same gallows. This reinforces the concept that the lives of men are indeed shaped by Divine Providence.

❦ HISTORY

THE ERA OF THE JUDGES CONTINUES

During the period of the Judges, an era of almost 400 years, all the Judges were temporary rulers whose power did not pass on to their sons. With the sole exception of Avimelech, no one seized power by force or arose by means of a coup d'état. Avshalom was not considered one of the Judges, but was a usurper who gained power by violence.

After the death of Avimelech, Tola was the Judge of Yisrael for twenty-three years (2737-2760/1024 B.C.E.-1001 B.C.E.). He was followed by Ya'ir, who judged for twenty-two years (2758-2779/1003 B.C.E.-982 B.C.E.). After his death, the Jews again forsook the righteous path and worshiped the idols of Tzidon, Mo'av, Ammon and the Pelishtites. Once again, God gave them over into the hands of their enemies. Ammon oppressed the Jews for eighteen years, until they cried out to God for deliverance. They repented for having forsaken God and worshiped idols.

Hashem reminded the Jews that He was the One Who had taken them out of Egypt and had chosen them as His people. He reminded them of all the other times He had saved them from their enemies, and still they chose to follow the strange gods of their neighbors. God, therefore, told them to cry to those gods for help from their oppressors. The Jews once again repented. They now sought a leader to break the oppressive hold of the Ammonites upon them.

YIFTACH (2779- 2785/982 B.C.E.-976 B.C.E.)

At that time, there lived a mighty warrior by the name of Yiftach, the son of Gilad, who was of questionable lineage. His brothers, born of a different mother, refused to allow him a share in their father's inheritance. Instead, they drove him out of the house and he went to live in the land of Tov. He did not try to fight back against his brothers, but rather sought peace.

When the Ammonites began to oppress the people of Yisrael, the elders of Gilad appealed to Yiftach to return and lead them in battle against the enemy. Yiftach hesitated to help them since they had not objected at the time his brothers had driven him from his home. He felt that they, too, hated him. The elders persisted that they wanted Yiftach to be their general and their ruler.

One learns an important lesson from this episode. At first, the people of Gilad had gone along with the humiliation and banishment of Yiftach from their town. Little did they suspect that they would need him as their leader and savior. One never knows when one may have to ask another for his assistance. We must be careful never to allow anyone in our midst to be embarrassed, for "There is no man who does not have his own hour."[10]

Yiftach sent messengers to the king of Ammon asking why he was attacking his country. Ammon responded that he sought to regain the land that the Jews had conquered at the time they had come across the Jordan River. If they returned the territory, they could live in peace.

Yiftach sent back messengers, explaining that the Israelites had not taken the land of Mo'av and Ammon. The kings of Edom and Mo'av had refused to grant them permission to pass through their land. Sichon, king of the Emorites, had not only refused to allow them to pass through, but had gone out to engage them in battle. It was then that God had helped the Jews to conquer all the land of the Emorites. Did Ammon now wish to conquer that which God had given to them? They had allowed three hundred years to pass without trying to recapture the land. Why were they trying to do so now? The king of Ammon ignored Yiftach's words.

The Spirit of God rested upon Yiftach, and he led the people in the fight against Ammon. However, before going into battle, he made a vow. If he emerged victorious, he would bring as a sacrifice to God the first thing that would come towards him upon his return home. When he arrived home after a successful campaign, his daughter, an only child, ran out to greet him. When he saw her, he tore his clothes and cried bitterly. He told her of his vow and she insisted that he keep his word. She asked to be given two months of solitude before he fulfilled it.

ETHICS II

The Punishment for Pride

Yiftach's pride as victor and newly proclaimed leader prevented his seeking out either the sages for their opinion, or Pinchas, the spiritual leader of that time. Pinchas felt that since Yiftach considered himself superior to the sages, he could not annul Yiftach's vow because an annulment is available only to people who personally come to the sages.

Since both Pinchas and Yiftach refused to seek each other out to annul Yiftach's vow, they were both punished for their haughtiness. Yiftach had to live with the consequences of his vow and was afflicted with boils on his limbs. Pinchas lost the Divine Presence which previously had helped him to lead the people.

Thereafter, the daughters of Yisrael would lament four days each year, in remembrance of this tragic event involving Yiftach's daughter.

❦ HISTORY

CONSEQUENCES OF CIVIL STRIFE

The people of Efrayim united against Yiftach, protesting the fact that he had not called upon them to join the fight against Ammon. They threatened to destroy him and burn down his house.

Yiftach explained that he and his people had been engaged in a bitter struggle against Ammon. They had called for help, but there had been no response. God had caused them to be victorious over their enemy. Why, then, did they now come to fight him?

Yiftach gathered his army to fight the men of Efrayim. The people of Efrayim sought to conceal their identities, but were tested by their pronunciation of the word, "*shibboles*." Those who pronounced it "*sibboles*" were from Efrayim, and 42,000 of them were killed.

We see a direct contrast between Yiftach's response and Gidon's response to the people of Efrayim. Gidon tried to placate them by praising their past achievements while lowering his own worth. On the other hand, Yiftach's response was one of confrontation. He put down the people of Efrayim while raising himself up. The result of both their actions was self-evident. Gidon was able to avoid bloodshed, while Yiftach had to fight a civil war which resulted in the deaths of 42,000 men from the tribe of Efrayim.

Yiftach continued to judge for six more years. He was buried in Gilad. He was followed by Ivtzan (Bo'az) who judged for seven years (2785-2792/976 B.C.E.- 969 B.C.E.).

❦ Key People, Places and Things

AVIMELECH: Gidon's wicked son by a concubine, who slew sixty-nine of his brothers. He had the support of the people of Shechem, from where his mother came.

DEVORAH: the prophetess who, together with Barak, led the Jews against Sisera.

EHUD: the courageous Judge with a shriveled right hand, who killed Eglon, king of Mo'av.

GIDON: a great leader who led the fight against Midyan and Amalek. As a result of God's help, he needed only 300 people to wage this battle.

KIBBUD AV V'EM: the mitzvah of honoring one's parents.

OSNIEL BEN KENAZ: the first of the Judges. A courageous and learned man from the tribe of Yehudah, who married the daughter of Kalev.

SHOFTIM: Judges, the leaders of the Jews following the death of Yehoshua and the Elders. This era lasted approximately 400 years until the era of the Prophets.

YIFTACH: a leader and Judge who defended and protected the Jews against their enemies.

YOSAM: the lone survivor of Avimelech's slaughter of his sixty-nine brothers.

NOTES

1. *Talmud Shabbos*, 104b.
2. *Midrash Masechtos Semachos, perek* 8.
3. *Shemos* 23:33.
4. *Devarim* 7:2.
5. *Devarim* 12:31.
6. *Talmud Yerushalmi, Pe'ah, perek* 1; Rashi, *Talmud Kiddushin*, 31b.
7. *Talmud Kiddushin*, 31b.
8. *Talmud Kiddushin*, 31b.
9. *Kitzur Shulchan Aruch, Hilchos Kibbud Av v'Em*.
10. *Pirkei Avos*, 4:3.

CHAPTER 13

Shoftim (Judges) (Part II)
From Ruth to Eli the Kohen
(2785 – 2830/976 B.C.E. – 931 B.C.E.)

❦ HISTORY

THE STORY OF RUTH

During the time of the Judges, there was a famine in the land of Yehudah. A wealthy man named Elimelech, along with his wife Naomi and their two sons, moved to the land of Mo'av. Because they had left the Holy Land, the family was punished by God and Elimelech and his two sons died in Mo'av. Naomi was left with her two daughters-in-law, Orpah and Ruth, who were Moavite princesses. They were sisters, who were descendants of Eglon, king of Mo'av.

When Naomi heard that God had listened to the prayers of the Jews and the famine had ceased, she left Mo'av together with her daughters-in-law, to return to her own country. As they set out, Naomi then thanked them for all of their assistance to her, and tried to discourage them from going to Eretz Yisrael with her. After some resistance, Orpah kissed her mother-in-law goodbye, but Ruth remained with her.

Ruth said, "Don't implore me to leave you and to turn back from following you. Wherever you go, I will go; wherever you stay, I will stay; your people shall be my people, and your God shall be my God; wherever you die, I will die, and there will I be buried. May the Lord punish me time and again if anything but death parts me from you!" When Naomi saw that she was determined to remain with her, she said no more.

The two went on until they came to Beis Lechem, where the barley harvest was just beginning.

Ruth went and gleaned in the fields after the harvesters, as was the custom of the poor people. She happened to come to the field belonging to Bo'az, a relative of Naomi's husband.

Bo'az gave Ruth advice and was very kind to her. Ruth returned to Naomi and told her all that had transpired. Upon Naomi's advice, Ruth married the aged Bo'az. She bore a son named Oved, who became the grandfather of King David.

Ruth's faithfulness, loyalty and self-sacrifice to her mother-in-law and the Jewish people made her deserving to become the mother of royalty from whose loins *Mashiach* (Messiah) will come.

ETHICS I

Treating a Convert Properly

The Torah commands us to love the convert living in our midst. The Rabbis explain Hashem's special concern for the convert. One may be inclined to take advantage of a convert since he has no relatives who will come to his defense. The Torah, therefore, reminds us that we, too, were strangers in Egypt. The Egyptians who oppressed our ancestors also thought that no one would come to help them, but the Almighty heard the cries of the oppressed and came to their aid, while severely punishing the Egyptians for their wickedness.

Our Sages teach us that Hashem regards the *ger tzedek* or *emes* (the sincere convert) as equal to an Israelite by descent. Moshe, in astonishment, asked Hashem, "Is a *ger* really to be regarded as a *levi?*"

Hashem answered Moshe, "How much did I toil for the Jews? I took them out of Egypt and lit their paths through the wilderness. I caused a well of water to come up for them and gave the Torah amidst splendor and glory. Then the Jews accepted my Torah. In contrast, this *ger* came to me of his own free will and accepted the commandments and Torah without having benefited from any miracle. Should he not be considered the equal of at least a *levi?*"

One must always be careful in dealing with converts. It is forbidden to remind a convert of his past. If you are angry at a convert, you are prohibited from saying, "Just a while ago you were an idol worshiper and ate pork. How dare you speak like that to me!"[1] The *ger* came to seek shelter under the wings of Judaism. Causing him anguish is a disgrace and desecration of God's Holy Name. It is incumbent upon us to make a convert feel welcome in his new community, for we must remember that we, too, were once strangers in a strange land.[2]

LESSON I

Be Considerate of Another Person's Predicament

The Sages say that the judge Ivtzan was Bo'az (2785 - 2792 / 976 B.C.E. - 969 B.C.E.). Ivtzan, who had thirty sons and thirty daughters, did not invite Mano'ach (the father of Shimshon) to partake in the wedding feasts of his children, since Mano'ach was childless and would not be able to reciprocate. Ivtzan was later punished for this and all of his children died during his lifetime. Afterwards he married Ruth the Moavite and was the progenitor of the Royal House of David.

The Maharal uses this example to point out the fact that one must be careful in his treatment of those less fortunate. Any wealth and blessings that an individual accumulates are solely gifts of the Almighty. If the individual does not properly recognize the source of his blessings, he may lose them.

The consequences of being inconsiderate are often unforseeable. There was once a wealthy man who enjoyed all the good graces of life: a successful business, a devoted wife, and a spacious, comfortable home. He was very content to continue this life of ease.

One day, as he was sitting down to a sumptuous meal, he heard a knock at the door. He opened it and found a wretched-looking beggar facing him. "Sir, I have not eaten in two days," the beggar pleaded. "Would you have a few morsels of food that you could spare?" He looked at the man hopefully.

The man responded with scorn. "Why don't you go out and earn a living instead of depending upon others to support you?" he said angrily, and shut the door in the beggar's face.

It was not long afterwards that the man noticed his business beginning to decline. Sales were not what they had once been and the man was forced to cut back on his lifestyle. First he shed his frills — his art collection and his extra wardrobes. But the business' downward turn continued unabated. Whatever the cause, the man eventually found himself pawning what he had once taken for granted. Out went his furniture, his clothing, and finally his house itself was lost. His wife volunteered to find work to help pay for food, but the man refused. He felt so ashamed at not being able to support her, that he gave her a divorce and she sadly agreed to it.

After some time, the wife found a new suitor. He was a well-to-do individual and had a fine home. One day, as they were preparing for dinner, a beggar appeared at their door and meekly asked for some food. The woman's new husband had a more charitable heart than her previous one. He invited the emaciated beggar inside and provided him with enough food and money to satisfy him for weeks. The beggar kept his eyes downcast, but he accepted the charity gratefully.

After the beggar had departed, the husband noticed that his wife had a strange expression on her face. He asked her if anything was wrong.

"I knew that beggar," she said in a shocked tone. "He was my first husband. He looked so thin and pale that I hardly recognized him. How sad to see a man sink so low."

The husband thought for a moment and said, "If that was your first husband, then I just realized something. Do you remember that a beggar once came to your previous home asking for bread and was turned away? Well, that beggar was me. Somehow, good fortune seemed to come my way after that, and I became quite wealthy. Do you suppose there was any reason why our fortunes became reversed?"

The wife nodded solemnly. "I most certainly think there was. One must always be sensitive to the needs of another person for one never knows when Hashem could punish one and take away what he has and give it to a more deserving individual."

Bo'az passed away (2792/969 B.C.E.) shortly after his marriage to Ruth. He was succeeded by Eilon, who judged for ten years (2792-2802), and then by Avdon, who judged for eight years (2802-2810).

❦ HISTORY

THE STORY OF SHIMSHON (2810-2830/951 B.C.E.-931 B.C.E.)

The Jews continued to sin against the Almighty and so were given into the hands of the Pelishtites (Philistines). At this time, there lived a man from the tribe of Dan, by the name of Mano'ach, who had no children. One day, an angel of God appeared to his wife with the news that she would conceive and bear a son. He warned her to abstain from alcoholic beverages and from unclean things during her pregnancy, for the son would grow up to be a *nazir* (one who abstains from drinking wine, from cutting his hair, and is totally devoted to God). He would save the Israelites from the hands of the Philistines. The wife related everything to her husband, saying that she did not know the name of the man who had spoken to her, nor where he had come from, only that he had been sent by God.

Mano'ach prayed to God that he, too, be allowed to see the angel and be instructed as to how to raise their son. God accepted his prayers and the angel appeared a second time to the wife, who ran to call her husband. The angel repeated to Mano'ach that his wife must abstain from wine and unclean foods. A son was born to Mano'ach's wife, and he was named Shimshon. The boy grew up and the spirit of God rested upon him.

Shimshon went down to Timnat, where he saw a Philistine woman. He asked his parents to arrange a marriage with her. They tried to discourage him from marrying a non-Jew but their arguments were to no avail. They did not know that all this was part of God's plan for Shimshon to find a pretense to fight the Pelishtites.

Shimshon and his parents traveled to Timnat to arrange the marriage. On the way there, a young lion roared at Shimshon. He killed it with his bare hands, but did not relate the incident to his parents. In Timnat, they spoke to the woman, and she agreed to marry Shimshon.

A few days later, Shimshon returned to look at the carcass of the lion and found a swarm of bees and honey inside it. Shimshon removed the honey and ate some of it. He also gave some to his parents, but did not tell them from where it had been obtained.

Shimshon married his Pelishtite bride in Timnat and arranged a great feast. At the feast, thirty Pelishtite relatives were present, and Shimshon made a bet with them. He would pose a riddle to them. If they guessed the answer, he would give them thirty linen sheets and suits of clothing. If, however, they could not guess the answer, then they would have to give these items to him.

The riddle was as follows: "From the eater came forth food, and out of the strong came sweetness." The Pelishtites could not figure out the answer. They sought to obtain the information from Shimshon's bride by threatening to burn her and her father's house down unless she found out the solution to the riddle.

Shimshon's bride spent the seven days of the wedding feast crying bitterly that Shimshon did not love her since he had not revealed the riddle's solution to her. He responded that he had not told the riddle to his parents, either. He told her the answer to the riddle and she quickly revealed it to her compatriots.

Shimshon responded that it was obvious who their source of information had been. He now had a reason to wage a personal battle against the Pelishtites without endangering the Jewish population at large, for it was obvious that he was waging a personal vendetta. Therefore, the Pelishtites would be unlikely to take revenge upon the entire Jewish nation. The spirit of God rested upon Shimshon and he went down to the Pelishtite city of Ashkelon where he killed thirty Pelishtites and took their suits of clothing. These he gave to the thirty Pelishtites who had answered his riddle.

Shimshon was angry with his wife for betraying him and returned to his father's home without her. In the meantime, her father gave her to another Pelishtite in marriage.

It should not enter one's mind that Shimshon, the savior of Yisrael, took gentile wives. Rather, he converted them to Judaism and married them. However, because they did not accept the Torah sincerely, as was subsequently seen, they were morally considered as gentiles, though legally they had the status of Jews.[3]

Shimshon had ulterior motives for marrying Pelishtite girls. It was his way of being able to fight the Pelishtites without causing reprisals against his fellow Jews. He also thought that by marrying and influencing a Pelishtite woman he would eventually influence all of the Pelishtites to subjugate themselves to the will of God.

There is a misconception about the greatness of Shimshon. He is looked upon as a mere warrior who, on occasion, strayed by succumbing to temptation. This is, of course, completely erroneous.

Shimshon was the leader and chief Judge of the Jewish people for twenty years. Shimshon judged judiciously, with complete impartiality. He never used his office for any personal gain. Proof of his greatness lies in the fact that there were two other great leaders who were his contemporaries — Pinchas the *Kohen Gadol*, and Eli, who was his successor. Yet Shimshon was the chief Judge and leader, elevated above everyone else. The Talmud states: "Shimshon in his generation was compared to Aharon in his generation."[4]

Based on how the Talmud and Midrash describe Shimshon, we see him as a great leader, totally dedicated to the salvation of his people. The only mistake that he made was marrying those Pelishtite women, despite his good intentions.

LESSON II

The Threat of Intermarriage

Every Jew is born with a Jewish spark in his *neshamah* (soul) which is a permanent bond to Judaism that never disappears. Jews have a special potential for holiness granted by God. Consequently, they must make sure not to dilute this holiness. They must live up to the rigorous standards of the Torah. They must keep certain laws and avoid certain acts that gentiles need not worry about.

"Neither shall you make marriages with them; your daughter you shall not give unto his son, nor his daughter shall you take unto your son. For they will turn away your son from following Me..."[5]

"It is not from hostility against members of other faiths that you should not intermarry with any non-Jews, but out of anxiety for Judaism, the sole treasure of your people. You must avoid mixed marriages on account of the obligation which God has laid upon you to transmit His law to your descendants and help to continue Yisrael's mission through them. Therefore, as long as Yisrael remains Yisrael, all marriage with non-Jews is forbidden... In order that the sons of Yisrael do not marry non-Jewish girls, nor the daughters of Yisrael non-Jewish youths,

God's law has also forbidden to Yisrael too great intimacy with other peoples."[6]

Throughout Jewish history we find that spiritual decay preceded physical destruction. Prior to the Spanish Inquisition and the expulsion of the Jews from Spain, they were already becoming assimilated. Likewise, before the terrible Holocaust of World War II, the rate of assimilation and intermarriage in Germany, Austria, and other countries was very high. The effect of intermarriage upon the Jewish people is clearly brought out in the following story related by the renowned Rabbi Avraham Yehoshua Heschel, the Kapitchinitzer Rebbe, after the war.

Rabbi Heschel was once arrested and detained overnight in prison by the Nazis, *yemach shemam* (may their names be obliterated). While in prison, he saw a young man bashing his head against a stone wall in an effort to commit suicide. The Rebbe spoke kindly to him in an attempt to stop such senseless self-destruction, explaining that this was forbidden for a Jew to do.

"One must never give up hope, no matter how desperate the situation is," said the Rebbe.

The young man explained that he was Jewish and married to a gentile woman. It was she who had handed him over to the Gestapo for arrest. The young man was so depressed that he saw no reason to continue living.

For some reason, the Kapitchinitzer Rebbe was released from prison the next day. He was never able to find out what had happened in the end to that young man and was not able to figure out the reason for his overnight imprisonment and sudden release.

Years later, when the Rebbe was living in Brooklyn, he was called by a Jewish mother, heartbroken over her son's impending marriage to a gentile girl. Her cries and pleas had fallen on deaf ears. The son was determined to go through with the marriage. After much pleading from the mother, the Rebbe agreed to speak to her son if he would come to the Rebbe's house. The latter did so, despite the fact that he was sure that no one could change his mind.

When the young man appeared before the Kapitchinitzer Rebbe, the latter suddenly recalled his own experience in prison many years earlier. He told the young man that he was not going to preach to him about the evils of intermarriage and the fact that it would break his mother's heart. He merely wanted to relate a true story to him, one that the Rebbe himself had witnessed.

When the young man left the Kapitchinitzer Rebbe's study after hearing the story, he was completely shaken. As soon as he returned home, his mother asked what had happened. Her son replied, "I nearly let my desires take control of my life, but the Rebbe set me straight. The wedding is off!"

❦ HISTORY

SHIMSHON'S BATTLES

It was during the wheat harvest that Shimshon sought to be reconciled with his wife. He brought a gift of a goat (kid) to her father's house, but her father would not admit him. He informed Shimshon that she had been given to another man, since he had assumed that Shimshon despised her after what had occurred. The father offered Shimshon her younger sister instead, but Shimshon refused.

Shimshon felt that this time he would be blameless in carrying out his revenge against the Pelishtites since his father-in-law had given away his wife. He used his brute strength and cunning to attack and destroy the Pelishtite oppressors of the Jews, and cause damage to their property.

When the Pelishtites learned that Shimshon had done this out of revenge for the wrongdoing by his father-in-law, they killed his wife and her father. When Shimshon heard this, he caused further destruction in the land of the Pelishtites.

Shimshon's marriage was a pretense to gain the opportunity to destroy the Pelishtites. In this way, the Jews were not held accountable and the Pelishtites did not seek revenge against them. They looked at Shimshon's acts of violence as a matter of personal hatred and animosity, rather than being on behalf of the Jewish nation. Shimshon did not wage war like the other Judges. He fought the enemy single-handedly, killing as many as 1,000 Pelishtites in a single battle.

The Pelishtites sought to capture Shimshon, who was hiding out among the rocks and clefts near the territory of Yehudah. They sent messengers to the people of Yehudah, demanding that they capture Shimshon and turn him over to them.

Three thousand people from the tribe of Yehudah went down to speak to Shimshon. They explained their own precarious position with regard to the Pelishtites who ruled over them. After obtaining their assurance that they would not harm him, Shimshon allowed them to bind him with two new ropes. They brought him up from the rock where he had been hiding.

When the Pelishtites saw him, they all shouted with joy. Their glee was short-lived, for the spirit of God rested upon Shimshon, and he was able to sever the ropes that bound him. He then found the jawbone of a donkey and used it to slay a thousand Pelishtites.

Afterwards, Shimshon became terribly thirsty, but no water was available to quench his thirst. Shimshon's desperate unnatural thirst was punishment for his arrogance after he slew the thousand Pelishtites. It is human nature that when one is successful he credits his own power, skill, and strength.[7] After he suffered great thirst, Shimshon realized that this was God's punishment for his pride. He prayed to Hashem, asking, "You have caused a great deliverance through the hands of Your servant. Will You now cause him to die and to fall into the hands of the uncircumcised [Pelishtites]?"

Since Shimshon recognized that God was his source of strength, then God found him worthy of a miracle, and water began to flow from the jawbone of the donkey. Shimshon drank and his spirit was revived.

Later, Shimshon visited a harlot in Aza (Gaza). When the Pelishtites learned of his presence in the city, they prepared an ambush at the gates of the city in order to seize him in the morning. Shimshon surprised them by leaving at midnight and carrying away the gates of the city on his shoulders to the top of a mountain.

Although Shimshon had a higher purpose in dealing with the Pelishtite women, he was still somewhat affected by his attraction to a woman named Delilah. He married her and when the Pelishtite leaders learned of this, they came to her with a request that she assist them. They persuaded her to ascertain and reveal to them the secret source of his great strength, so that they could capture and torture him. In return, they each offered her 1100 pieces of silver.

The first time Delilah nagged Shimshon to reveal his source of strength, he responded that if he were tied with seven moist bowstrings which had not been dried, his strength would fail him. The Pelishtites provided her with the moist bowstrings and then set up an ambush. Delilah tied up Shimshon and yelled, "The Pelishtites are upon you!" Shimshon easily ripped the bowstrings apart. Delilah realized that she had been fooled.

The second time she insisted on knowing the secret of his strength, he told her that if he were tied up with seven brand new ropes, then he would have the strength of any other normal man. Delilah tied him up with the new ropes while the Pelishtite ambushers were hiding in the room. When she yelled that the Pelishtites had come, Shimshon once again tore the ropes from his arms as if they were mere threads.

Delilah cried at Shimshon that he was mocking her with his lies. This time he told her that if she were to weave on a loom the seven locks of hair on his head, then his strength would ebb. Delilah tested him again, and once again found that she had been fooled. So strong was her nagging persistence that Shimshon finally weakened and told her the secret of his strength — the fact that since birth, he had been a *nazir* to God. As a result, no razor had ever come upon his head. If his head was shaved, all his strength would leave him. This time, Delilah felt in her heart that he had finally revealed the truth. She sent word to the Pelishtite lords to come prepared with the money they had promised her.

Delilah put Shimshon to sleep upon her knees and called a man to assist her. She proceeded to shave off the seven locks from Shimshon's head. When she yelled that the Pelishtites were upon him, he awoke from his sleep, thinking that he had his previous strength. He only realized that his God-given strength had departed from him when he was seized by the Pelishtites. They gouged out his eyes and then brought him in chains to the town of Aza. There, they forced him to do hard labor in the prison house.

The manner in which Shimson was punished — having his eyes put out — came about because he had allowed his eyes to stray. Therefore, he was punished with their loss (measure for measure).[8]

With the passage of time, the hair on his head grew back. The Pelishtites gathered to offer a great sacrifice to their god, Dagon, attributing to him the successful capture of their enemy, Shimshon. During the wild celebration, the Pelishtites decided to bring Shimshon from his prison cell in order to make sport of him. They positioned him between two pillars.

Shimshon asked the lad who was leading him by the hand to allow him to lean against the pillars. The house was full of men and women, with another 3,000 on the roof. They were all making sport of Shimshon's plight.

Shimshon prayed fervently to God, "Please remember me and strengthen me this one more time." With his last strength, he yelled, "Let me die with the Pelishtites," and pushed the two pillars apart. The entire building collapsed upon its inhabitants. With this one act, Shimshon killed more Pelishtites than he had during his entire lifetime.

Shimshon's brothers and all of his father's family came to retrieve his body. He was buried in his father's burial plot after having judged Yisrael for twenty years (2830/931 B.C.E.).

MITZVAH

Responsibilities for the Deceased

The Torah teaches us that the kindness shown to the dead is true kindness.[9] When dealing kindly with a person in life, one cannot know whether it was truly kindness, for many times that which one thinks is an act of mercy and kindness may have been done consciously or subconsciously with ulterior motives. But the kindness one shows to the dead is called "chesed shel emes" — true kindness — since the doer cannot expect to be repaid. This is not necessarily the case if the recipient is alive.

Burying the dead is a very great mitzvah, especially when there is no relative or Jewish burial society (chevrah kad-disha) to assume the responsibility.

Once, when Rabbi Yisrael Salanter was in the middle of the morning prayers, he heard a loud argument between the heads of two burial societies. A poor woman had died and each society claimed that it was the other's obligation to bury her.

In the middle of his prayers, Rabbi Yisrael Salanter removed his tallis and tefillin, gathered together a few of his students and followers, and told them to join him in the burial of the woman. Since neither society wanted to perform the burial, it was a mes mitzvah (when no one else is available to perform the burial) and everyone must drop whatever he is doing to perform this final *chesed* (kindness) for the deceased.

The most important religious law with regard to burial pertains to the honor and respect given to the deceased. The body must be clothed in white garments after having been carefully washed and cleansed by a group of trained and pious individuals from the *chevrah kaddisha*. The male deceased is also wrapped in a *tallis*.

The deceased should not be left alone, even at night in the mortuary. Someone should be designated to stay with him. So great is this duty that if that person has no one to relieve him, he is exempted from reading the *Shema* and all other religious obligations. The face of the deceased is covered with a sheet as a sign of respect. Displaying the dead in an open casket is considered a dishonor. Embalming is forbidden because the blood of the deceased is considered part of him and must be buried with him and not discarded.

Burial must take place as soon as possible following death, unless there are certain mitigating circumstances. It is forbidden to bury the dead on Shabbos, Yom Kippur, or on the first day of *Yom Tov*.

Cremation is forbidden and is considered a desecration of the dead. Aboveground burial is also prohibited by Jewish law. Burial must be within the ground.

Tearing one's garment, according to Halachah, is the proper way to express grief for the dead. For a deceased parent, one tears on the left side near the heart. For all other relatives it is done on the right side. One tears the jacket, possibly the shirt (depending on custom), but not the undershirt.

It is customary for neighbors to prepare the first meal for the mourners after they return home from the funeral. This is a comforting sign to the mourners that there are others who will help them. The meal should include hard-boiled eggs, as a symbol that there is no beginning nor end to life, just as there is no beginning nor end to an egg.

It is proper for a family to observe mourning together in the home where the deceased lived. Included in the family for whom one must observe a week of mourning (*shivah*) are the following relations: father, mother, spouse, son, daughter, brother or sister. A son is duty-bound to recite the Kaddish prayer at daily prayer services for a period of eleven months. It is a reverence and a comfort for the deceased parent. Kaddish is recited for eleven months, for only the wicked are subject to judgment for twelve months.

During the week of *shivah*, both the mourners and those who come to comfort them are forbidden to greet each other. It is a mitzvah to comfort the mourners after burial. Upon taking leave of the mourners, we say to them, "May the Lord comfort you among the mourners of Tzion and Yerushalayim." Some people add the wish that the mourners be spared knowing any more sorrow.

There are different customs for when and how a tombstone should be put up. Some do it after seven days, thirty days, or after a year.

The yahrtzeit refers to the anniversary of the day of death, according to the

Jewish calendar. It is customary to light a candle on the eve of the yahrtzeit, one that will burn the entire twenty-four hour period. Sons say Kaddish, lead the services and give charity on this day. Some have the custom to fast on that day, to visit the gravesite, and say prayers there. It must be remembered that prayers recited at the cemetery are not recited to the dead who are buried there, but to God, that He may show mercy on the living for the sake of the merits of the pious dead. We also pray that the deceased will serve as a defender on our behalf before the Almighty.

❧ HISTORY

TWO TRAGIC EVENTS DURING THE PERIOD OF THE JUDGES

There are varying opinions concerning when the following two episodes (the graven image and the concubine of Givah) actually took place. Some sages, including Rav Ya'akov Kamenecki, state that they occurred before the installation of Osniel ben Kenaz as the first Judge of Yisrael. Others state that these incidents occurred either while Shimshon was incarcerated or after his death. It is possible that the precise years of these events were deliberately not listed by the Prophet, to indicate that their lessons are timeless. The Jew in every age must know the tragic consequences that result when people do not respond to their leaders and do not accept authority. These episodes serve as admonitions to the entire Jewish nation, calling for proper conduct as befits God's Chosen People.

There was a man from the mountain of Efrayim by the name of Michayahu or Michah. He admitted to his mother that he was the one who had taken 1100 pieces of silver from her. After he returned the silver to her, she used it to make a graven and molten image. Michah's house became a house of idolatry, and he appointed one of his sons to serve as priest.

In those days, there was no king in Yisrael, and every man did as he saw fit. There was a lad, a Levite from Beis Lechem, who traveled about. When he happened to arrive at Michah's house, Michah invited him to stay with his family and to serve as their instructor and priest. Michah was pleased with himself that he now had a Levite to serve as his priest.

At this time, the tribe of Dan was still in the process of conquering territory that was part of their inheritance in the Land. Five men were sent from Dan to investigate the possibility of acquiring some additional territory to the north of Yisrael for their tribe. They happened upon the house of Michah, and recognized the voice of the Levite. They questioned his presence there and he explained that he had been hired as Michah's priest.

Subsequently, the tribe of Dan sent out 600 warriors to capture the territory. On their way north, they passed Michah's house. The five men who had gone earlier to spy out the area informed them that it was a house containing a graven image. They entered Michah's house and took the graven image. When the Levite tried to stop them, they ordered him to be quiet and throw in his lot with them.

They asked him, "Is it better for you to be the priest to one man, or to a whole tribe in Yisrael?"

This appealed to the young Levite and he joined them. Michah and his followers tried to overtake the people of Dan and retrieve what had been confiscated from them. Michah realized, however, that they were stronger than he, and turned back.

The graven image that Michah had made was worshiped throughout the period that the Tabernacle was in Shiloh.

LESSON III

The Necessity for Concern for All Jews Includes the Estranged

These people of Dan were not typical of the mainstream of Jews who inhabited the land at this time. Their search for further territory all the way up north indicates that they were like rough frontiersmen. Their rough language and the threatening and crude manner in which they stole the graven image showed that they were on the "fringe" of society. Perhaps that is why the people of Dan were able to continue with their idol worship without being rebuked by the rest of the nation. They were looked upon as a group of unusual characters and consequently were left alone. Such indifference on the part of the rest of the nation to these people from the tribe of Dan was wrong. This indifference — which was later punished with a civil war and much loss of life — came as a result of the following episode.

A Levite who lived near the mountain of Efrayim took a concubine from Beis Lechem in Yehudah. She subsequently left him to return to her father's home. After four months, the man traveled to his father-in-law's home to ask that she return. His father-in-law was very happy to see him and provided him with food and shelter for three days. When the man wanted to leave on the fourth day, his father-in-law delayed him a while longer. On the fifth day, the man no longer wanted to tarry. Despite the fact that it was late in the day, he insisted upon departing with his concubine.

They arrived in Givah, in the territory of Binyamin. Although they sat in the street, no one came out to offer lodging to these strangers, except for one old man returning from his field at night. He brought them to his home, offered them food and drink for themselves and their donkeys, and water with which to wash themselves.

While the guests were refreshing themselves, the wicked people of the city surrounded the house, banging on the door. They demanded of the old man that he send out his male guest to them. The old man went out to try to appease them by offering his own daughter and the man's concubine. He pleaded with them not to commit any disgraceful act. They took away the concubine. When she returned in the morning, she collapsed, dead, on the doorstep of the old man's house.

In the morning, the Levite opened the door, preparing to leave. He saw his concubine lying there and called to her to get up and to join him. When she didn't respond, he realized that she was dead. He put her body on his donkey and returned to his home. There he took a knife and proceeded to dismember her into twelve parts, one of which he sent to each of the tribes of Yisrael. He did this bizarre act to awaken the entire nation to this great tragedy. People were shocked to hear what had occurred in a city of Yisrael. From the time that the Jews had left Egypt, until that day, no such abomination had ever occurred.

ETHICS II

Don't Display Anger and Create Unnecessary Fear in Your Household

The commentaries on the *Tanach* and the Talmud[10] state that the whole sequence of events that developed was the result of the Levite's anger and impatience with his concubine after a fly had been found in food that she had prepared. After this she left her house to return to her father's house. The tragic events were thus set in motion. Had the Levite been more patient and understanding, this tragic incident could have been avoided.

Rav Chisda, a great rabbi mentioned in the Talmud, stated that one must be careful not to strike unnecessary fear into the hearts of one's household (as the Levite was guilty of doing), since it can lead to tragedy. In the case of the *pilegesh b'Givah* (concubine in Givah) we will learn that it resulted in the deaths of thousands of Jews.

Adam's deep sleep during the creation of Chavah demonstrated that a husband should sometimes act as if he were asleep and unaware of his wife's shortcomings. He should overlook minor faults in order to avoid domestic quarrels.

The famed rabbi known as the Seer of Lublin once wanted to rise especially early to attend to an important matter. The day before, he had asked his wife to prepare his evening meal earlier than usual so that he could go to bed earlier, but it was prepared much later than usual. He said, "It would be natural for me to become angry now. But the only reason I wanted to have the meal early was to do the will of my Creator, and it is also the will of my Creator that I should not become angry."

❦ HISTORY

CIVIL WAR IN YISRAEL

The Children of Yisrael were united in their anger against the abomination that had been committed. Over 400,000 warriors assembled from all the tribes of Yisrael, except Binyamin, in order to eradicate the evil from their midst. The people from Binyamin chose not to join them, but rather to defend their tribesmen from Givah. By their inaction, the people of Binyamin showed that they condoned the evil perpetrated in Givah and, therefore, were to be held responsible for that abominable act.[11]

The tribes of Yisrael demanded that the men of Givah be handed over to them for justice, but the people of Binyamin refused to comply. Instead, 26,000 gathered from Binyamin, and 700 from Givah.

When the tribes inquired of God through the *urim v'tumim* who should lead them, they were told that Yehudah should be at the forefront. Terrible battles were fought in which tens of thousands from the tribes of Yisrael perished.

On the opposing side, some 25,000 people from Binyamin were killed. The remaining soldiers from Binyamin continued to fight until they saw a pillar of smoke rising from their burning city. Then when they attempted to flee, another 18,000 of them were killed. The cities of Binyamin were totally devastated. According to the commentaries, one day 25,100 men fell, the next day an additional 1,000 men were killed, and then 18,900 more men were killed. Approximately 600 men escaped.

This entire tragedy and misfortune was attributed to the Great Sanhedrin (Supreme Court) led by the High Priest, Pinchas. They were busy pursuing perfection for themselves, and neglected the needs of the generation. Instead of the Elders traveling around throughout the towns of Yisrael, disseminating Torah and justice, they chose instead to remain in their own towns.[12]

SAVING OF THE TRIBE OF BINYAMIN

Before the war against Binyamin, the warriors of the tribes of Yisrael had assembled in Mitzpah. There, they all took an oath that they would not give their daughters in marriage to the men of Binyamin. Since the men of Givah (which was part of Binyamin) had acted in such a degenerate manner, the whole tribe was deemed unworthy of intermarrying with the rest of the tribes of Yisrael.

The Jews gathered at Beis El to mourn before the Almighty the great tragedy that had befallen their people. They were deeply anguished at the thought that now one tribe from the nation of Yisrael would, in effect, be missing. The leadership devised two methods for Binyamin to marry the daughters of Yisrael and thereby remain part of Yisrael. One was that the fathers in Yisrael not actually give their daughters to them; rather, they would be taken. The second was that the daughters of Gilad would be permitted as wives, since they were never part of the oath, as we will now explain.

It was the custom in those days that when a great sacrifice was brought in Shiloh (place of the Tabernacle) on a certain Festival, the daughters of Shiloh would come out to dance in the vineyards. The date of that Festival was the 15th day of the Hebrew month of *Av*. It was suggested to the people of Binyamin that they come to the vineyards at that time and that each man take one of the girls who was dancing. In this manner it could not be said that their fathers had given them willingly in marriage to the men of Binyamin, and therefore, they had not broken their oath.

Our Sages have stated that there was no greater holiday in Yisrael than the 15th day of *Av*[13] — the day that the tribe of Binyamin was once again permitted to enter the nation of Yisrael by marrying the daughters of Yavesh Gilad (who had come to dance in the vineyards of Shiloh). They were able to circumvent the oath taken in Mitzpah since the people of Yavesh Gilad were not present at the time the oath was taken. This was done, and the men of Binyamin were able to marry, and to proceed to rebuild their tribe and their cities.

These tragedies occurred because there was no strong leadership that was able to control and lead the entire nation.

❧ Key People, Places and Things

BINYAMIN: the tribe of Benjamin, that was almost totally decimated in the civil war among the tribes.

BO'AZ: the elderly Judge in Yisrael who married Ruth. He was also known as Ivtzan.

DELILAH: a Pelishtite who converted to Judaism and married Shimshon. She betrayed him to the Pelishtites and caused his downfall.

GIVAH: a town within the territory of Binyamin.

MEGILLAS RUTH: the Book of Ruth, which is read on Shavuos and is part of *Kesuvim.* It details the story of the convert, Ruth.

NAOMI: the saintly mother-in-law of Ruth, who was compassionate during a difficult time of trials and tribulations.

PESEL MICHAH: a graven image made by Michah which served as an idol. It was the cause of great suffering for the Jews.

PILEGESH B'GIVAH: the tragic story of the killing of a concubine that resulted in a civil war among the tribes of Yisrael.

RUTH: the Moavite princess who converted to Judaism, married Bo'az and merited having the dynasty of King David descend from her.

SHIMSHON: Samson, a Nazirite since birth, who became a great Judge and defender of the Jewish People.

NOTES

1. *Talmud Bava Metzia,* 58b.

2. *Sefer Ha-Chinnuch,* 431; Chafetz Chaim, *Sefer Ha-Mitzvos Ha-Katzar.*

3. Rambam, *Mishneh Torah, Hilchos Issurei Bi'ah,* 13:14.

4. *Talmud Rosh Hashanah,* 25b.

5. *Devarim* 7:3-4.

6. Rabbi Samson Raphael Hirsch, *Horeb.*

7. *Me'am Lo'ez, Shoftim,* 15:18.

8. *Talmud Sotah,* 9b.

9. Rashi, *Bereshis* 47:29.

10. *Talmud Gittin,* 6b.

11. *Talmud Shabbos,* 54b.

12. *Tanna d'Vei Eliyahu,* as cited by the Chafetz Chaim, *Chomos Ha-Da'as, perek* 1.

13. *Talmud Bava Basra,* 91b.

❧ Introduction to Chapters 14 - 19

The spiritual well-being of the Jews throughout the Era of the Kings was enhanced by the presence of the prophets (*nevi'im*) who served as God's messengers to the kings and to the populace and encouraged them to observe God's Torah.

The main message of all the prophets was that Jews must keep the commandments as presented in the Torah. God said to His prophets, "Remember the Torah of Moses, My servant, which I commanded him...." The authority of every prophet is derived only from the Torah. Therefore, no prophet could contradict a single word of the Torah, even if he produced a miracle to enhance his credibility. Any prophet who contradicted the Torah in any way was assumed to be a false prophet and was judged accordingly. In no case could a prophet introduce or take away a law of the Torah based upon his prophecy. The usual reason for God to send a prophet was to admonish the people to keep the Torah.

The prophets, as messengers of God, demanded more of the Jewish people than other nations expected of themselves — and this fact is reflected in the critical manner, unparalleled among the nations of the world, in which they wrote the historical chronicles of their people. Thus we must not look down upon those times ... even though the nation failed to achieve spiritual perfection. Indeed, we need only remember the positive response of the people to any king that arose who was willing to restore the rule of the Torah over the land.

The task of the prophets was to remind the Jewish people of their Divine mission, in the face of the tempting but disastrous lure of paganism. Paganism pictures the world as being dominated by mysterious natural forces and gods who terrify man by the arbitrary use of their invincible power. They do not require obedience to some moral law, but only "appeasement" through sacrifices and other rites. Otherwise a follower is free to pursue the same desire for pleasure and domination which he ascribes to and idealizes in his gods. Paganism gained many Jewish followers, primarily among the ruling classes. Kings found in it a means to justify the unrestrained use of their powers and the full expression of their arbitrary whims. Ultimately, pagan influences served to undermine public respect for the law, and thus the kings frequently became the victims of intrigues and assassinations.

It was in opposition to this state of affairs that the prophets lifted their voices. They warned that the kingdoms of both Yehudah and Yisrael were, during certain historical periods, rotten to the core because they lacked righteousness, and they proclaimed that only a state ruled by the Torah could flourish. They emphasized that pagan reliance on material power was fruitless — royal glory and national survival should be sought through loyalty to the Divine law. The first need was for the Holy Land to be cleansed of the worship of pagan idols and of the evils this had bred: exhausting power politics, perversion of justice, class oppression, and immoral practices. Again and again it was emphasized that failure to adhere to the Torah would result in domination by other powers and the exile of the Jewish people.

❦ Introduction to Chapter 14

The beginning of the Era of the Prophets and Kings covers the history of the Jews from Eli, the High Priest, who was the last of the Judges, through the decline of King Sha'ul's reign. Most of the events during this period are centered around three great personalities: Shemuel, Sha'ul and David.

Shemuel was the first of the prophets, a leader who maintained an extraordinarily high spiritual level. He was extremely honest and dedicated in his service to the Jewish nation.

As a result of the pressures of the neighboring nations, such as Mo'av and Midyan, there emerged a popular desire for a unified monarchy, "as possessed by all other nations." This demand was received by the prophet Shemuel with great trepidation. He feared that the nation or its leaders might attempt to imitate "the other nations," and strive for sovereign power and independence. Thus, the creation of a monarchy would become a danger, by permitting the emergence of a despotic ruler to whom the Divine law would be secondary to his own will. This would cause the collapse and destruction of the Jewish nation and their mission.

On the other hand, a monarch who considered himself first and foremost a servant of God, who would lead the nation in the observance and protection of the law, could make a vast contribution to the rise of a holy nation. In fact, Sha'ul was chosen by God to be king of the Jews because, despite his great stature, he was extremely humble. This humility was accompanied by a deep loyalty to the Torah. The Torah addresses itself to the establishment of a monarchy in Yisrael in the following manner: "You shall surely set him king over you.... And it shall be when he sits upon the throne of his kingdom, he shall have for himself a double copy of this law.... And it shall be with him and he shall read it therein all the days of his life, that he may learn to fear the Lord his God."

CHAPTER 14

Shemuel I
The Prophet Shemuel and
The Reign of Sha'ul, First King of Yisrael
(2830 – 2883/931 B.C.E. – 878 B.C.E.)

❦ HISTORY

ELKANAH

During the tenure of Eli the High Priest (2830-2870/931 B.C.E.-891 B.C.E.), there lived a great man named Elkanah, from the tribe of Efrayim, who had two wives, Channah and Peninah. Peninah had children, but Channah did not. Year after year, on the *Shalosh Regalim* (the three Festivals of Pesach, Shavuos, and Sukkos) Elkanah would go up from his home town to worship and sacrifice to Hashem at the *Mishkan* in Shiloh.[1] He always tried to travel using different routes, thereby encouraging people along the route to join him in his pilgrimage to Shiloh. Elkanah was responsible for awakening a feeling for Judaism in many families who were scattered all across the land. He was ultimately rewarded with a son, Shemuel, who became a great leader and prophet and who also traveled throughout the land, spreading God's Torah and teachings to the populace.

LESSON I

The Reward for Spreading Judaism

The name Elkanah means "God has acquired," for he inspired the people to worship Hashem and to participate in the pilgrimage festivals. He spread God's word among the people.

This story about Elkanah is written in the Book of Shemuel right after the terrible tragedy of the *pilegesh b'Givah*. Pinchas the *Kohen Gadol*, and the members of the Sanhedrin were considered directly responsible for the incident, for they did not go out among the people to disseminate Judaism. Elkanah, on the other hand, made sure to use different routes every time he traveled to the Tabernacle in Shiloh in order to revive Judaism among the people. In this way he was very similar to our patriarch Avraham. Although there were other righteous people who lived before and during the lifetime of Avraham, only he is considered the founder of the Jewish religion, for he was the one who went out and disseminated both the idea of monotheism and

God's teachings.

Rabbi Shimon bar Yochai taught,[2] "We are all like men on a ship. If someone were to take a drill and begin drilling through the deck beneath his feet, everyone would be sure to yell, 'Stop! You can't do that.' If he retorts, 'What business is this of yours? I'm drilling under my own seat,' would we all agree passively? Of course not. We would all shout at him that the water rushing through his hole would drown us all." With this parable in mind, we understand how every Jew is responsible for his fellow Jew. We cannot sit back passively and allow other Jews to drift away from Judaism. We must jump into action and do everything we can to bring them back.[3]

❦ HISTORY

CHANNAH'S DESIRE TO HAVE CHILDREN

Elkanah traveled on these journeys with his wives and children. Elkanah distributed portions from the sacrifice to all the members of his family. But to his wife, Channah, he gave a special portion because he especially loved her, and to compensate for the fact that she was childless.

Elkanah's other wife, Peninah, would provoke and embarrass Channah in an attempt to encourage her to pray more fervently to Hashem. Channah would then cry and refuse to eat. Elkanah always tried to console her by asking, "Why do you weep? Am I not worth more to you than ten sons?"

CHANNAH'S SILENT PRAYERS ARE ANSWERED

Channah prayed to God while Eli the High Priest was sitting near the doorpost of the *Mishkan*. With a sad heart, she prayed and wept bitterly, saying, "If You will remember me and grant me a son, I will give him to You for the rest of his life."

As Channah prayed, Eli watched her. She was speaking inwardly; her lips moved but no sound was heard by others. Channah is credited with initiating the silent prayer which came to be known as the *Shemoneh Esreh* (prayer of Eighteen Benedictions recited three times a day). She prayed silently because she wanted her prayers to be private, communicating directly with God without anyone else hearing.

Observing her strange conduct, Eli assumed that she was drunk and rebuked her. Channah convinced him that she was not drunk, but was very distressed and was praying silently. Eli then blessed her and prayed that Hashem would answer her prayers.

God responded to Channah's prayers, and at the end of the year she bore a son whom she named Shemuel, because, as she explained, "I asked God for him."

MITZVAH

Shemoneh Esreh
The Special Silent Prayer

Channah's silent prayer was answered. It marked the beginning of the special prayer called the *Shemoneh Esreh*. This prayer consists of eighteen benedictions compiled by the men of the Great Assembly (*Anshei Knesses Ha-Gedolah*). At a later date, another benediction was included, pleading for the destruction of the traitors within the fold of Yisrael who conspired against their own people. The name, however, continues to be the Eighteen Benedictions despite the additional prayer. On the whole, the *Shemoneh Esreh* contains praise of God and prayers for understanding, repentance, health, prosperity, peace, resurrection of the dead, and the restoration of Jewish spiritual life in Eretz Yisrael.

The *Shemoneh Esreh* is recited quietly while standing erect and with both feet together. The reason it is said quietly is because it is like a personal letter to God. The makeup of the *Shemoneh Esreh* is similar to a personal letter of request. The first three blessings are praise. The next thirteen are requests. The last three express gratitude to God.

The *Shemoneh Esreh* must be recited in a place where the person is free from distractions and will be able to concentrate on his prayers. The person should be dressed appropriately for prayers as if he were speaking to a high official, for after all, he is speaking to God! The

importance of the *Shemoneh Esreh* can be illustrated by the following story:

A pious man was traveling along a road when dusk fell. He then stopped at the edge of the road in order to pray. While he was in the middle of the *Shemoneh Esreh*, an officer approached him and asked what he was doing. The officer looked very important, but the Jew did not respond and simply continued praying.

After he had finished, the officer shouted at him angrily, "You fool! Why didn't you answer me on the spot? I could have killed you for your insolence!"

The Jew replied, "Permit me to explain my behavior. If you were standing before the King, would you have interrupted your speech to greet a friend?"

"Of course not," said the officer.

"Then you can certainly understand what I did. If you'd be afraid to interrupt your speech to a mere mortal king, then how much more so should I be afraid of interrupting my prayers to the eternal King of Kings. When I speak to God, I have to devote all my concentration to this. How, then, could I have interrupted my prayers to answer you?"[4]

The officer nodded his head in satisfaction.

(The man knew that he would not be harmed if he did not respond. If, however, there is a question of life or death, a person should interrupt his prayers to respond.)

At both the beginning and the conclusion of the *Shemoneh Esreh*, we take three steps backward and three steps forward. During the recitation of the *Shemoneh Esreh* we bow four times, at the following places:

(a) *"Baruch Attah"* (at the beginning of the first paragraph)

(b) *"Baruch Attah (Hashem magen Avraham)"*

(c) *"Modim"*

(d) *"Baruch Attah (Hashem, ha-tov Shimcha u'l'cha na'eh l'hodos)"*

When one prays with a *minyan* (quorum), the *Shemoneh Esreh* is repeated by the cantor and everyone listens and answers amen after each blessing. The repetition of the *Shemoneh Esreh* is said only during the morning and afternoon services — not at night. During the repetition of the *Shemoneh Esreh*, the special prayer of *Kedushah* is recited by the entire congregation.

❦ HISTORY

THE RULE OF ELI THE KOHEN GADOL (2830-2870/931 B.C.E.-891 B.C.E.)

Channah devoted herself to her son, Shemuel, for the first two years of his life. She then brought him to Eli the High Priest at the Sanctuary in Shiloh.

Channah said to Eli, "As sure as you live, I am the woman who stood beside you praying for this boy. God has granted my request. I give him over to the Lord for as long as he shall live."

Channah sang a song of praise to God, expressing her great awe of God's power, knowledge and strength — how God has the power to give life and to take it and to raise up people from the depths of despair. She reaffirmed the belief that God rewards and punishes everyone on this earth.

Eli blessed Elkanah and Channah that because of what she had done in dedicating her son to God's service, Hashem would further remember her. She subsequently bore three more sons and two daughters.

It was during this time that Eli's sons, Chofni and Pinchas, were the ministering *kohanim* in the *Mishkan* in Shiloh. They were not sufficiently humble, scrupulous and meticulous in their holy work, and thus incurred God's wrath. Due to their sins, the offerings brought by Chofni and Pinchas were as abominations before God.

Eli, the aged High Priest, became aware of his sons' public transgressions and admonished them. He showed them the gravity of their evil — that everyone was speaking badly of them and that they were sinning directly against God. Since they had attained a prestigious position of power, they would be judged by the Almighty more stringently than others. However, despite the harsh reproof, they did not completely change their ways. Thereafter, a prophecy came to both Eli and Shemuel that since Chofni's and Pinchas's actions had disgraced God's sacrifices, Hashem would punish them severely. Most of their descendants would never reach old age. As an indication of the veracity of this prediction, Eli was told that both of his sons would die on the same day, and the new prophet Shemuel would be chosen. Those surviving from the families of Chofni and Pinchas would humble themselves before him.

During this time, the young Shemuel was growing up and improving himself in the eyes of God. One night, while he was sleeping, Shemuel received a Divine inspiration. At first he did not know what to make of it. He thought that he was being called by Eli and ran to inquire what he wanted from him. Eli responded that he had not called him and told him to go back to sleep. After this happened three times, Eli realized that it was the voice of God calling to Shemuel. He instructed Shemuel to go back to his bed and if he were called again, to respond, "Speak oh Lord, for Your servant is listening!"

The Almighty called to Shemuel and repeated the prophecy that had been foretold previously to Eli. He further stated that no offerings would ever wipe out the sins of the House of Eli, which were the sins of desecrating the honor of God's Holy Name.

Eli summoned Shemuel to find out what God had told him. After some hesitation, Shemuel repeated the prophecy that had been told to him. When Eli heard this, his response was, "He is the Lord. May He do what is good in His eyes." (This statement indicates the superior level of Eli. He accepted God's sad decree upon his family without complaint.) God continued to prophesy to Shemuel, who was the first in a new era of prophets.

ETHICS I

Respect for One's Teachers and Elders

When Shemuel was two years old, Channah brought him to the *Mishkan* in Shiloh in order to fulfill her vow. She also brought along three bullocks to be sacrificed to Hashem. When Eli saw the bullocks, he ordered a *kohen* to be brought to slaughter them. The two-year-old Shemuel, who had the developed mind of an adult, heard the command and declared that it was halachically permissible for a non-*kohen* to also perform the act of slaughtering the animals.

"You have stated the law correctly," admitted the High Priest Eli. "However, one who formulates the Halachah in front of his teacher is liable to the death penalty." Channah begged Eli to forgive her child. Eli did pardon Shemuel's transgression. He grew up to become the famous leader and prophet who inspired his people in the service of Hashem.

Why does a person deserve to die if he renders a *halachic* decision in front of his rebbe? Our Sages teach us that one who publicly shames another is likened to a murderer and deserves to die. A student who puts his rebbe to shame by acting in his presence as if the latter were incapable of a decision, becomes deserving of death.

A student of Rabbi Eliezer once pronounced a Torah decision in his rebbe's presence. Rabbi Eliezer later remarked to his wife that he doubted if that young man would live until the end of the year.

The student did pass away before the year was over, and Rabbi Eliezer's wife wondered if her husband was indeed a prophet.

"I am not a prophet nor the son of a prophet," he said to his wife. "However I know by tradition that someone who teaches Halachah in front of his rebbe is punished by death."[5]

In addition to the prohibition of issuing a decision in the presence of one's rebbe, one is not allowed to contradict one's rebbe. This, too, would be disrespectful. One must remember to give proper respect to his rebbe in every possible way because he is the one who has opened up before him the eternal world of wisdom and truth, *Olam Ha-Ba*.

❧ HISTORY

THE END OF ELI'S DYNASTY AND THE RISE OF SHEMUEL HA-NAVI

(The Conclusion of the Period of the Judges and the Beginning of the Era of the Prophets)

At this time, Yisrael went out to fight against the Pelishtites who were encamped in Afek. The Pelishtites were victorious and slew 4,000 Israelites. The people decided that in the next battle, they would bring the Holy Ark from Shiloh into their midst, thereby assuring themselves of victory. Eli's two sons, Chofni and Pinchas, accompanied the Ark in the next battle.

At first the Pelishtites feared God's power. However, they decided to continue the battle and were victorious in defeating the Jews. They slew 30,000 Israelites, including the two sons of Eli, and captured the Ark. A man from the tribe of Binyamin fled from the battlefield and came to Shiloh with his clothes torn and earth upon his head. Eli was sitting beside the road, for he was worried about what might have happened to the Holy Ark. When he heard the commotion caused by the appearance of this person, he asked what was happening. Eli, at that time was ninety-eight years old and blind.

The man related to Eli that Yisrael had lost the battle, his two sons had been killed, and the Holy Ark had been captured. When he heard what had happened to the Ark, Eli fell over backward from his seat, broke his neck, and died. His pregnant daughter-in-law, the wife of Pinchas, heard the news of the tragedies and died in childbirth, after having given birth to a son whom she called E-Kavod ("Honor has been exiled from Yisrael because the Ark of God has been taken"). Thus ended forty years of Eli's leadership, the glorious era of the Sanctuary of Shiloh, and the era of the Judges (2870/891 B.C.E.).

Eli was the Judge who succeeded Shimshon and preceded Shemuel. His greatness is evident from his acceptance of the Divine will after the doom of his dynasty was prophesied by Shemuel. "He is God," said Eli. "May He do whatever is good in His eyes." Also, his death came after he heard that the Holy Ark had been captured by the Pelishtites. This news was such a shock that he fell from his seat and died. This devoted leader and teacher trained Shemuel and prepared him for his role as a prophet in Yisrael.

THE SPECIAL POWERS OF THE HOLY ARK

The Pelishtites brought the Holy Ark to the city of Ashdod and placed it beside the House of Dagon. When the people of Ashdod awoke in the morning, they saw that their god, Dagon, had fallen on his face. They restored him to his place, but the following morning they not only found Dagon on his face, but his head and hands were cut off as well. Only his trunk remained.

Hashem punished the people of Ashdod and made them ill. The people realized that their sufferings were due to the presence of the Holy Ark in their midst, and they sent it to the Pelishtite city of Gas. There, too, irritating diseases spread. The people of Gas sent the Ark on to Ekron, whose people were immediately punished with sickness and sought to get rid of the Ark. They sent it out to the fields.

After it had remained in the fields for seven months, the Pelishtites decided to send the Ark back to Yisrael accompanied by gifts of gold. They placed these on a wagon along with the Ark. The wagon was drawn by two cows upon which no yoke had ever been placed. They allowed the wagon to go by itself. The Pelishtites said, "If the Ark goes toward Beis Shemesh (the border of Yisrael), then we will know that it was the Ark that caused all the punishments. However, if it goes in any other direction, then we will know that all this was just coincidence."

The wagon carrying the Holy Ark went straight to Beis Shemesh. When the people of Beis Shemesh, who were in the fields reaping the harvest, saw the approaching Ark, they rejoiced.

The Levites placed the Ark on top of a huge stone and offered sacrifices to the Almighty. The Ark remained in that field. Because their rejoicing had included a bit of levity, inconsistent with the holiness and dignity of the Ark of God, a terrible plague struck the people of Beis Shemesh, and 50,000 died. The people of Beis Shemesh sent messengers to Kiryas Ye'arim requesting that they take custody of the Holy Ark. The people of Kiryas Ye'arim brought the Ark to the house of Avinadav, where his son, Eliezer, took charge. Seeing all that had transpired, the people of Yisrael once again followed the Almighty.

THE LEADERSHIP OF SHEMUEL HA-NAVI (2871-2883/890 B.C.E.-878 B.C.E.)

Shemuel spoke to the people, warning them to remove the idols from their midst and to return wholeheartedly to the Almighty. Since the Jews were aware of the plagues which had struck down the Pelishtites before they had released the Ark, they were inspired with renewed enthusiasm for the service of Hashem. The Jews listened to the words of Shemuel and abandoned their idols. They assembled at Mitzpah, fasted and prayed to Hashem.

When the Pelishtites heard that the Israelites were assembled at Mitzpah, they went out in battle against the Jews. The Jews were frightened, but Shemuel assured them that if they continued praying to God they would have no reason to fear.

As Shemuel was offering a sacrifice to Hashem, the Pelishtites were about to attack. Suddenly, God created a very loud noise, which threw the Pelishtites into a panic. The Israelites defeated them, and the Pelishtites fled. Shemuel set up a stone in Mitzpah as a monument to God. He called it *even ha-ezer* (the stone of God's assistance), in remembrance of the place where God had helped them.

The Pelishtites remained subdued all the years that Shemuel lived. Yisrael gained back the territory that it had previously lost, and its boundaries were restored to what they had been.

In Yisrael, no idol worship was practiced until many generations later. So great had been the impact of both the miracle of the plagues upon the Pelishtites and the miraculous victory at Mitzpah, that the Jews began to totally devote themselves to the service of God. No remnant remained of their idols anywhere.

Shemuel devoted his life to traveling throughout the land, judging the people, and exhorting them to remain faithful to God.

THE JEWS' REQUEST FOR A KING

When Shemuel grew old, he made his sons, Yoel and Aviyah, judges over Yisrael. They did not follow in the path of their father. Following in the footsteps of the earlier great leaders of Yisrael meant living a life devoid of any personal gains and having complete devotion to serving God and His people. Unfortunately, Shemuel's sons did not live up to these criteria. Consequently, the people demanded of Shemuel a king to rule over them like other nations of the world had.

This request displeased Shemuel very much. He prayed to Hashem for guidance. Hashem responded that He would listen to the voice of the people and grant their request. However, Shemuel should give them due warning as to what a monarch's rule would mean.

Shemuel warned the people that the king who would rule over them would take away their sons to be horsemen or to plow his land. He would take their daughters to cook and bake for him. He would take their fields, vineyards and grain and give it to his servants. He would use their cattle and their servants for his benefit. However, the people refused to heed the voice of Shemuel and said, "No, we must have a king over us!"

The reason that this request was so displeasing to God and to Shemuel, even though the Torah makes allowances for a king, was that it was made in a complaining manner, rather than for the purpose of complying with the Divine commandment. Also, their request showed a lack of trust in the Almighty, especially when they said they wanted a king "like all the nations." This was objectionable since they did not need a king like all other nations to wage their wars. Hashem was their King and would wage war for them, as He had done in the past. Hashem, however, told Shemuel to honor the request of the people.

THE CHOOSING OF A KING

In the latter years of Shemuel's rule, there lived a man named Kish from the tribe of Binyamin. He had a son by the name of Sha'ul, a very tall, good-looking young man, who tended his father's flocks. One day, some donkeys belonging to Kish got lost and Sha'ul was sent to find them.

Sha'ul went with a servant to look for the lost animals, but they couldn't find them.

Sha'ul considered turning back and said to his servant, "Come, let us return, lest my father cease to worry about his donkeys and worry about us." Sha'ul showed concern that his father might worry about them. He also showed sensitivity by stating that his father might worry about his servant as well. The servant responded that there was a respected holy man living in that area whose words always came true. Perhaps he would tell them what to do.

Hashem had revealed to Shemuel that he would send a man to him from the tribe of Binyamin whom he would anoint as the new ruler of Yisrael. He would save the Yisraelites from the Pelishtites.

When Shemuel saw Sha'ul, God told him, "This is the person!"

Sha'ul approached Shemuel, not knowing for sure who the prophet was. Shemuel identified himself and asked Sha'ul to eat with him. He told Sha'ul that the donkeys which had been missing for three days had already been found. He also told him that he was destined to be the new king of Yisrael.

Sha'ul answered him modestly that he was from the smallest tribe of Yisrael and from the family that was least important in that tribe. He could not understand why he was being chosen for such an honor.

After Sha'ul sent his servant ahead, Shemuel anointed Sha'ul to be the new king of Yisrael (2881/880 B.C.E.). He took a vial of olive oil, poured it over Sha'ul's head and kissed him. He said to Sha'ul, "God has appointed you to be the ruler over His inheritance. When you leave me today, you will meet two men at the tomb of Rachel. They will tell you that the donkeys which you seek have been found, and that your father is concerned about you. You will proceed from there to the Plain of Tabor, and you will see three people going up to Beis El. One of them will be carrying three goats, the second — three loaves of bread, and the third — a jug of wine. They will greet you and give you two loaves of bread. You will take them from their hands. Thereafter, you will go to the Hill of God and you will see a band of prophets coming down from the hill who will be prophesying. The Spirit of God will rest upon you and you will prophesy along with them. You will become like another man, and you will find that God is constantly with you."

Everything that Shemuel predicted occurred to Sha'ul on that day, and for a short period of time Sha'ul became one of the prophets.

Shemuel assembled all the people in Mitzpah and spoke to them in the name of God. He reminded them that the Almighty had brought them out of Egypt and had saved them from the hands of all who sought to destroy them. Now, the people chose to have a human king.

Shemuel told them that the new king would be Sha'ul, the son of Kish. When they went to look for him, they found him hiding. He was humble, God-fearing and very loyal to Hashem and His Torah. When Sha'ul stood up, he was taller than any of his fellow Israelites. The people shouted, "Long live the king!"

SHA'UL'S LEADERSHIP

Nachash, king of Ammon, camped at Yavesh Gilad, waiting for the opportune time to attack the Jews. The people of Yavesh Gilad wanted to sign a treaty with him, consenting to serve him. Nachash agreed, but only on condition that every Israelite from Yavesh Gilad gouge out his right eye. This was intended as an embarrassment for all of Yisrael. They requested seven days to consider the matter, and also hoped someone would come to their aid. Messengers were sent all over the land.

Sha'ul had been grazing the cattle in the fields when he heard people crying. They were messengers from Yavesh Gilad lamenting their terrible plight. Sha'ul became very angry and cut oxen into pieces. He then sent pieces of the oxen to his countrymen throughout the land, warning them that this was what would be done to their oxen if they did not come to the aid of their brethren in Yavesh Gilad.

The people of Yisrael responded to Sha'ul's urgent call. They were 300,000 in number, and 30,000 were from the tribe of Yehudah. They sent a message to Yavesh Gilad that assistance was on the way. Sha'ul's army attacked the Ammonites and defeated them.

After the victory, the people were so enthused over Sha'ul's leadership that they wanted to punish those who had been skeptical about it earlier. Sha'ul did not want anyone punished. Under the direction of Shemuel, they all went to Gilgal to renew the kingdom. Shemuel declared to the people of Yisrael that he had fulfilled their wish for a king. He reminded them that in all his years of leadership he had never wronged anyone. Yet, despite all that God had done for them, they had still requested that a king be appointed to rule over them. He further cautioned them that if they obeyed their king, all would be well. If they didn't, they would be punished. Shemuel assured them that Hashem would be with them as long as they continued to walk in His path and follow the Torah.

After ruling for one year, Sha'ul chose people from all over the land to make up his army. They succeeded in overcoming the Pelishtites in Givah. Sha'ul warned the people that the Pelishtites would seek revenge for this attack. They camped in Gilgal and waited for seven days for the Prophet Shemuel to appear to offer a sacrifice to Hashem. The people started getting restless and some wanted to leave. Giving in to public pressure, Sha'ul took it upon himself to bring the sacrifice instead of waiting for the prophet. Shemuel arrived just as Sha'ul was completing the service.

Sha'ul went out to greet Shemuel, and the latter asked him what he had done. Sha'ul responded that he had been pressured and was worried that the people would leave him, since the prophet had not arrived on time and the enemy was prepared to attack.

Shemuel responded that Sha'ul had acted foolishly. Had he followed the prophet's commandment and waited for him to appear on the seventh day, then he might have been assured that his kingdom would rule Yisrael forever. However, since he instead listened to the request of the people, he was destined to lose his reign.

In response to the people's pressuring, Sha'ul had consented to their request. He thereby denied Shemuel's prophecy in which he had stated that he would appear in seven days and offer the sacrifice to the Almighty. Sha'ul feared that the Almighty would desert him in his time of need. As a king, he should have imposed his authority upon the people, thereby bringing them under the rule of the Almighty. Instead, he allowed the people to dictate to him, bringing God's wrath down upon himself.

Together with his son, Yonasan, Sha'ul waged war against Ammon, Edom, and the king of Tzova and the Pelishtites, as well as parts of Amalek. Sha'ul protected Yisrael from its enemies, who trembled in fear of him.

Sha'ul had three sons, Yonasan, Yishvi and Malchishua; and two daughters, Michal and Merav. Sha'ul's commander-in-chief of the army was Avner. Sha'ul, who was constantly engaged in battles, was always on the lookout for brave men and drafted them into the army.

The prophet Shemuel instructed King Sha'ul to seek revenge against Amalek and to annihilate them completely — men, women, and children, as well as all of their possessions.

Sha'ul led a huge army of 200,000 foot soldiers and 10,000 of the strongest warriors from Yehudah. Sha'ul and his army destroyed Amalek, except for King Agag, whom he held prisoner, and the best of the cattle, which he felt was a pity to destroy.

God spoke to Shemuel and told him that he regretted having made Sha'ul king. Shemuel cried to the Almighty all night. In the morning, a messenger arrived telling him that Sha'ul was in Karmel.

Shemuel met Sha'ul, who felt satisfied that he had fulfilled all that God had commanded. Shemuel then asked, "What is that sound I hear of bleating animals?"

Sha'ul responded, "We had pity on the best of the sheep and left them over to be used for sacrifices to God."

Shemuel then said that Sha'ul had not hearkened to the commandment of God, Who had ordered the total destruction of Amalek. Instead, Sha'ul had allowed them to leave the sheep and cattle alive.

Sha'ul tried to explain that he had the best of intentions, and that his motives were to serve God by using the best sheep for sacrifices to the Almighty.

Shemuel asked Sha'ul, "Does God want your peace offerings more than He wants you to listen to Him? You have rebelled against God. Since you have rejected His words, He has rejected you as king."

Sha'ul admitted that he had sinned — he had feared the people and had listened to their voices instead of to God.

LESSON II

Sha'ul's Grave Mistake: Giving in to Pressure

Although humility and mercy are admirable and desirable qualities, a king must be strong and unyielding when appropriate. Unfortunately, Sha'ul, who had these qualities in abundance, was not able to overcome his nature and fulfill God's instructions. He was, therefore, found unfit to be the king of Yisrael, who must put aside all his personal feelings and obey the will of Hashem.

Three lessons are learned from this incident:

(1) "Be not overly righteous."[6] By allowing Agag, king of Amalek, to remain alive that one night, Agag was able to father a child. That child continued the accursed nation of Amalek, and was the ancestor of Haman, who sought to totally annihilate the Jewish nation. Since Sha'ul had pity on Agag, the seed that has tried to destroy Jews throughout the ages remained alive.

(2) The Sages teach us, "One who has mercy on the cruel will in the end be cruel to the merciful."[7] Sha'ul exhibited misplaced compassion towards Agag. Later, when he was pursuing David, and discovered that the latter had been given

bread by Achimelech, a priest in the city of Nov, Sha'ul ordered that city and all of its inhabitants to be wiped out. Imagine! A city of priests, women, and children, was destroyed because David had passed through there and been offered food!

(3) Unfortunately, we find two instances where Sha'ul blamed the people for his own deficiencies. The first was at the time of the sacrifice in Gilgal, when Sha'ul did not wait for the Prophet Shemuel to arrive and brought the sacrifice himself. The second involved disregarding the command to totally destroy Amalek, including all of their cattle. Sha'ul left alive Agag and the best of the sheep.

In both instances, Sha'ul blamed the people for his own failure to completely fulfill God's command. This was unlike other great leaders of Yisrael who not only accepted blame for their own shortcomings, but also accepted blame for the misdeeds of the people as well. This was the quality that Hashem was seeking in a king. Since Sha'ul seemed to be lacking it, Hashem subsequently gave the kingdom over to David.

Sha'ul asked Shemuel to return with him to Gilgal, and to ask forgiveness for him from the Almighty. Shemuel responded that he would not be able to return with Sha'ul because the latter had rejected the words of God, and consequently, God had rejected him as king.

As Shemuel turned to leave, Sha'ul seized his cloak and it tore. Shemuel said to Sha'ul, "God has today torn your kingdom from you and given it to someone better than you."

Despite Sha'ul's grave mistake, he was still a very righteous man. In fact, he again requested that Shemuel return with him to Gilgal, and the prophet complied with his request. One sees here the greatness of Sha'ul. Despite the harsh words that Shemuel had spoken to Sha'ul, foretelling the loss of his kingdom, the latter did not complain and still deferred to the prophet. He understood his guilt and accepted the consequences.

Shemuel ordered Agag to be brought before him, and said, "Just as your sword caused bereavement to so many women, so, too, your mother will grieve today." Shemuel himself executed the cruel Agag. Agag represented the archenemy of the Jews, from a nation that symbolized extreme cruelty. Amalek was the first nation to attack the defenseless Jews who had just come out of slavery in Egypt. Their attack was without provocation or purpose. Amalek, represented by Agag, was the personification of evil. They sowed the seeds of destruction that gave rise to Haman. The greatness of Shemuel lies in the fact that he was able to change his very nature, which was kind and merciful, and rise to the occasion that necessitated the execution of Agag. Shemuel and Sha'ul parted ways and Sha'ul did not see him again until Shemuel's death (2883/878 B.C.E.)

❦ HISTORY

DAVID, THE EMERGENCE OF A NEW LEADER

God commanded Shemuel to fill a horn with olive oil and go anoint a new king from the sons of Yishai. Shemuel feared that such an action would incur the wrath of Sha'ul, who might then try to kill him. He camouflaged his real intentions by inviting Yishai and his family to a feast.

When Yishai's family arrived at the feast, Shemuel saw Eliav, the eldest son, and thought that surely he was the one Hashem intended since he was tall and of regal bearing. However, Hashem told Shemuel not to look at the person's appearance. Shemuel realized that the one whom God intended was not among the sons of Yishai. He asked whether the entire family was present, and was told that David, the youngest, was occupied tending the sheep. Shemuel explained that he would not be able to sit down to the feast until the youngest son appeared. As soon as Shemuel saw David, he realized that he was chosen to be king and Shemuel obeyed God's command to anoint him.

ETHICS II

Don't Judge a Book by Its Cover

Originally, Shemuel thought that Eliav, the oldest son, was the one intended by Hashem to be the next king. He was a handsome, impressive individual, with the appearance of a leader. Shemuel was deceived by Eliav's appearance and jumped to the conclusion that he was to be the new monarch. On the other hand, when Shemuel saw David, he was surprised because of his ruddy complexion, and could not imagine that this was God's chosen.

There is a strong lesson to be learned here. One must not judge a person by his looks. This important concept can be further illustrated by the following story:[8]

The daughter of an emperor once approached a Torah Sage who had a rather homely appearance and asked, "Why did God insert so much wisdom into such an ugly vessel?"

The Torah Sage replied by asking, "Where do you keep your wine?"

"In earthen vessels," was the response.

"But why not keep the wine in precious gold containers which would be more fitting?"

The princess thought this over and decided it was a good idea. She immediately went home and transferred all the wine in the royal household from earthenware to gold containers. Two weeks later, she held a party and she ordered that the butlers bring the wine in their new, glistening containers. However, with the very first taste, all the guests came to the same conclusion: the wine had turned sour. The golden vessels looked magnificent, but they had provided poor protection for the wine.

The princess went directly to the Sage the next day and asked him to explain what had happened. "What you have just learned," replied the Sage, "is how unimportant outward appearances are. The earthen container may have appeared drab, but it kept the wine tasting sweet, something that the shiny gold vessels could not do, for all their splendor. The same is true of the appearance of humans. Some individuals might be good-looking. Yet, this does not mean that their inner spirit is just as beautiful. In fact, their interest in their own appearance may cause them to become preoccupied with themselves. On the other hand, one who is ugly may appear repulsive, but he might also be kind and wise and inwardly beautiful. Appearances can be deceiving. Therefore, do not always assume that if something looks unimpressive, it must be inferior. Sometimes it is the humble-looking item or individual that is the greater treasure."

❦ HISTORY

DAVID'S GREATNESS

After the spirit of God departed from Sha'ul, he became depressed. The servants noticed it and suggested that someone be asked to play a harp before the king, and perhaps that would soothe his depression. Sha'ul agreed. The youngest son of Yishai was chosen because, in addition to being a superb harpist, he was a brave and handsome young man, a warrior who acted with caution, and God was with him. David appeared before Sha'ul, and the king was impressed with him. David became Sha'ul's weapon-bearer, and his playing relieved Sha'ul's painful moods of depression.

The Pelishtites had assembled to wage war once again upon Yisrael. Sha'ul prepared his people to do battle with the enemy. The two camps faced each other from two mountains with a valley between them. One day, Golyas, a great and mighty warrior, emerged from the camp of the Pelishtites. Golyas taunted the Jews by cynically asking where their Divine assistance was. He then issued a challenge that the Jews send someone to fight him. If Golyas was victorious, the Jews would be enslaved to the Pelishtites. If his opponent won, then they would be enslaved to the Jews.

The Jews were panic-stricken at the sight of the giant in the valley before them. For forty days, the situation was at a stalemate. No one would accept the challenge.

David had three older brothers, Eliav, Avinadav, and Shammah, who were serving in Sha'ul's army. Yishai sent David with food to give to his brothers, and to find out what was new at the battlefield.

David entrusted his flock of sheep to someone else. He then went to the battlefield, as instructed to by his father. When he arrived, Golyas once again was voicing his challenge. No one from the Jewish camp responded. A reward was offered to the one who would be willing to fight Golyas. Besides great riches, he would also be given King Sha'ul's daughter in marriage.

David professed an interest, and made several inquiries among the soldiers. When word reached King Sha'ul that David was interested in confronting Golyas, Sha'ul tried to dissuade him, stating that he was too young. When Sha'ul saw that David was persistent, he consented for him to go, and gave him his coat of armor and helmet. David, however, was not accustomed to wearing armor, and removed it before going to the battlefield. All that he took along was his staff in his hand, a slingshot and five smooth pebbles.

As Golyas saw David approaching, he expressed his disdain for the young lad. "Am I a dog that you come at me with sticks?" roared Golyas. "Come closer," he shouted, "so that I may feed your flesh to the birds."

David responded, "You come with your spear and javelin, but I come with the Name of the Lord, my God, Who will deliver you into my hands. Everyone will then know that the Lord is God of the Jews. God does not need weapons to deliver you into our hands."

As the Pelishtite was coming closer, David put a smooth stone into his slingshot and struck Golyas in the forehead. David killed Golyas, despite the fact that he didn't even have a sword in his hand. He ran and removed Golyas's sword and used it to sever the Pelishtite's head. When the Pelishtites saw their hero was dead, they fled in panic. David brought the severed head of Golyas and the weapons taken from the Pelishtite to Yerushalayim.

After the victory, David was brought to the palace of Sha'ul. It was there that he became very close friends with Yonasan, the son of Sha'ul.

LESSON III

The Reward for Perseverance

At this juncture, it is important to mention that Golyas was a great-grandson of Orpah, daughter-in-law of Naomi who returned to her Mo'avite home. David was a great-grandson of Ruth, the pious daughter-in-law of Naomi. It is interesting to note that both daughters-in-law had wanted to return with Naomi. Orpah had even taken forty steps to return with Naomi back to Yisrael. However, Naomi tried to discourage both women. This was in keeping with the law pertaining to a gentile who wishes to convert to Judaism. At first one must try to dissuade him. Orpah then returned to her former home in Mo'av with its pagan culture. It was her grandchild, Golyas, who taunted the army of the Jews for forty days. He was unharmed and spared for these forty days as a reward for the forty steps Orpah took to accompany Naomi.

Ruth, on the other hand, persisted in

staying with Naomi, and eventually converted to Judaism. This was in spite of the fact that Naomi did everything she could to discourage her. Ruth understood all of the difficulties that she was going to encounter, but nevertheless wanted to be a Jewess. As reward for her great perseverance, Ruth became the great-grandmother of David Ha-Melech and progenitor of the Messiah. Imagine! Two people were at the same crossroads, faced with the same difficult decision. One persevered for Judaism and one did not.

❦ HISTORY

SHA'UL'S RAGE AGAINST DAVID

Sha'ul did not allow David to return to his home. He remained at Sha'ul's palace. Meanwhile, David and Yonasan became fast friends.

Whenever Sha'ul sent David to fight, he would be victorious, and was, therefore, put in charge of the army, where he gained quick acceptance. Each time that David returned victorious, the women would sing victory songs praising his heroism. They sang, "Sha'ul killed thousands and David killed tens of thousands."

Sha'ul became jealous and enraged by David's popularity. A mood of depression descended upon Sha'ul, and he asked cynically, "What more can he have, but the kingdom?"

One day, while David was playing for Sha'ul, as he normally did, Sha'ul went berserk, took his spear and threw it at David, saying, "I will pin David to the wall." Twice David turned away, unaware that Sha'ul sought to kill him.

Sha'ul feared David because he knew that God was with him. He dismissed David from his house and made him a captain over a thousand soldiers. Sha'ul noted David's success and the fact that he was favored by everyone.

Sha'ul offered his daughter, Merav, in marriage to David if he would continue to be his warrior. He hoped that in this way the Pelishtites would get rid of David. But Hashem was with David and he was always victorious. In the meantime, Sha'ul gave Merav to someone else to marry. Sha'ul's daughter Michal, however, loved David. When this was told to Sha'ul, he saw the opportunity to get rid of David. He offered his daughter Michal in marriage if David would kill one hundred Pelishtites for him. Again, Hashem was with David, and he succeeded in going beyond Sha'ul's request, and killing two hundred Pelishtites. Thereupon, Sha'ul gave his daughter, Michal, in marriage to David.

Nevertheless, he grew even more hostile and afraid of David after seeing all of his successes.

Sha'ul spoke to Yonasan and all his servants about putting David to death. Yonasan's friendship for David, however, led him to warn David to go into hiding. Sha'ul sent messengers to David's house in an attempt to capture and kill him. Michal warned him to flee immediately that night, for he was in mortal danger. She helped David escape by lowering him from the window. Michal then put something in his bed that made it look as if he were still sleeping there. In response to Sha'ul's messengers, Michal told them that David was ill.

At a party in honor of *Rosh Chodesh*, Yonasan used the opportunity to inquire as to how the king felt about David. Sha'ul became so enraged that he even attempted to kill his own son, Yonasan. The latter then signaled to David who was hiding in the field, by using the secret sign that they had previously agreed upon which indicated that David was still in grave danger. When the coast was clear, David came out of his hiding place. He and Yonasan embraced and they wept. Yonasan bade David to go in peace and to remember the oath between them and between their descendants after them.

After Yonasan and David parted ways, David went to Achimelech, a priest in the city of Nov. Achimelech was surprised that such an important individual as David was all alone. David told him that he was on a secret mission for the king and that he had sent his men ahead to a secret place. He requested whatever food he had on hand. Achimelech complied by giving him some bread. This scene was witnessed by Do'eg the Edomite, one of Sha'ul's high officials. David asked Achimelech if he could give him a sword or spear, since he had left in great haste and had not taken his own. Achimelech gave him the only sword he had available. It happened to be the one that David had used to behead the Pelishtite giant, Golyas.

In the meantime, Do'eg the Edomite reported to King Sha'ul all that he had seen in Nov. Sha'ul, furious at the news, summoned Achimelech and all the priests of Nov before him. Achimelech responded to the king's accusations, "Who is so faithful among all your servants as David, who is your son-in-law and does all of your bidding?" But Sha'ul, in his madness, ordered the execution of all of the inhabitants of Nov, for he insisted that they were guilty of rebelling against him. Do'eg the Edomite carried out this horrible command, for no other Jew was willing to harm the innocent people of Nov. One man alone escaped — Evyasar, the son of Achimelech. He fled and joined David's group in hiding.

LESSON IV

The Importance of Providing Food to a Wayfarer

One lesson that is learned from this entire horrible episode is that it is important to remember to provide food to one who is about to set out on a journey. One should not take it for granted that the traveler will be able to fend for himself. He might end up in some difficulty, without any food at all.

This is learned from the above episode of David, departing from Yonasan and going to Nov, where he asked Achimelech for food. The Talmud relates that Yonasan was negligent in not providing his friend, David, with food before the latter continued his flight from Sha'ul. Had Yonasan provided David with food, he would not have had to go to Nov, and the massacre of the innocent priests and inhabitants of that city would never have taken place.[9]

❦ Key People, Places and Things

AMALEK: the nation that the Jews are commanded to destroy. Sha'ul neglected to follow Hashem's command to completely eradicate them.

CHANNAH: Hannah, Shemuel's mother, whose prayers were answered.

DAVID: a member of the tribe of Yehudah; he was anointed by Shemuel and founded the dynasty of the House of David. He rose to fame after he killed the giant, Golyas.

DO'EG THE EDOMITE: the evil informer who saw Achimelech give food to David and reported it to Sha'ul. He was the one who carried out the death sentence against the inhabitants of Nov.

ELI: the High Priest who promised Channah that her prayers would be answered. His death marked the end of the era of the Judges.

ELKANAH: the father of the prophet, Shemuel.

GOLYAS: Goliath, the Pelishtite giant who taunted the Jews and was slain by David.

HOLY ARK: the sacred chest which contained the Ten Commandments, the essence of Judaism.

KEDUSHAH: the prayer of special praise, stressing the holiness of God, which is said during the repetition of the *Shemoneh Esreh,* at the completion of the second benediction.

MICHAL: Sha'ul's daughter, who married David after he killed Golyas. She protected her husband from her father.

MODIM: a prayer in the *Shemoneh Esreh* in which we bow in deference to the Almighty.

NOV: a city inhabited by priests. One priest, Achimelech, offered food and a sword to David. They all were subsequently punished by Sha'ul, and the entire city was destroyed.

SHA'UL: Saul, first king of Yisrael. He came from the tribe of Binyamin. He was a great and modest king, but due to a serious error in judgment ended up losing his kingdom.

SHEMONEH ESREH: a special silent private prayer, containing eighteen benedictions (an additional one was added, for a total of nineteen blessings).

SHEMUEL: the great leader Samuel, first in the era of the Prophets. He led the Jews through perilous times and anointed the first king.

YONASAN: Jonathan, son of Sha'ul and very close friend of David, whom he protected from his father's wrath.

NOTES

1. Ramban, end of *Parashas Re'eh*.

2. *Vayikra Rabbah*, 4:6.

3. Rambam, *Mishneh Torah, Hilchos Ma'amarim, perek* 3.

4. *Talmud Berachos*, 32b.

5. *Talmud Eruvin*, 63.

6. *Koheles* 7:16.

7. *Me-am Lo'ez*, Shemuel I, 274.

8. *Talmud Nedarim*, 50b.

9. *Talmud Sanhedrin*, 104.

❦ *Introduction to Chapter 15*

In this chapter we describe the greatness of David, his trials and tribulations.

David said to Hashem, "Show me the open gate which leads a man straight into the World to Come." Hashem replied, "David, if eternal life is your wish, then affliction must be your lot" (*Vayikra Rabbah* 30).

In all of the Torah we find no one who was afflicted as much as David. David's life was an endless succession of misfortune, leading him to lament, "My soul drips from agony" (*Tehillim* 119:28). *Sifri* elaborates: My soul drips from the disasters which overwhelm me. No year passes without calamity. No month goes by without bad tidings. There is no day without misfortune.

Throughout his life, David constantly begged God to care for him as a father cares for his son, and to guide him along the straight path. God responded to this sincere plea. "I will be like a father to him, and he will be like a son to Me. If he will go astray I will rebuke him with the rod of men and with the plagues of mankind. But My kindness shall not depart from him..." (*Shemuel* II 7:14-15).

There is no kindness which surpasses that of the father who cares so for his child that he will punish him if that is the way to guide him to perfection. Any time the son strays or loses sight of his father's instructions, he receives a punishment to forcefully remind him that he must correct himself. Thus David's sufferings were in reality an indication of Hashem's concern for his aspirations toward perfection.

David was a man of Torah, courage and humility. Throughout his lifetime he delved deeply into Torah study during virtually all hours of the night. The Talmud states that the Almighty said to David, "One day of your Torah study is more precious to Me than a thousand sacrifices that your son Shelomo will sacrifice before Me" (*Berachos* 3b).

The ascension of David ushered in a golden age for the Jewish People. The Bible does not gloss over any of his weaknesses. Yet there still emerges from its account the picture of a towering personality, longing for closeness to God through the purging of his imperfections, and achieving greatness through the sheer power of his penitent service of God. The Psalms are an expression of this personality, and so is David's planning for the construction of the Temple. Yet they also reveal the profound religiosity of his generation, which resulted from his strong leadership.

CHAPTER 15

The Trials and Tribulations of David
David's Flight from Sha'ul – Death of David Ha-Melech
(2884 – 2924/877 B.C.E. – 837 B.C.E.)

❦ HISTORY

DAVID'S FLIGHT

During the period that David was hiding from Sha'ul, he had many perilous episodes during which he was nearly captured. The people of Zif informed Sha'ul that David was hiding in their midst. David and his men were on one side of the mountain and were about to be encircled by Sha'ul and his men. Suddenly, a messenger arrived to tell Sha'ul of a new threat by the Philistines, who were about to attack. Sha'ul immediately turned away from his pursuit of David in order to defend Yisrael.

In Ein Gedi, with 3,000 soldiers at his side, Sha'ul came very close to capturing David. David discovered that Sha'ul was camped nearby in a cave and was sleeping. He was urged by his men to kill the king. David merely cut a piece from his royal cloak. Afterward, he called to Sha'ul and held up the piece of cloak as proof of the fact that he had had the opportunity to kill the king but didn't do so. Didn't this in itself prove David's loyalty to Sha'ul?

Sha'ul wept and admitted that David was more righteous than he. He told David that he felt that he would be the next king of Yisrael and begged him not to destroy his family. David promised, and the two men parted.

LESSON I

Everything Has a Purpose

Everything in creation has a purpose. Even such seemingly insignificant creatures as flies, fleas, and mosquitoes in reality play an important role in the functioning of the world. For example, the wicked Roman Emperor Titus, who conquered Yerushalayim and caused great destruction, once arrogantly exclaimed concerning the Almighty, "I overcame the King in his own palace!" A small gnat flew into his nostril and subsequently penetrated his brain, causing Titus great suffering until his death.[1]

Even the great David wondered about the need for certain creatures. He was particularly curious about the purpose of the wasp, which seems to do nothing but sting and harm individuals, and the spider which apparently does nothing but spin a web to catch prey.

"Master of the Universe, what is the purpose of these creatures that You have created?" asked David. He also questioned God's purpose in creating an insane individual. In time, David learned the answers to these questions.

On several occasions, when David was forced to flee from the wrath of King Sha'ul who sought to kill him, his life was saved by these seemingly useless creatures. Once, while fleeing from Sha'ul's soldiers, David hid in a cave. Just as he thought the soldiers would enter the cave and find him, the Almighty sent a spider to spin a web across the cave's entrance. When Sha'ul and his soldiers arrived at the cave and saw the unbroken spider's web, they assumed that the cave had not been recently entered, and went looking elsewhere.

During one of his expeditions in pursuit of David, King Sha'ul retired to a cave while Avner, his chief of staff, guarded the entrance of the cave. Both fell soundly asleep. David crawled into the cave, careful not to awaken the sleeping figure of Avner. He then took the king's water pitcher as proof that he could have killed Sha'ul, but didn't. Leaving the cave, however, was not as simple as entering had been. Avner had shifted his position in his sleep, and his feet blocked the exit from the cave. David was trapped![2]

He prayed to the Almighty, "O Lord, my God, why did You forsake me?"[3] Just then a wasp started buzzing around the sleeping Avner. Without awakening,

Avner moved, and again changed his position away from the cave's opening. David was thus able to flee undetected from the cave.

At another time when David was fleeing from King Sha'ul, he fled to the Philistine city of Gas. King Achish was informed that David, the youth who had slain the giant, Golyas, was in the city. His soldiers sought to capture him and bring him before the king.

David feigned madness, acting like a fool in the streets of Gas. When Achish heard about this and that his soldiers wanted to bring David to his palace, he angrily shouted, "Am I lacking imbeciles that you seek to bring another to my palace?" It was known that Achish had an insane wife and daughter. He did not care to have another insane individual in his palace.

David saw the wonders of God's creations and gave thanks to Him for having created them.

If we insist that everything in creation has a purpose, what reason can there be for people growing old or getting sick? In reality, sickness and old age are important in a human being's life. They cause him to reflect on his own mortality and to ponder his existence.[4] If a person is eternally young and healthy, what would force him to look beyond his present state and to think about his place in creation? By aging or by falling ill from time to time, a person truly appreciates what he has and starts reflecting on his life beyond the materialistic. When we look around and see handicapped people making the best of what they have, isn't it an inspiration to others — handicapped and non-handicapped alike?

There is no denying that there were many who achieved greatness in their own way, managed to overcome their severe handicaps and to serve as an inspiration to countless numbers of people everywhere. Encountering the sick and the handicapped as we go about our everyday affairs causes us to be more appreciative and grateful to the Almighty for the blessings of good health that He has bestowed upon us.

LESSON II

The Importance of Fulfilling Mitzvos

David had cut the corner of Sha'ul's coat as evidence that he'd had the opportunity to harm Sha'ul but chose not to do so. Afterward, David regretted his action, since by tearing the corner of the king's coat, he had removed the *tzitzis* (fringes), thereby preventing Sha'ul from fulfilling the mitzvah of *tzitzis*. David considered the damaging of Sha'ul's *tzitzis* tantamount to injuring Sha'ul himself.

It was a reflection of David's greatness that he understood the value of a mitzvah. His remorse was deep because he realized how important it was to fulfill the mitzvos every minute of the day. A simple parable illustrates this:

A plain, penniless Jew was blessed with a family of many children, but alas, had no way of providing for them properly. He struggled against hardships in an effort to find work so that he could support himself and his family, but he never succeeded in earning even barely enough.

One day he was walking along the road in bitter despair, knowing that there was no food in his house for his hungry children. As he walked on with his head bowed, he saw a brilliantly colored object lying at the roadside. He thought it was a piece of broken glass — nothing worth bothering about. He was about to continue walking, but decided to stop and look at it. Maybe it had some small value and he could use it to buy a piece of bread for his children.

The man stooped down and picked it up — and could hardly believe his eyes. It was a sparkling polished jewel set in precious metal, and it flashed, glinted and blazed in all the colors of the rainbow as he turned it in his hands.

The man stopped to consider his situation. He was on a main road between two towns. Whoever had lost it had probably lost hope of recovering it, since he was not likely to know where to look for it. Therefore, the jewel was now his. But what sort of precious stone was it? And how much was it worth?

As fast as his legs could carry him, he headed for a jeweler in his town. The jeweler examined the stone under his enlarging glass, and whistled in amazement. "I have never seen a gem like this," he said. "It belongs in the king's crown. I will write the royal palace about it, and let's see what happens."

In a short while the king's messengers came to take the poor man and his jewel to the palace. There the king and his advisors examined the stone, and they, too, were greatly impressed. They found it so beautiful and flawless that they could hardly stop praising it. At last the king called the poor man to him.

"Well, my good fellow," he said, "how much do you want for it ?"

The man shrugged his shoulders. "Your majesty, how could I possibly know what price to ask? Until I brought it to the jeweler, I did not even know it was valuable."

"Very well," said the king, and at his order the poor man went home a rich man, the owner of a small fortune.

Righteous Jews keep the mitzvah of *tzitzis* with no idea at all of what its full worth will be to them.[5] They know that

Divine reward is promised for keeping the mitzvos — a reward more precious than gold and jewels. Yet this is not what they have in mind, because mitzvos have to be observed for their own sake, and not just for a reward. Jews are commanded to pick up every such precious gem that they find by the road of life, without ever really knowing how much or little it may be worth, or how much recompense will be awaiting them in the afterlife.

MITZVAH

Tzitzis

The Torah stipulated that any male wearing a garment with four or more corners is required to attach *tzitzis* to each of the four corners, as a reminder of his allegiance to God and His mitzvos. A person should be very careful in the observance of this commandment, since the *tzitzis* symbolize a Jew's willingness to adhere to God, His Torah, and all His mitzvos. The word *tzitzis* in Hebrew numerically equals 600, which together with the 8 strings and 5 knots in the *tzitzis* adds up to 613, the total number of Biblical commandments. Therefore, by looking at one's *tzitzis*, a person is reminded to fulfill all of God's commandments.

The *tzitzis* are attached to the garment as follows: 4 strings are inserted into the hole in each corner of the garment and folded in half, forming 8 strings. The strings are double-knotted and the longest string is wound 7 times around the others and a double-knot is made. This process is repeated three more times with the following variation. The long string is wound around 8, ll, and 13 times respec-

tively; each winding is followed by a double knot. The number of windings is symbolic. The numbers 7, 8, and 11 add up to 26, which is the numerical value of one of the Names of the Almighty; while 13 is equivalent to the word *"Echad"* (one) signifying God's unity. The *tzitzis* thus symbolize that God is One!

It is customary for married men (in some communities, boys also wear *talleisim*) to wear a *tallis* (prayer shawl) during the morning service prayers. It is a four-cornered garment that has *tzitzis* in each of the four corners. It should be large enough to cover most of the body. It should be worn with two corners in the front and two corners in the back, and must be handled with proper respect. According to some customs, a *tallis* is worn only after marriage. According to others, it is worn after *bar mitzvah*. The *tallis* is put on first before one puts on his *tefillin*.

If any one of the four corners of the *tzitzis* are torn off, the garment should be immediately removed and the *tzitzis* replaced. If one of the strings is torn, then a rabbi should immediately be consulted. One should bear in mind that even if the *tzitzis* are torn, they are still considered ritual and sacred items and must be shown appropriate respect.

The Vilna Gaon, in the last moments before his death, was crying as he held his *tzitzis*. When asked what was troubling him, he remarked that once a person dies, he no longer has the obligation of *tzitzis*. How hard it is to separate from this world of deeds! With such an easy commandment as *tzitzis*, man could receive a spiritual uplift. In the next world,

there is no way one can achieve this advancement.

The reason for Hashem giving us this commandment was to add holiness to us at all times of the day. The *tzitzis* show the degree of our attachment to Hashem. We accept our yoke of service to God, and attach ourselves to Him.

"Because of the sin of disregarding this mitzvah [*tzitzis*] children die."[6]

"For the merit of the mitzvah of *tzitzis*, the prophets Chananyah, Misha'el, and Azaryah were saved from the fiery furnace" (Midrash).

❧ HISTORY

THE DEATH OF THE PROPHET SHEMUEL

The prophet Shemuel passed away at the age of fifty-two (2883/878 B.C.E.). He judged his people for twelve years, after having lived forty years in the household of Eli the High Priest. Shemuel's beginning was exceptionally holy, having been born in answer to his mother's special prayers. She had made a vow to give him over to the house of God for the rest of his life. He was a *nazir* who served in the *Mishkan* under the supervision of Eli the *Kohen Gadol*. While Shemuel judged the people, he traveled throughout Eretz Yisrael to help them with their affairs and to exhort them to greater efforts in the observance of Torah. That is what is meant by the statement that Shemuel judged "all Yisrael" (traveling throughout the entire nation), and he judged "all the days of his life" (without any leisure for himself). He also started a campaign to cleanse the land of idolatry. Finally, he attained such a lofty degree of prophecy that he became known as the leading prophet of his generation.

When Shemuel died, Jews gathered from all over the land to bury him and to mourn for their leader who had shown such devotion to his people all his life.

THE WICKEDNESS OF NAVAL

During this time there lived a wealthy man by the name of Naval. David and his men, while hiding from Sha'ul, helped Naval's shepherds protect his huge flocks. When David learned Naval was in the area, he sent ten of his youths to him, reminding him of all the kindnesses that he and his men had shown to Naval's men and possessions. David, in turn, requested some food for himself and his men. Although Naval was distantly related (being from the tribe of Yehudah), he responded in a haughty manner, as if David were a runaway slave. Naval was a wicked and ungrateful individual who not only disgraced his own relative, but refused to recognize the favors that had been performed for his own shepherds and flocks.

David, in his anger, was prepared to severely punish Naval and his household. However, Naval had a beautiful and clever wife named Avigayil, whose wisdom saved his life. She quickly assembled bread, sheep, jugs of wine, flour and grains, and had her servants bring them to David and his men. She took the blame for Naval's behavior upon herself, explaining that she had not seen David's youths when they came asking for food.

Avigayil returned to her home, where she found Naval feasting like a king and too drunk to talk. After he sobered up, she told him what she had done and he became like stone. Ten days later he died. Upon hearing of Naval's death, David sent his men to ask Avigayil to become his wife. She modestly considered herself unworthy of the honor, but did consent to marry David. At that time, David also married Achino'am from Yizre'el, while Sha'ul took away David's wife, Michal, who was Sha'ul's daughter.

SHA'UL'S LAST BATTLES

The people of Zif came to inform Sha'ul a second time where David was hiding. Sha'ul came with an army to capture David. Once again David happened upon Sha'ul in a cave. The latter was sleeping, while Avner, his commander-in-chief, and the rest of the army were encamped around him. Hashem caused a deep sleep to descend upon the camp so that they heard nothing. David again resisted the urgings of his followers to kill Sha'ul. Instead, he took away the spear and jug of water that were near Sha'ul's head.

David crossed back over to the other side of the mountain, from where he taunted Sha'ul's servants for not guarding their king properly. David asked Sha'ul why he persisted in seeking his life. The two parted, and Sha'ul returned to his palace.

David and his group of men continued to defend the Jews from the Pelishtites.

PHILISTINE ASSAULT AGAINST THE JEWS AND THE DEATH OF KING SHA'UL AND HIS SONS

The Philistines gathered to wage war against Yisrael. Sha'ul's heart trembled at the sight of the huge Pelishtite encampment. Because of Sha'ul's action against the priests of Nov, he could not obtain any response from Hashem through the *urim v'tumim*.

Sha'ul was desperate. Despite the fact that witchcraft and sorcery are strictly prohibited by Jewish law, Sha'ul asked a sorceress to evoke the spirit of the prophet Shemuel. Shemuel told him that there was no use in seeking his help and advice since Hashem had turned away from Sha'ul. All this came upon him for not following Hashem's directive to exterminate Amalek. Shemuel's spirit revealed that Sha'ul and his men would be defeated by the Pelishtites.

During this time, David was waging war against the Amalekites, who set his city of Tziklag afire and captured all of the women and children. David destroyed most of the Amalekites in the camp, but four hundred of them managed to escape. David then freed all of the captured women and children.

The Pelishtites fought the Jews on Mount Gilboa. Many Israelites fled and many fell in battle. The Pelishtites killed three of Sha'ul's sons. As the battle grew heavier, Sha'ul realized that the enemy's archers had found him. He therefore asked his weapon-bearer to kill him with his sword, rather than allow the king of Yisrael to fall into the hands of the Pelishtites. The weapon-bearer was afraid to do so, and Sha'ul fell upon his own sword. When the lad saw that Sha'ul had died, he, too, fell upon his sword. When the Jews on the other side of the valley and on the other side of the Jordan saw what had occurred, they left their cities and fled. The Pelishtites came and occupied them.

On the following morning, when the Pelishtites came to strip the dead soldiers of their weapons, they found Sha'ul and his sons. The people of Yavesh Gilad heard what had transpired and wanted to prevent Sha'ul and his sons' bodies from being dishonored (which was normal practice by the enemies of the Jews). They came at night, succeeded in rescuing the bodies of Sha'ul and his sons, and brought them home for burial (2884/877 B.C.E.).

ETHICS I

Hakaras Ha-Tov (Showing Gratitude)

Why did the people of Yavesh Gilad risk their lives to retrieve the bodies of Sha'ul and his sons? It was in return for the *chesed* (kindness) that Sha'ul had done for them when they were being threatened by Nachash, king of Ammon. At that time, Nachash sought to subdue the people of Yavesh Gilad under his rule and further sought to humiliate them by blinding the right eye of every Jew in that city. In desperation, they turned to Sha'ul, who had only recently been anointed king of Yisrael. Sha'ul united all of the tribes and came to the aid of the people of Yavesh Gilad. Now they, in turn, showed kindness and their gratitude to Sha'ul and his sons.

The mitzvah of *hakaras ha-tov,* to recognize and reciprocate the good that was done by someone, is a very important one. Sometimes one gets an opportunity to show his gratitude many years after the favor.

A student, new to the school, moved into the yeshivah's dormitory. Unfortunately, his behavior left much to be desired, and his antics caused many disturbances in the dormitory. It was decided that, while the student could continue his studies in the yeshivah, he would have to live elsewhere. But where would he find lodging? The school authorities were stumped until they received a surprise offer. The head of the academy himself suggested that the student live in his own house and dine with his own family.

The offer created quite a stir. Why would the dean of the academy take such a special interest in a student who had proved to be so disruptive? Soon, though, the reason became known. When the dean himself had been a young man, he had studied in a yeshivah that had been founded by the rebellious student's great-grandfather. Though the dean had never known the founder of the yeshivah, he nevertheless felt a sense of gratitude toward him. Now, at last, he had found the means to express it, by welcoming the unruly student into his own home. This favor, given in return for a previous favor, had a very gratifying effect, for the student who had caused so much trouble eventually became a highly respected rabbi in his own right.

LESSON III

The Greatness of Sha'ul

When Sha'ul was chosen to be king of the Jews, he was extremely humble. In fact, it was because of this humility that God chose him. Shemuel had even stated about Sha'ul that "he was little in his own eyes." This humility was accompanied by a deep loyalty to the Torah.

Sha'ul was a monarch whose dynasty was temporary. He was a guardian of the kingdom of Yisrael until someone from the tribe of Yehudah would be ready to occupy the throne, as had been previously promised by Hashem. The Almighty was very exacting and strict with Sha'ul, punishing him for any infraction of the law, and thereby ultimately causing him to lose his kingdom.

Sha'ul's two major transgressions were that he disobeyed the command of the prophet Shemuel to wait for him to offer the sacrifice, and he disobeyed the prophet when he failed to destroy Agog and the livestock of Amalek. In the first case, one must keep in mind that when Sha'ul did finally bring the offering, he did so at a very late hour and only because of the pressure put on him by the people. In the second case, Sha'ul had destroyed all of Amalek and was guilty of leaving alive only Agog and the livestock.

Sha'ul's sins and mistakes were in the lack of execution of his kingly duties. Therefore, his punishment was the loss of his kingdom, unlike David's sins (to be discussed further on), which were personal and did not warrant dismissal from his position.[7]

Among Sha'ul's other mistakes, was the destruction of Nov, the city of priests, for he considered them rebels who had sided with David against the king. Also, Sha'ul consulted a sorceress out of desperation when he felt he was on the brink of destruction by the Philistines. Because of his behavior toward Nov, the *urim v'tumim* did not answer him.

One must remember that despite the knowledge that he was going to die in battle, Sha'ul led his people. Knowing full well that this battle would be his last, this devoted king took three of his sons and went forth to do whatever he could. As our Commentaries have stated: Seven righteous men were killed by the Philistines — Chofni and Pinchas (the two sons of Eli), Shimshon, Sha'ul and his three sons.

❦ HISTORY

DAVID HA-MELECH'S REIGN OVER YEHUDAH (2884-2892/877 B.C.E.-869 B.C.E.)

David was informed that the Jews had fled from the battlefield, where many had been killed, and that Sha'ul and his sons were among those who had died in battle. Upon hearing this terrible news, David and his men rent their garments, mourned and fasted until evening. David mourned and eulogized the great Sha'ul and Yonasan.

The men of the tribe of Yehudah anointed David king of all of Yisrael. Avner, commander-in-chief of Sha'ul's army, crowned Ish-Boshes, son of Sha'ul, as king of Yisrael. He reigned for two years. In an unfortunate situation, play-fighting turned to violence and Avner struck down the younger brother of Yo'av, the general of David's army. This resulted in fighting, where over 360 people lost their lives. All this caused great friction between the two camps. Avner became angry at Ish-Boshes because of accusations made against him [Avner], and he decided to make a pact with David. David agreed to the pact and sent him off in peace. Without David's knowledge, Yo'av sent his men to bring Avner to him and then murdered him.

Upon hearing of Avner's murder, David declared his innocence of all involvement. He cursed Yo'av and his father's house for spilling innocent blood. David ordered Yo'av and all the people with him to rend their clothes and don sackcloth in mourning for Avner. David Ha-Melech himself escorted Avner's bier to its eternal resting place, while mourning the death of a great man who had fallen victim to wicked men. After the funeral, the people brought bread to David, but he refused to eat. He swore that he would eat no bread or anything else that day. David's sincere mourning for Avner was appreciated by the people, who now realized that he was completely blameless in his death.

Two brothers in the army of Ish-Boshes assassinated him in the middle of the night. This left Mefiboshes, the lame son of Yonasan, as the sole survivor of the house of Sha'ul. The two brothers thought they would be rewarded by David. Instead, he had them executed for their betrayal.

DAVID PROCLAIMED KING OVER ALL OF YISRAEL (2892-2924/869 B.C.E.-837 B.C.E.)

David was now anointed king over all of Yisrael. He had ruled for seven and a half years over Yehudah, and now ruled thirty-three additional years over all of the tribes of Yisrael. He waged fierce battles to wipe out the Pelishtites, who continually attacked the Jews.

David Ha-Melech and the people went to Givah to bring the Holy Ark to Yerushalayim. David and the people of Yisrael walked in front of it, dancing and rejoicing with assorted instruments. Along the way, the oxen leading the cart stumbled, causing the Ark to sway. Uzzah the priest feared that the Ark might fall, and reached out his hand to steady it. He was punished by Hashem and died on the spot. It was disrespectful for Uzzah to touch the Holy Ark, for it showed a lack of faith in the ability of the Ark to protect itself.

After three months, the people's repentance for his disrespect to the Ark was accepted by the Almighty. They were then ready to bring the Ark to Yerushalayim, the City of David. The Ark was carried on the shoulders of the *leviyim*, the bearers of the Ark. David and the people of Yisrael danced and rejoiced in front of the Ark. He then made a feast for those who had participated in this great, joyous event.

David's wife, Michal, daughter of Sha'ul, observed how David was dancing before the Lord, in front of all the people. As a result of her royal upbringing, she loathed his behavior and scolded him for dancing in front of all of his servants. David responded that he was dancing in front of Hashem and Hashem's Ark.

Respect for the Sefer Torah and Holy Articles

One must show the utmost respect for the Holy *sefer Torah* and other Jewish religious articles. When a *sefer Torah* is removed from the *Aron Kodesh* (Holy Ark), one must stand and walk towards the *sefer Torah* as if one is greeting a great leader. When it is being returned to the Ark, one escorts it, walking behind the Torah. One should not stand with his back to the *sefer Torah*. One should not even leave the shul until the *sefer Torah* has been returned to the *Aron Kodesh*. Whoever drops a *sefer Torah*, as well as those who witness it fall, must fast.

One must go to great lengths to protect the honor of the *sefer Torah*. If it is damaged, it may not be discarded, but must be buried. If, God forbid, a *sefer Torah* was burned, it is treated as if it were a human being who had passed away and must be buried.

The first thing the Germans did when they entered a Jewish community in Europe was to set fire to the local synagogue. The purpose of this act was to terrorize and demoralize the Jews. It was done openly, in broad daylight, sometimes to the accompaniment of a German army band. On occasion, the enemy would gather the local Jews and force them to watch the destruction. More than once, though, one of the oppressed and persecuted Jews would defy death and rush forth into the shul to rescue the sacred scrolls of the Torah.

In the community of Pshevorsky, Poland, both the synagogue and *beis hamidrash* (house of study) were engulfed in flames. Hordes of German soldiers and officers stood there enjoying the spectacle. Many Jews were gathered behind them, their heads bowed in pain and humiliation. The rabbi of the community had been ordered to stand in the front row, himself the object of scorn and derision. Suddenly the rabbi broke away and began to run. Two more Jews were seen running after him. The Germans stopped laughing and shouted after him to halt. The rabbi did not hear a thing. Nothing could stop him, not even the flames. He and the other two disappeared inside the burning building. The Germans were speechless with astonishment. A few moments later the rabbi reappeared. His clothes were singed, but his face shone with a triumphant smile as his hands lovingly held a *sefer Torah*.

"Jewish impudence!" the German commander grumbled, accompanied by the rest of the men. They pointed their rifles at the burning synagoguge, so that the two men who assisted the rabbi would not be able to come out. They attacked the rabbi with the butts of their rifles, but the rabbi held on to the Torah as if he and the scroll were one and inseparable, as, in fact, they were.

❦ HISTORY

DAVID'S DESIRE TO BUILD HASHEM'S TEMPLE

David approached the prophet Nasan to express his desire to build a permanent Sanctuary for God. Hashem responded that David was both a faithful servant of God and a faithful leader of his people. However, he was a warrior who had shed much blood on the field of battle, and therefore could not personally build the Temple. David was upset that he was considered a shedder of blood, and for that reason had been disqualified to build the Sanctuary. God reassured him with the following prophecy:

"Do not fear, David. Everything you did is considered as a sacrifice before Me. If you were to build the Temple, it would last forever, never to be destroyed even though Yisrael would sin. I know that Yisrael will sin and, because the Temple will not be built by you, it will be possible to punish them by destroying the Temple instead of destroying them."

The Almighty promised that He would establish David's throne and kingdom forever. The *Beis Ha-Mikdash* was to be built by his very own son, Shelomo, but it would be called the Temple of David. The Temple was dedicated with a psalm authored by David. David was grateful for Hashem's promise.

David Ha-Melech was not only a man of courage, Torah, and humility, but he was also a prophet, a man of God, leader of the Sanhedrin (Supreme Jewish Court of Law), and author of *Tehillim* (Book of Psalms).

ETHICS II

Keeping a Vow

David searched for survivors from the house of Sha'ul to whom he could show kindness for the sake of his friend Yonasan. He was informed that Yonasan left a son, Mefiboshes, who was lame. When Mefiboshes was brought before David, the king promised to show kindness to him in the *zechus* (merit) of his father, Yonasan, with whom he had made a pact of friendship.

David went to great lengths to fulfill his vow to Yonasan. The Talmud says that for the sin of unfulfilled vows, chil-dren die.[8]

The Talmud[9] relates that a woman once went to her neighbor's house to knead dough. She had three dinars with her, which she put aside, rolled up in her shawl, for safekeeping. During the course of the baking activity, the three dinars somehow slipped out of the shawl, ended up in the dough, and were baked into the bread.

When the woman was ready to go home, she looked for her coins, but they were nowhere to be found. She was very upset and accused her neighbor of stealing them. The latter was so eager to prove her innocence of such petty theft, that she swore by the life of her youngest son that she had not touched the three dinars.

When the Heavenly Court examined her record, it was found that the woman was not free of sin, and was in fact deserving of punishment. It was decreed that her youngest son would pass away as a result of her oath.

When the woman whose dinars were missing heard of the tragedy, she felt this confirmed her suspicions, and that the neighbor had indeed taken her money. Her husband, meanwhile, counseled her to go over to her neighbor and comfort her. The woman took along two loaves from the bread she had baked, as a meal of consolation (*seudas havra'ah*). As they cut the bread, the three dinars fell to the floor.

Everyone involved realized how careful one should be about making an oath.

❦ HISTORY

DAVID'S MISTAKE

David realized that a beautiful woman named Bas-sheva was destined to be his wife and the mother of the future king of Yisrael. Because her husband had rebelled against him, he sent him to the front battle lines and he was killed. After the mourning period was over, David sent for Bas-sheva and took her for his wife. What David had done was displeasing in the eyes of Hashem.

The prophet Nasan explained to him his grave misdeed through a parable. David did not get angry at the prophet for rebuking him. Instead, he repented and felt great remorse for his deed. A child was born to Bas-sheva and became deathly ill. David fasted for seven days while the child was in critical condition, hoping that he could beseech the Almighty to be gracious to the child. Once the child died and his fasting could no longer bring it back to life, he comforted his wife, Bas-sheva. They later had another son, whom he named Shelomo.

AVSHALOM'S REBELLION AGAINST DAVID

David Ha-Melech had many wives and children. One of his sons, Avshalom, was an extremely handsome and vain young man, with beautiful long curly hair.

Amnon, another son, had done a terrible misdeed to his stepsister, Tamar, who was Avshalom's sister. Avshalom didn't say a word to Amnon, but he bore a terrible hatred against him. Two years later, when the opportunity arose, he had his brother killed.

When David heard about this, Avshalom was forced to flee until he was pardoned by his father, David. Avshalom was an opportunist who would position himself by the gate of the court and convince the masses that he was the perfect person to succeed his father David. When the opportunity lent itself, he led an uprising against David, and forced his father to leave the throne and flee for his life.

Achitofel was David's power-hungry chief counselor. He eventually joined Avshalom and became his chief advisor.

While David was on the run, a man by the name of Shimi ben Gera from the tribe of Binyamin, came out to throw stones and curse David. The king's men requested permission to execute Shimi as a rebel. However, David ordered his men not to kill him. In the most bitter hour of his life, with the ability and opportunity at hand to slay his tormentor, David recognized Shimi as a messenger of God, and he accepted his taunting and curses as God's will. This was proven the correct thing to do because a descendant of Shimi was the great Mordechai. Together with his niece, Queen Esther, they saved the Jewish nation from Haman's plot to destroy them.

ETHICS III

Holding Back Anger

One sees the greatness of David Ha-Me-lech, who held back his anger and did not have Shimi ben Gera executed. David exercised great self-control in allowing him to live. The following stories show the importance of self-control and restraining one's anger.

A man once bought a beautiful *esrog* for a considerable sum of money. Someone asked to borrow the *esrog* so that he, too, could fulfill the mitzvah of reciting the blessing on the Four Species. The borrower accidentally dropped the *esrog* and it was damaged, rendering it unfit for use. Understandably, the owner of the *esrog* felt upset, but thought to himself, If I show anger towards someone who tried to fulfill Hashem's mitzvah, this will surely be displeasing to the Almighty. He, therefore, accepted the damaged *esrog* without a word of reproach.

A great rabbi known as the Sefas Emes once gave a powerful spiritual message to his followers. "Do you know why the locomotive has the power to pull all those carriages? Because it keeps the steam inside! Remember, the one who is wise in the hour of his anger will leave room for love, and remember at the beginning of his actions what the end will bring."

LESSON V

Avshalom and his Punishment for Being Proud

Avshalom's rebellion lasted six months. After David successfully defended his throne, he gave orders to spare Avshalom's life. While Avshalom was escaping, his long hair got caught on some low-hanging branches. He was lifted off his horse and remained suspended in the air, at the mercy of his pursuers, who refused to harm him because of the king's command. However, Yo'av, David's general, came and killed him. Avshalom displayed excessive pride in his beautiful hair; therefore that same hair was the instrument of his downfall.[10]

There are people on this earth who have great power and come to believe in themselves as being the source of their own power. But a person must at all times realize that Hashem is the source of his strength. Should He desire, He could abruptly withdraw His support, making a once powerful individual into a feeble weakling.

Avimelech, the son of Gidon, was a tremendously strong warrior who had killed seventy brothers at one time in order to consolidate his own power. He seemed invincible at the time. Yet, he was killed by a millstone thrown onto his head by a woman. One can learn from this that our powers on earth emanate from heaven and cannot be taken for granted.

❦ HISTORY

THE INHERENT CRUELTY OF THE GIVONITES

During the reign of David Ha-Melech, there was a terrible famine in the land that lasted for three years. When David inquired of the *urim v'tumim* the cause for the famine, he was informed that it was due to two transgressions by the Jewish people: (1) their failure to eulogize King Sha'ul properly, and (2) the breach of Yehoshua's promise to the Givonites. Sha'ul was guilty of killing the Givonites. The Talmud[11] explains that actually he was guilty of depriving them of their source of livelihood and food when he ordered the execution of the *kohanim* in the city of Nov, for the Givonites worked for the *kohanim*.

When David asked the Givonites what could be done to atone for the wrongdoing of Sha'ul Ha-Melech, they requested that seven of Sha'ul's sons be handed over to them to be hanged. Nothing else would appease them. They exhibited the characteristic of being merciless — a clear indication that they were not part of the Jewish nation, despite having lived among them for several centuries.

The fear of intermarriage with and the adverse influence of the Givonites was amply justified. Even after four centuries under the influence of the *kohanim*, the Givonites demonstrated by their extreme cruelty that "they were not of the Children of Yisrael."[12]

THE REBELLION OF ADONIYAHU AND YO'AV

David Ha-Melech had decided that the one to succeed him would be Shelomo, the son of Bas-sheva. Toward the end of David's reign, when he was old and weak, Yo'av decided to join forces with Adoniyahu, another son of David. They attempted to gain the throne despite David's decision that Shelomo should reign. When David heard from Bas-sheva that Adoniyahu was attempting to rule, despite his old age and infirmities, he took immediate action that prevented Adoniyahu and Yo'av from assuming power.

On his deathbed, David commanded Shelomo to punish Shimi ben Gera and Yo'av. At a time when men usually harbor no vengeance and forgive their enemies, he did not neglect his duty to punish rebels in accordance with the laws of the Torah. All his life, he had been both humble and strong, each at the right time. Therefore, the Almighty called him "My servant, David." He did justice and righteousness to all his people. His highest aspiration was to sit in the House of God all his days. David Ha-Melech died at the age of seventy, after a reign of forty years (2924 - 837 B.C.E.).

LESSON VI

The Greatness of David

David was a gifted, courageous warrior and a benevolent ruler with an extreme love for Hashem. Despite all his difficulties, his devotion to Hashem was undiminished. One of his most outstanding characteristics was his single-minded devotion to Torah study. Throughout his lifetime, he delved deeply into Torah study, during virtually all hours of the night. So beloved was the Torah study of King David to Hashem, that the Almighty said to him, "Devote yourself to Torah study and I will wage your battles."

David's flight from Sha'ul into the wilderness, constantly running for his life in this forced exile, was part of Hashem's plan for his historic role as the author of the book of *Tehillim* (Psalms). Living a life which required unwaivering trust in the Almighty and eventual intense gratitude for being saved from death gave David the special ability to write *Tehillim*. In the book of *Tehillim*, every man can find some passages to suit his own circumstances and special problems. The entire nation of Yisrael can especially identify with the Psalms of David Ha-Melech. David, the chosen of God, was unjustly persecuted so that he was forced to flee for his life. Despite that, he persisted in his flaming love for and un-yielding trust in Hashem. This is also true of the Jewish nation, which is constantly persecuted and exiled, but remains faithful to Hashem.

Even after David overcame all of his difficulties, his devotion to Hashem remained undiminished. Unlike those who remember Hashem in times of need but not in prosperity, David continued to be a humble servant of Hashem even when he became a powerful monarch.

Like Avraham before him, David was tested to prove his devotion to Hashem. When, on rare occasions his decisions or actions failed to meet the high standards Hashem sets for the righteous, he listened to the harsh messages of the prophets and sought immediate repentance. For many years, he was deeply remorseful about an act which was only a sin in the eyes of God, and for which he found no rest all the days of his life.

David earned the title of "Servant of Hashem" because he used all of his abilities solely in God's service. The Almighty bestowed the mantle of royalty upon David for all future generations as well. He became the progenitor of the Davidic dynasty, which will once again reign in all its glory with the coming of Mashiach ben David.

NOTES

1. *Talmud Gittin,* 56b.

2. *Me-am Lo'ez, Shemuel I.*

3. *Tehillim* 34.

4. Rav Sa'adyah Gaon, *Sefer Emunos v'De'os.*

5. Rambam, *Mishneh Torah, Hilchos Teshuvah, perek* 10.

6. *Talmud Shabbos,* 32.

7. *Meshech Chochmah, Parashas Va-yelech.*

8. *Talmud Shabbos,* 32b.

9. *Talmud Gittin,* 35.

10. *Talmud Sotah,* 9b.

11. *Talmud Yevamos,* 78b and *Talmud Bava Kama,* 119.

12. *Shemuel II* 21:2.

❦ Key People, Places and Things

ACHITOFEL: advisor to David, who later joined forces with Avshalom.

ADONIYAHU: one of David's sons, who attempted to usurp the throne. One of his supporters was Yo'av, David's general.

AVIGAYIL: Naval's wife, who sought to correct her husband's misdeeds and injustice toward David and his men. She offered food to David, and after her husband died, married him.

AVSHALOM: David's rebellious son who caused his father to flee from Yerushalayim.

BAS-SHEVA: a woman whom David married after her husband was killed at the battlefront. She was the mother of Shelomo Ha-Melech.

GIVONITES: the nation that made peace with Yehoshua through trickery. They were a cruel nation that later demanded the death of Sha'ul's sons for an injustice done to them.

NASAN: Nathan, the prophet and advisor to David Ha-Melech.

NAVAL: the wicked man who refused to return David's kindness of providing him with food.

SHIMI BEN GERA: a member of the tribe of Binyamin who cursed David when he was fleeing from Avshalom.

TALLIS: a prayer shawl that has fringes on its four corners, and is worn by male Jews.

TZITZIS: fringes attached to the four corners of a garment that is worn by male Jews. It is sometimes referred to as *tallis katan* (small *tallis*) or *arba kanfos* (four corners).

YO'AV: David's general. On two occasions he disobeyed his king. He killed Avner as well as Avshalom, and sided with Adoniyahu.

❦ Introduction to Chapter 16

"Behold, a son shall be born to you, who shall be a man of tranquillity, and I will give him rest from all his surrounding enemies. For Shelomo shall be his name, and peace and quietness I will give to Yisrael in his days" (*Divrei Ha-Yamim* I 22:9).

Shelomo succeeded his father David as king of Yisrael, and his rule marked the period of Yisrael's supreme glory. He organized a strong army and kept his country out of war for forty years. King Shelomo's fame and wisdom were widespread. Other nations far and wide came to honor the majestic and scholarly king. This era was one of tranquillity that allowed time for intense learning. Shelomo built the Temple, and through his wisdom and inspiration advanced devotion to the Torah and its laws.

With the completion of the holy Temple in Yerushalayim, all eyes turned toward king and Temple — each representing the Divine spirit. Shelomo (*shalom*) is a name of God, because He is the ultimate source of all peace. Shelomo dedicated his wisdom only to the service of God. After amassing great wealth, Shelomo said, "*Havel havalim* (futility of futilities)," since only Torah wisdom matters.

Unfortunately, Shelomo fell short of being the ideal leader. Because of his greatness, his lapses were considered equivalent to idol worship. Royal pomp and the splendid public works required him to impose heavy taxes and forced labor on his resentful people. Also, alliances with the neighboring countries increased the local influence of foreigners and with them their pagan ideas and beliefs. Thus, the seeds of trouble were sown.

The people's dissatisfaction with the heavy burdens put on them led to a rebellion, and after the king's death, to the secession of the northern provinces. Yarovam made himself king of Yisrael and even called in Egyptian aid against the southern kingdom, Yehudah. To destroy the hold which Yerushalayim had on the minds of his subjects, he erected two golden calves to serve as the national sanctuaries of Yisrael. Thus, the unity of the Jewish state was destroyed, and its religious foundation, which had given it cohesion and the power of survival, was lost.

The fate of the kingdoms of Yehudah and Yisrael was sealed when they disregarded the teaching of the prophets. In the midst of the continuing quarrels as to what Yisrael was and what it ought to be, the kingdom was shattered. Only a few decades before the destruction of the First Temple, an invasion occurred which tore the larger part of the nation away.

The last king of the kingdom of Yisrael was Hoshea, who was defeated by Assyria. The Jews of his kingdom were exiled to distant lands, and lost without a trace to this day. They are known as the Ten Lost Tribes of Israel.

CHAPTER 16

King Shelomo's Reign and the Kingdom of Yisrael
From the Rule of Shelomo to the Exile of the Ten Tribes
(2924 – 3205/837 B.C.E. – 556 B.C.E.)

❦ HISTORY

SHELOMO IS CROWNED KING (2924/837 B.C.E.)

Shelomo's reign began in 2924/837 B.C.E. when he was only twelve years old. His father, David Ha-Melech, had imbued him with a great love of Hashem and devotion to his people. Shelomo was guided by very wise and God-fearing men whom David Ha-Melech had personally chosen to advise the young monarch. After he assumed the throne, Shelomo brought the people to Givon to offer sacrifices to the Almighty. He generated great enthusiasm for the worship of God, and inspired a new excellence of spirit. Hashem then appeared to Shelomo and offered him the fulfillment of one request. Shelomo requested the gift of an understanding heart and wisdom in judging his people. Hashem blessed Shelomo with great wisdom. He was admired by monarchs from around the world for it.

LESSON I

David and Shelomo:
Great Kings with Different Missions

David and Shelomo, father and son, were the greatest kings Yisrael ever had, but they were very different personalities with very different missions.

David was the king who, true to the example of his ancestor, Yehudah, lived not for himself at all. He saw none of his greatness as belonging to himself; everything was for the service of his people.

The name of David begins and ends with the letter *dalet*, which means poverty. David remained a pauper. Nothing that he achieved was his own. All was a heavenly gift to be held in safekeeping for the people because the king belongs to the people. On the other hand, Shelomo's mission was to bring holiness into every aspect of living. Wealth did not affect Shelomo. In fact, he utilized it to carry out his holy mission.

❦ HISTORY

THE BUILDING OF THE BEIS HA-MIKDASH (2928/833 B.C.E.)

In the fourth year of his reign, Shelomo built the *Beis Ha-Mikdash.* The *Beis Ha-Mikdash* was the heart and nerve center of the Jewish community. It was the seat of the *Sanhedrin,* and served as a constant source of spiritual inspiration. It served as a house of worship where the prayers of the Jews would be favorably received. For as long as the *Beis Ha-Mikdash* remained standing, the *Shechinah* (Divine Presence) rested within its walls.

The Temple was to serve as the prime source of spiritual inspiration for the people. It was for this reason that the windows of the *Beis Ha-Mikdash* were narrow within and broad without, for light shone forth from them to the outside world. During the Temple dedication ceremony, Shelomo Ha-Melech prayed that the *Beis Ha-Mikdash* should serve as a house of worship, where the prayers of all the Jews would be favorably received. He also requested that the Temple sacrifices would serve to atone for the sins of Yisrael.

MITZVAH

Beis Ha-Knesses (Synagogue)

In the time of the Tabernacle and the Temple, a person was able to bring a sacrifice there to atone for his sins, and was also able to pray there. The Temple is no longer standing, but man still has a direct link to God through prayer.

Jews gather to pray together in a synagogue. It is a place set aside for prayer, and is referred to as a *Beis Ha-Knesses* (House of Assembly). In areas where the synagogue is also used as a place to learn Torah, it is called a *Beis Midrash.*

The synagogue becomes not only a gathering place for worship but also an instrument to promote Jewish values and Torah. Therefore, when choosing a synagogue to pray in, one should be careful to pick one whose worshipers adhere to God's commandments. That is the most accurate barometer of measuring the faith of a Jew.

MITZVAH

Praying with a Minyan

One should pray with a quorum of ten males in a synagogue. The quorum of ten required for public prayer is called a *minyan* (which means a number). If there is no synagogue, one should still make an effort to pray with a *minyan.* The concept of a *minyan* has its source in the Torah, where it is written that God must be sanctified in an assembly of Jews.[1]

One should select a God-fearing congregation with which to pray. It is not the aesthetic beauty of the building that is important, but rather what is conducted inside it that counts.

We see the importance of a *minyan* in the following parable: A king was once asked to decide which of two towns deserved a certain royal privilege. Both towns sent letters of merit to the king listing their past deeds, in the hope that their requests would be answered. The members of the first town sent their letters individually at different times. As each letter arrived, the king examined it and usually managed to find fault with each one. The second town, however, sent their letters in one shipment. When this bundle arrived, the king looked at them all collectively. What some lacked, the others compensated for. Seen together, the second town presented their needs more effectively, and therefore won the favor of the king. As would be expected, the second town won the privilege.

In a similar vein, if each of us would pray separately, God would examine each of us on an individual basis and would no doubt find us deficient. On the other hand, if we pray in a group, as part of a *minyan*, then our combined prayers are conveyed to God, and hopefully the merits of the entire group will outweigh the deficiencies of each individual in the group.

The fact that the synagogue is a miniature sanctuary calls not only for frequent attendance, but also proper decorum and respect. Prayers must be said with sincerity and concentration, not as a habit. It should not be as if we are saying mere words, without meaning or thought.

MITZVAH

Contents and Description of the Synagogue

The synagogue contains a holy ark where the scrolls of the Torah are kept. It should be placed against the eastern wall, facing toward Yerushalayim, and that is the direction toward which we pray.

Adjacent to the holy ark is a *ner tamid* (eternal light) that burns continuously. There is a table in the center of the synagogue upon which the Torah is read to the congregation. Candleholders are usually placed on the table where the cantor prays. This is symbolic of the seven-branched menorah of the Temple.

The *chazan* (cantor) fills the role of emissary for the congregation. It is he who leads the congregation in prayer before the Almighty. The sexton, or *shamash*, is the person who attends to the many maintenance needs of the synagogue.

Having an *ezras nashim* (women's section) follows the same tradition of separation that was observed in the Temple.

❧ HISTORY

SHELOMO HA-MELECH'S WISDOM

Because David Ha-Melech had vanquished Yisrael's enemies, Shelomo's rule was one of tranquillity, intense Torah learning, and great wealth. Rulers of nations from far and wide came to honor the wise and scholarly king. Among them was the Queen of Sheba (Sheva). She had heard of the great wisdom and wealth of Shelomo Ha-Melech, and so she came to witness it herself. She appeared before Shelomo with many difficult questions and riddles that she had prepared to test his unique wisdom.

Among the riddles of the Queen of Sheva were the following: She presented Shelomo Ha-Melech with bunches of the most beautiful flowers. However, some were real and some were artificial. Shelomo had to find the real flowers but, of course, without touching them. Shelomo Ha-Melech ordered that the window be opened and a little bumble bee flew in, buzzing from one real flower to the next.

The Queen of Sheva also tested Shelomo by having a large group of boys and girls, all dressed identically, presented before the king. Shelomo had to decide which were the boys and which were the girls.

Shelomo Ha-Melech ordered that basins of water be brought in, and asked all the children to wash their hands. However, he did not provide towels with which to dry their hands. The girls instinctively wiped their hands on their long robes, while the boys did not know what to do with their wet hands. Once again, Shelomo had proved his great wisdom.

Following many more riddles with which she tested Shelomo Ha-Melech, the Queen of Sheva declared, "It was a true report that I heard in my own land of your acts and of your wisdom. But I did not believe the words until I came and my own eyes had seen; and behold, the half of it was not told me — thy wisdom and thy wealth exceed the fame which I heard.

With the completion of the Holy Temple, offerings to God came from rulers everywhere. God's blessing made Shelomo the wisest man on earth. We see segments of his wisdom in his books: *Mishlei* (Book of Proverbs), *Shir Ha-Shirim* (Song of Songs) and *Koheles* (Ecclesiastes), which are incorporated into the holy books of the *Tanach*.

SHELOMO'S MISCALCULATION

Although Shelomo was a great man, he made the mistake of marrying too many wives, owning too many horses, and acquiring too much wealth. He felt that although these actions were prohibited by the Torah, they allowed for certain exceptions. Reasons were given along with each of these prohibitions, and Shelomo felt that it meant that one whose character was strong enough to withstand the temptation was exempt. He was strong enough to withstand the risks in his younger years. Unfortunately, when he grew older he was unable to control his wives' actions. Since he should have prevented his wives from continuing to serve their own foreign gods, he is held accountable as if he had worshiped them himself.

The Talmud[2] states that Shelomo did not sin, and of course never worshiped idols. However, since it was his responsibility to control everything in his house, he shares the blame for the outcome. It also shows that even the wisest king must yield to the Torah and accept its precautions. No man is above the Torah. Because of his harmful influence, God sent a prophet to inform Shelomo that part of his kingdom would be taken away from his son. Unlike heroes and leaders of the gentile world who are worshiped by the populace regardless of their faults and flaws, Jewish leaders are subject to a higher standard. It is by this standard alone that Shelomo fell short and therefore spent his last years in decline. The severity of his punishment should not blind us to the true greatness of Shelomo Ha-Melech. Shelomo Ha-Melech's reign ended after forty years.

YAROVAM BEN NEVAT'S REPROOF OF SHELOMO HA-MELECH

During his reign, Shelomo Ha-Melech sealed certain openings in the wall surrounding Yerushalayim. David Ha-Melech had left these open to provide easy access into Yerushalayim for Jews coming from all over the land. Shelomo's action was for the purpose of strengthening the fortifications of the city.

Yarovam, from the tribe of Efrayim, was an officer appointed by Shelomo Ha-Melech. He rebuked the king by stating, "Your father opened additional gates to allow easy access to the city from all sides, but you closed them and left only one gate open in order to put a toll collector there to raise money to build a palace for the daughter of Paroh (his wife)." Yarovam was suspected of fomenting opposition against the king and was forced to flee to Egypt, where he remained until after the death of Shelomo.

The Almighty gave Yarovam the power to fulfill the prophecy concerning Shelomo's punishment for the damage done by his many wives. This prophecy had been foretold to Yarovam by Achiyah Ha-Shiloni. The prophet took his cloak and tore it into twelve pieces. He then gave ten of the pieces to Yarovam, symbolizing the fact that ten of the twelve tribes would be torn away from Shelomo and given to him.

The gall and audacity displayed by Yarovam against Shelomo Ha-Melech, although for a virtuous cause, proved his undoing, as will be seen later on. He could have attempted to counsel Shelomo privately, instead of lashing out at him in a public forum.

THE SPLIT IN THE KINGDOM

After Shelomo's death (2964/797 B.C.E.), his son and successor, Rechavam, rejected the advice of the elder statesmen who wanted him to be humble and conciliatory toward the people. He favored the advice of his youthful friends who recommended increasing the taxes and burdens on the people. This aroused the wrath of the populace, and many forsook the new king.

The people encouraged Yarovam ben Nevat to lead ten of the twelve tribes in secession. Yarovam was chosen because of his greatness, and also because of his courage when he rebuked Shelomo for closing up some of the gates leading to Yerushalayim. He was rewarded by Hashem for this legitimate complaint by becoming king of the ten tribes. Henceforth, the Jewish nation consisted of two kingdoms: the kingdom of Yehudah (*malchus Yehudah*) under Rechavam, and the kingdom of Yisrael (*malchus Yisrael*) under Yarovam. However, although Yarovam was correct, the anger and audacity he displayed proved his undoing.

During the *Shalosh Regalim* (three festivals of Pesach, Shavuos and Sukkos) all the Jews from the land would go up to Yerushalayim to offer sacrifices to Hashem. Yerushalayim was within the territory belonging to Rechavam. Yarovam feared that once the Jews would go to Yerushalayim, it would awaken their old loyalties to the kingdom of the House of David. He could not abide the thought of being inferior in dignity to Rechavam. This resulted in Yarovam committing a tremendous transgression. The man who had so angrily protested against closing the gates that led to Yerushalayim, now set up guarded barriers on all roads leading to Yerushalayim.

ETHICS I

Heeding the Advice of Elders

Rechavam's downfall came about because he did not heed the advice of the elders. He should have learned from the teachings of his father, Shelomo, as it is written in *Mishlei*,[3] "Where there is no wise guidance a people must fall; but salvation is through the multitude of counselors." "The way of a fool is straight in his own eyes; but he who listens to good advice is wise."[4]

Even afterward, when the Prophet Shemayah cautioned him not to wage war against the seceding tribes, since this was the will of Hashem, Rechavam listened only temporarily. Had he heeded the prophet's words, the ten tribes might not have remained estranged. Eventually the ten tribes might have returned to the House of David, but the continuous war caused the ten tribes to be permanently split off from the rest of the Jewish nation.

Every individual needs advice, for it is impossible for a man to be experienced with all aspects of a problem and make the appropriate objective decision needed. It is foolish and arrogant to refuse advice from others. Naturally, the most reliable and expert advice would come from scholars and elders who have benefited from the experiences of life.[5]

In the course of his long life, the saintly Chafetz Chaim gave advice to countless numbers of individuals. The following story is an example of the advice he gave to a young man, a merchant, who was a former yeshivah student:

The latter bought a lottery ticket and made the special trip all the way to Radin to ask the Chafetz Chaim for his blessing. However, a friend advised him not to mention a word about the lottery, of which the rabbi disapproved. He took this advice.

The Chafetz Chaim wished him a comfortable living and that he be successful in educating his children to grow into good and faithful Jews. But this blessing did not satisfy the young man, and he stayed another day at Radin. The next day he went again to the rabbi, but after the latter repeated his former blessings, the young man remained in the room, discomfited.

The rabbi immediately noticed that, and began to speak, as it were, his thoughts aloud: "Some people, whenever they are asked how they are faring, always answer: 'Quite well, but it could be better.' Now, how can they know that it could be better? The Almighty knows better and can do better, and if He does not do better — it is only because we already have the better!

"Many people come to me for advice, but what they really want is for me to agree with their wishes, and that I can't always do!" Saying this, he rose and came close to the young man, putting his hand on the man's shoulder. He continued: "A young man once came to me who wanted to win in the lottery, but if the Almighty wishes to grant him meritorious children, who are indeed the greatest treasure on earth, wealth can only interfere with their education. Be content with what you have."

LESSON II

Averah Goreres Averah
(One Sin Prompts Another)

Yarovam was a very proud and ambitious person. Thus he openly reprimanded Shelomo, and ultimately became the leader of the ten tribes. But this was still not enough. He was jealous that the people were going up to Yerushalayim. He therefore set up guards to prevent them from going. That was still not enough. He had to find a substitute place for the people to bring their offerings. He set up two temples of idol worship for the people to bring their offerings. To legitimize these temples, Yarovam revived the people's desire for idol worship. He set up two golden calves, and quoted the same words that had been used to introduce the Golden Calf in the wilderness. Most of the *Kohanim* and *Leviyim*, as well as other important Israelites from other tribes, did not want to have anything to do with Yarovam and they rejoined Rechavam.

Yarovam intended for the golden calves to be used solely as symbols of the worship of the true God. His motives were selfish and political; he was not interested in worshiping idols. This, however, led the entire Jewish nation astray and was the beginning of idol worship among the Jewish people. Instead of remaining the man exalted by God, Yarovam became the symbol of one who sinned and caused the multitude to sin. Consequently, he lost his share in the World to Come. Because of him, the kingdom of Yisrael began to deteriorate until, finally, they were sent into exile, to be lost among the nations.

❦ HISTORY

TURMOIL IN THE KINGDOM OF YISRAEL; CONTINUITY IN THE KINGDOM OF YEHUDAH

Yarovam was succeeded by his son, Nadav (2985/776 B.C.E.), who was assassinated after a short reign. The entire family of Yarovam was destroyed, as foretold by the prophets. The succeeding family of Basha was also totally wiped out. While the kingdom of Yisrael was rocked by intrigue and assassinations, the kingdom of Yehudah enjoyed stability and relative tranquility. On the whole, they remained faithful to the House of David, with the throne passing from father to son.

During this time there was sporadic fighting between the kingdom of Yisrael and the kingdom of Yehudah. Asa, the grandson of Rechavam, ruled justly over the kingdom of Yehudah. However, he made one mistake. He made a pact with Ben Hadad, king of Syria. He was rebuked by the Prophet Chanani for not trusting in Hashem. Asa yielded to anger and put the prophet in prison. He also did not treat the Torah scholars in the proper manner, as he did not exempt them from work and taxation, a practice followed by David and Shelomo. His punishment was that he became crippled. Nevertheless, he was still considered a good ruler and reigned for forty-one years (2983 - 3024/778 B.C.E. - 737 B.C.E.).

Asa was succeeded by his son, Yehoshafat, who followed in his father's footsteps and was a just king. Unlike his father, Yehoshafat did honor

Torah scholars.[6] However, he, too, made a grave mistake. In an attempt to unify the two Jewish kingdoms, Yehoshafat gave his son in marriage to the daughter of the wicked King Achav and the evil Queen Izevel. Although he had virtuous intentions, we see that subsequent developments were catastrophic. Instead of improving the ten tribes, Yehoshafat brought great misfortune upon his own kingdom of Yehudah.

The kingdom of Yisrael was ruled by evil men, idol worshipers who totally misled the populace. The most evil of them all was the wicked King Achav. Under the influence of his even more wicked queen, he erected a temple to Ba'al and caused many of the people to adopt this new religion. Achav and Izevel had reached such a degree of wickedness that they slaughtered many of God's prophets. It was through the efforts of a saintly prophet, Ovadyah, that one hundred prophets did remain alive. He hid them in two caves and supplied them with bread and water. This was at a time when food was very scarce in the land.

THE GREATNESS OF ELIYAHU HA-NAVI (ELIJAH THE PROPHET)

Hashem sent a terrible famine on the kingdom of Yisrael as punishment for the widespread practice of idolatry. It was during the third year of the famine that God allowed Eliyahu Ha-Navi to appear and challenge Achav to a demonstration of the power of the Ba'al. The Jews of the kingdom of Yisrael assembled on Mt. Karmel, where Eliyahu spoke to them. "How long will you hedge between two opinions? If Hashem is God, go after Him." The people's response was one of hesitation, for they did not want to openly oppose King Achav.

A contest was arranged between the priests of the Ba'al and Eliyahu Ha-Navi. Each faction erected an altar upon which a sacrifice was to be brought. However, no fire was lit. The fire would have to descend from heaven, and that would prove who was the real God.

The priests of Ba'al prepared their sacrificial offering and prayed to Ba'al. They cried and screamed out to Ba'al, but to no avail. They cut themselves with knives in frenzied ecstasy, but their god did not respond. They tried subterfuge to get the fire going, but nothing happened.

Then it was Eliyahu's turn. Before placing the sacrifice on the altar, he poured water on the wood, making it soaking wet. This would make the miracle even greater. Then he prayed to Hashem that He grant a miracle so that all the Jews would see who is the true God. A fire came down from heaven and consumed Eliyahu's offering. The Jews were overwhelmed by the miracle that they had just witnessed, and they all proclaimed, "*Hashem Hu Ha-Elokim, Hashem Hu Ha-Elokim* (The Lord He is God, The Lord He is God)."

Eliyahu then ordered the Jews to kill all the priests of the Ba'al. After that was done, Eliyahu informed the king that the famine was over and rain would fall.

THE WICKED KING ACHAV AND QUEEN IZEVEL (3021-3041/740 B.C.E.-720 B.C.E.)

When Izevel heard that her priests of Ba'al had been slaughtered, she flew into a rage and again sought to kill Eliyahu. Once again, he had to flee for his life and hide in a mountain cave.

Among the wicked things that Izevel perpetrated was the terrible injustice against a man named Navos Ha-Karmeli. The latter had a beautiful vineyard that was adjoining King Achav's palace. Achav desired the vineyard, but Navos refused to sell the land that was his family's inheritance. Izevel arranged for two men to bear false witness against Navos, stating that he had blasphemed God and the king. Izevel arranged for her court to condemn Navos to death. This was the only time during the period of the prophets that a *beis din* was forced to act so wickedly. Navos was stoned, and Achav took possession of the vineyard that he had coveted. Eliyahu Ha-Navi appeared afterward to Achav, rebuking him severely for the murder he had arranged. In turn, Eliyahu predicted a violent death for both Achav and Izevel. Achav was frightened by the prophet's words and he sincerely repented for his misdeeds. For this he merited that the evil that was to befall his household would come during the reign of his son. As for Achav, he fell heroically in the field of battle when an enemy archer's random arrow struck him between the joints of his armor.

ETHICS II

Making a Bride and Groom Happy

The wicked Izevel was killed later on during a palace coup d'état. The officers threw her from a window, and she was trampled to death by passing horses. Dogs then devoured her body, leaving only her skull, feet and the palms of her hands. This was in merit of the fact that she used to help make merry in front of a bride and groom. She sang with her lips, clapped with her palms, and stamped with her feet.[7]

From the episode related in the *Tanach* about the death of Izevel, we learn about the importance of celebrating in front of a bride and groom and making them happy. On their wedding day, a bride and groom have the status of a king and queen. They are dressed in finery. They are escorted everywhere and are kept happy by all the guests around them.[8]

A story is told about Rabbi Mendlowitz (who, because of his modesty, allowed people to call him only Mr. Mendlowitz), the leader of Mesivta Torah Vodaath, that he had been dancing in front of the bride and groom despite the fact that he had a heart condition. Someone attempted to stop him, reminding him of his illness. His response was, "Never mind. I feel fine. We must teach the students how important it is to dance in front of the *chasan* and *kallah.*"

This period of keeping the bride and groom happy extends for seven whole days, for the seven day period after the marriage ceremony parallels the seven days of creation. During the bridal week known as *sheva berachos*, it is customary for close relatives or friends to make special meals in honor of the couple.

❦ HISTORY

THE GREATNESS OF THE PROPHET ELISHA

It was at this time that the great Prophet Eliyahu fulfilled his mission and departed this world in a most miraculous fashion, leaving his faithful disciple, Elisha, as his successor. Unfortunately, the people had strayed once more and were again worshiping idols.

Elisha, the successor of Eliyahu, soon became renowned for performing miracles just as his master had done. He came to Yericho, where he was told that the water was tainted, causing people to become sick. He asked for some salt, which he threw into a well, and the water became sweet and good.

From Yericho Elisha went to Beis El, where he was met by a crowd of young men shouting abusive words at him. It was their way of displaying their anger for his causing them a loss of income. These young men used to supply Yericho with fresh, pure drinking water, and made a handsome profit at the expense of their fellow Jews. When Elisha made the water sweet, they lost their business, and they, therefore, shouted at him. Elisha cursed them, and suddenly ferocious bears appeared from a forest that had not even been standing there before. The bears killed the young men. Elisha continued on his way.

King Achav was succeeded by his son, Achazyah, who reigned for only two years and died childless. He was succeeded by his brother Yehoram (Yoram). Neither one interfered with the widespread idolatry in the land. Yehoram declared war against Mo'av, and enlisted the help of Yehoshafat. Yehoram was worried about their chances of success in the war, and Yehoshafat suggested that they go to the prophet Elisha. Elisha rebuked Yehoram for his idol worship, but predicted that he would be victorious nevertheless in a most miraculous manner.

During Yehoram's reign, there was war and famine, and the population suffered greatly. It was at this time that Hashem sent the Prophet Elisha to bring comfort and courage to the people.

ELISHA'S MIRACLES (3043/718 B.C.E.)

(1) Elisha and the miracle of the oil

One day, the widow of the Prophet Ovadyah came to Elisha to ask his help in saving her two sons. Her husband had died, leaving overwhelming debts, and now the creditors wanted to take her two sons as slaves unless the debts were repaid immediately. Elisha was well aware of the kindnesses of the God-fearing Ovadyah. Under the very eyes of the wicked Izevel, he had sheltered and fed one hundred true prophets of God whom the evil queen had sought to exterminate. Ovadyah sustained them at his own expense, and when his money ran out, he borrowed and incurred tremendous debts. Now his widow was faced with the terrible threat of her sons being sold as slaves in order to repay those debts.

Elisha asked the widow what she had in her house, and she replied that all that she had left was a small cruse of oil. The prophet told her to borrow as many vessels as possible from her neighbors, and then to shut herself in her house with her two sons. She was then to pour the cruse of oil into the vessels.

The woman went home and did exactly as the prophet had told her to. In the privacy of her home, she began to pour from the small cruse of oil into the vessels that her sons handed to her. Vessel after vessel was filled to the brim with what appeared to be an endless supply of oil. When all the vessels had been filled, the supply ceased. The widow ran to Elisha to tell him what had happened. He told her to sell all the oil and pay off her debts, and she would still have enough to support herself and her sons. All that the prophet had said was fulfilled.

(2) Elisha and the Shunamite woman

Elisha used to visit the town of Shunem, where an aged couple were especially hospitable to him. They even built a special chamber with a bed, table, lamp, and chair, so that the prophet would always have a room at his disposal during his travels.

Elisha saw to what great lengths the hostess went to please him, and he inquired if there was anything he could do for her. The woman replied that there wasn't anything they needed. Elisha noticed, however, that the couple had no children, and so he blessed them with a son. A year later, a son was born to the aged couple. This was a miracle similar to the one that happened to Avraham and Sarah.

One day, when the boy was a few years old, he complained of a headache while in the fields with his father. He was sent home to his mother, where he died shortly thereafter. The mother placed the lifeless body of her son on the bed in the prophet's room, and hurried off to Mt. Karmel to the Prophet Elisha. When the prophet heard the tragic news, he quickly sent his servant Gechazi with his own staff, and told him to place the staff upon the dead child and thus restore him to life. He warned him, however, that he was not to speak to anyone along the way. Gechazi did not obey these instructions, and told everyone whom he met that he was going to restore life to a dead child with the prophet's staff. When he reached the woman's house, Gechazi, of course, was not able to revive the child because he had not followed the instructions of the prophet.

Elisha had to come himself, and after uttering a sincere prayer to the Almighty, he did revive the dead child. This very child was later to become the prophet Chavakkuk.

(3) Elisha and Na'aman

Na'aman was a great Syrian general who had both fame and fortune, but who was afflicted with a most dreaded disease — leprosy. His wife's maidservant, a Jewish captive girl, told her of the miracles performed by the Prophet Elisha, and suggested that her master, Na'aman, go to him and ask the prophet to pray for him.

Na'aman took many expensive presents with him, and set off to see the Prophet Elisha. When he arrived at the prophet's door, the latter sent out one of his disciples to tell Na'aman to immerse himself seven times in the Jordan River. Na'aman was highly insulted that the prophet had not come out personally to bless him, and refused to follow the prophet's instructions. While he was on his way back to Syria, however, his servants convinced him to immerse himself in the Jordan River, since they were passing it anyway. Na'aman agreed, immersed himself seven times, and emerged with the clean, unblemished skin of a baby.

Na'aman went back to Elisha and, with sincere gratitude for his miraculous recovery, declared, "Now I know that there is no other God on the entire earth but the God of Yisrael!" Elisha refused Na'aman's offer of a gift of thousands of pieces of gold and silver and ten changes of clothing. Had he accepted the gift, it would have minimized the effect of the miracle upon the people.

Gechazi, Elisha's servant, was a learned man, but possessed a vile character. He greedily thought about all the expensive gifts that his master had declined, and devised a plan whereby he would obtain them instead. He rode after Na'aman and told him that his master had reconsidered, in view of the fact that two new students of the prophet had arrived and were in need.

Na'aman was suspicious of Gechazi's story and asked him to take an oath, which the latter immediately did. Na'aman then gave Gechazi a huge gift of silver and two changes of clothing. When Gechazi returned to Elisha, the prophet asked where he had been. Gechazi denied having been anywhere, whereupon Elisha replied that although he had not been present physically at that moment, he was aware of all that had taken place between Gechazi and Na'aman. Elisha was furious with Gechazi for having committed a *chillul Hashem* (desecration of God's holy Name) by transgressing the oath that Elisha had made not to accept any gift from Na'aman.

"Take his leprosy too!" said the prophet. "You and your sons shall never be healed from it."[9]

REMOVING THE IDOLS

At God's request, Elisha sent the Prophet Yonah ben Amitai to anoint Yehu as the next king of Yisrael. Yehu killed King Yehoram and the entire house of Achav, including his seventy sons. The only survivor was Achav's daughter, Asalyah, who was the wife of Yehoram, king of the kingdom of Yehudah. Thus was fulfilled the prophecy of Eliyahu concerning the destruction of the house of Achav.

Yehu destroyed the worshipers of the Ba'al, slaughtered all of its priests, and destroyed their temples. Although he destroyed the Ba'al, Yehu still allowed the two golden calves to remain. He only considered them as a symbol of the true God, but in the eyes of God this was no excuse and He considered them idol worship anyway.

Yehu reigned for twenty-eight years over the kingdom of Yisrael, and was followed by Yehoachaz, who lost most of his army in battle with Aram (Syria). Yehoash inherited the weakened kingdom which was surrounded by its enemies.

THE PROPHET YONAH

Yonah was a great prophet and disciple of Eliyahu and then Elisha. Hashem appeared to Yonah and told him to go to Ninveh, the capital city of Assyria, and exhort them to repent.

Yonah did not wish to go to Ninveh, for if its people would actually listen to him and repent, they would make the ten tribes of Yisrael, by comparison, appear evil. In effect, it would be a terrible condemnation of Yisrael, which still had refused to repent. Yonah had to choose between obeying God and defending Yisrael. In order to shield Yisrael from the wrath of God, Yonah chose not to go to Ninveh.

Yonah was ready to forfeit his stature and even his life to commit a transgression for the sake of Yisrael. Like Moshe *Rabbenu*, he was ready to accept any fate — exile, degradation, and even death — rather than hurt the Jewish people.

Yonah fled on a boat. Hashem caused a terrible storm at sea which threatened to capsize the boat. Yonah knew that he was the cause of the storm, and asked the sailors to throw him overboard. At first they refused to do so, knowing that he was a holy and pious person. However, when he persisted, they lowered him into the sea and the waters calmed down. The sailors then realized that Yonah was correct in his assessment, and consequently, they threw him into the ocean.

Hashem sent a whale to swallow Yonah. He cried out to Hashem, and after three days and three nights, the whale spit him out onto dry land.

Yonah went to Ninveh and warned the people of impending doom if they did not repent. They took heed and proclaimed a fast. They prayed and donned sackcloth in sincere repentance to God. Even the king put on sackcloth and ashes as an example for all the people to follow. Hashem accepted the sincere repentance of the people of Ninveh, and He annulled the evil decree against them. Yonah left Ninveh, waiting to see what would happen to it.

Yonah was extremely grieved by the fact that a strange nation took his words to heart and repented sincerely, while his own people would not do so. He asked Hashem to take his life.

Hashem caused a special tree to grow overnight in order to provide

Yonah with shade and relief from the heat of the day. Yonah rested under the tree until it suddenly began to wither. Hashem had designated a worm to attack the tree, causing it to wither and die. The hot sun was beating on Yonah, and he felt faint. He felt tremendous sorrow over the loss of the tree.

Hashem responded, "You took pity on the tree for which you did not labor nor did you make it grow; it materialized overnight and perished overnight. Shall I not take pity upon Ninveh, that great city in which there are more than 120,000 children who do not know their right hand from their left, and many cattle as well?"

Although Scripture does not explicitly record Yonah's response, the commentaries do: "At that moment he [Yonah] fell upon his face and said, 'Conduct Your world according to the attribute of mercy, as it is written: To Hashem our God, are mercy and forgiveness.'"

LESSON III

The Important Lesson Learned from the Story of Yonah

The Book of Yonah teaches us many important lessons that should serve as a basis for our lives.

(1) God's Providence extends to the entire earth. No one is excluded from His Providence or removed from His mercy.

(2) No one can run away from God. When it is His wish, a ship's crew, a storm, a fish, even a worm, can retrieve or bring about the return of whomever He desires.

(3) Repentance (*teshuvah*) is never too late. The decree against the city of Ninveh had been issued, but they were able to save themselves through true repentance.

(4) God's mercy knows no bounds.

❦ HISTORY

THE KINGDOMS IN TURMOIL (3041-3205/720 B.C.E.-556 B.C.E.)

During this time, in the kingdom of Yehudah, Yehoram ruled for eight years. His mistake was following the wicked advice of his evil wife Asalyah, daughter of Izevel, and killing his brothers. The Prophet Eliyahu, who had already risen to the heavens, sent a letter down that said that Yehoram would suffer a tragic ending. Yehoram's family was ravaged by the Philistines. Of his immediate family, only he and his son Achazyah, remained alive. Eliyahu's prophecy came true and Yehoram fell seriously ill with an intestinal disease. When he died, he was not buried in the tomb of the other kings of the Davidic dynasty, as a result of his evil actions.

Yehoram was succeeded by his only son, Achazyah. The latter reigned only one year, and was killed along with the other children of Achav at the hands of Yehu. Queen Asalyah, who killed all of David's descendants except for one infant son, then continued to reign for six more years. Yoash, the only surviving infant son of Achazyah, was hidden by Yehoyada the *Kohen Gadol,* until the age of seven, when he was declared king. His grandmother, the wicked Asalyah, was overthrown and killed.

As long as Yehoyada the *Kohen Gadol* and great Torah leader was alive, Yoash was a righteous and God-fearing king. He strengthened Torah learning throughout the kingdom. He repaired the *Beis Ha-Mikdash.* He destroyed any remnants of idol worship throughout the land. However, when Yehoyada died, Yoash came under the influence of new advisors who led him astray. The prophet Zecharyah, son of Yehoyada the High Priest, publicly rebuked the king and his advisors for transgressing the laws of God. Yoash became so incensed at this public rebuke that he ordered his men to kill Zecharyah. Imagine! Zecharyah's father, Yehoyada, had saved Yoash's life and established him as king. Yet, Yoash ordered the cold-blooded murder of Zecharyah. He was killed in the courtyard of the *Beis Ha-Mikdash,* and on that spot his blood continued to bubble and to boil without cease until the conquest of Yerushalayim by Nevuchadnetzar. The fact that Zecharyah, a holy individual who was both a prophet and a priest, was killed in cold blood had tremendous repercussions later on for the Jewish people.

Punishment came quickly. The enemy defeated Yoash's army and brutally tortured him. Two of the king's servants then avenged the blood of Zecharyah and assassinated the king in his own bed. He, too, was not buried with the righteous kings of the House of David.

Yoash was succeeded by his son, Amatzyahu. At first, he acted righteously and God rewarded him with victory over his enemies, but Amatzyahu returned from battle bearing their idols. God turned Amatzyahu's victory into his own undoing. He was rendered so confident by his success that he challenged Yeho'ash, king of Yisrael, to battle. Yeho'ash defeated Amatzyahu in the war and then proceeded to plunder the *Beis Ha-Mikdash,* taking gold and silver. Although Amatzyahu was not killed by Yeho'ash, he had already lost the respect of the people because he brought back idol worship, and that caused his defeat.

When Elisha lay on his deathbed after being prophet for sixty years,

Yeho'ash wept, referring to him as his father. After Yeho'ash's death, his son Yarovam II became king and ruled for forty-one prosperous years over the kingdom of Yisrael. During his reign the prophets Hoshea, Amos and Yonah prophesied. The land enjoyed relative prosperity. Even when Hoshea foretold the evil that would befall Yarovam's household, the king did nothing to punish the prophet. Yarovam II was urged to kill him, but he responded, "What should I do, if God told him to say these words?"

After Yarovam, his son Zecharyah ruled for six months and was assassinated by Shallum, as prophesied by the prophet Amos. In turn, Shallum was assassinated by Menachem after ruling only one month. Menachem was succeeded by his son, Pekachyah, who was killed by Pekach. Pekach ruled for twenty years. However, his enemies got the upper hand and took over much of the land that was held by the kingdom of Yisrael. Hoshea slew Pekach and made himself king.

On the 15th day of Av, Hoshea removed the guards that blocked the roads leading to Yehudah. For the first time in two hundred years, it was possible to go up to the Sanctuary in Yerushalayim. However, it was too little, too late. Hoshea was unable to undo the evil of Yarovam ben Nevat.

Shalmaneser, king of Assyria, laid siege to the powerful city of Shomron, capital of the kingdom of Yisrael, for three years until it fell. He then took the ten tribes into exile, and they were dispersed among the nations of the world. In the kingdom of Yehudah there was great mourning for the ten tribes that were now lost (3205/556 B.C.E.).

There are various views concerning what ultimately happened to the ten tribes. Many nations of the world claim to be descended from those tribes. However, every one of those lost tribes has descendants among us.[10]

Yisrael waits for the day when a great shofar will sound and "there will come those who were lost in the land of Assyria and those who were cast away in the land of Egypt, and they will bow down to God on the holy mountain, at Yerushalayim," together with their brothers from Yehudah and Binyamin.

❦ *Key People, Places and Things*

BEIS HA-MIKDASH: the holy and majestic Temple, which was the resting place of the *Shechinah* (Divine Presence).

ELISHA HA-NAVI: a disciple of Eliyahu who performed wondrous miracles, especially during a period of drought and famine.

ELIYAHU HA-NAVI: Elijah, a great prophet who performed wondrous miracles. On Mount Karmel he publicly demonstrated the greatness of God and the falseness of the Ba'al.

HOSHEA: the last king of the kingdom of Yisrael. The king reopened the roads leading to Yerushalayim. However, it was too little, too late.

HOSHEA, AMOS AND OVADYAH: three of the Twelve Prophets (*Trei-Asar*) who prophesied during the period of the two kingdoms.

KING ACHAV AND QUEEN IZEVEL: the most evil rulers of the kingdom of Yisrael. They erected a temple to Ba'al and caused widespread idol worship. They killed the true prophets of Hashem. During their reign, God caused a terrible famine in the land.

KINGDOM OF YEHUDAH: the two tribes of Yehudah and Binyamin. When the nation of Yisrael split into two kingdoms, the kingdom of Yehudah remained faithful to the dynasty of David.

KINGDOM OF YISRAEL: the ten tribes that first seceded under the leadership of Yarovam. The history of this kingdom is filled with idol worship, turmoil, and assassinations. They were exiled from the land much earlier than the kingdom of Yehudah, and were dispersed among the nations of the world.

RECHAVAM: successor to Shelomo, who did not heed the warning of the elders, resulting in the secession of the ten tribes from his kingdom.

SHALMANESER: king of Assyria who conquered the kingdom of Yisrael and took the ten tribes into exile.

SHELOMO HA-MELECH: David's son and successor, who built the *Beis Ha-Mikdash*. He was renowned for his great wisdom and justice.

YAROVAM: the leader of the secession of the ten tribes from Rechavam's kingdom, and the establishment of the kingdom of Yisrael. He closed the roads leading to Yerushalayim, and set up golden calves for idol worship. He is one of those who has no share in the World to Come.

YONAH: Jonah, the prophet who tried to flee from his mission to prophesy at Ninveh. He was swallowed by a whale. He reluctantly went to Ninveh and exhorted them to repent, which they did. He was taught a valuable lesson by Hashem concerning the value of mercy.

ZECHARYAH: a priest and prophet who was killed in the courtyard of the Temple on the orders of King Yoash.

NOTES

1. *Vayikra* 22:32.

2. *Talmud Shabbos,* 56b.

3. *Mishlei* 11:14.

4. *Mishlei* 12:20.

5. *Devarim* 32:7.

6. *Talmud Makkos,* 24.

7. *Pirkei D'Rabbi Eliezer, perek* 17.

8. *Pirkei D'Rabbi Eliezer, perek* 16.

9. *Melachim II,* 5.

10. *Talmud Arachin,* 33.

❦ *Introduction to Chapter 17*

The kingdom of Yehudah, like its counterpart in the north, also suffered from the unstable rule of self-serving monarchs. In place of the Divine protection on which the Jewish nation had previously relied, it now became deeply dependent on idol worship and political power. A sequence of catastrophes which should have inspired the Jews to return to God instead allowed them to drift further away from Him.

It is remarkable that the northern kingdom disappeared first; it had been larger, stronger and richer. However, Yehudah, tied to the Temple and the House of David, had a closer attachment to the spiritual heritage of the Jewish people. Indeed, at the time of Yisrael's destruction, Yehudah was enjoying a period of unparalleled spiritual flourishing under King Chizkiyahu. Several generations later, however, it too faced destruction. Neither the labors of the pious King Yoshiyahu, nor the warnings of the Prophet Yirmeyahu succeeded in regenerating the kingdom. Forsaken by its allies, Yehudah soon found Yerushalayim besieged by the Babylonians. Yet, even at that moment, the prophets' plea to the people to repent was not hearkened to. Unrepentant, the populace led Yehudah to its doom.

The declining years of the kingdom of Yehudah were turbulent and bloody. They marked the end of a glorious period that had reached its greatest heights during the reigns of David and Shelomo. After an extended period of time, the walls of Yerushalayim were breached. Many thousands of the inhabitants were slaughtered, and the *Beis Ha-Mikdash* was set afire. Thousands were exiled to Babylonia. Nevuchadnetzar, ruler of Babylonia, eventually appointed Gedalyah as the governor over the remaining inhabitants. After he was assassinated, the remnant of the Jews lost hope and fled to Egypt.

Out of that struggle and tragedy there has come to us the story of the prophets, those men of God who constantly reminded the Jewish people of their mission. It was they who once again exemplified those moral standards which put Judaism above both country and ruler. The ideals taken from the deepest sources of God's teachings and put into words by prophets like Amos, Michah, Yirmeyahu and Yeshayahu became the watchwords of the nation, as it struggled onward. They became the eternal possession of the people, to comfort them through long centuries of oppression and suffering.

CHAPTER 17

Beginning of the Fall of Yerushalayim and the Destruction of the Beis Ha-Mikdash
(3115 - 3338/646 B.C.E.-423 B.C.E.)

❦ HISTORY

THE RULE OF THE KINGDOM OF YEHUDAH CONTINUES

After the death of Amatzyah (3115/646 B.C.E.), his son Uzziyah ascended to the throne of the kingdom of Yehudah. During this period, the great prophets Hoshea, Amos, and Yeshayahu were active. They demanded the fulfillment of all the laws of the Torah, and reprimanded those who strayed.

Uzziyah reigned for fifty-two years and was a righteous man in every respect. Once, however, he became proud and wanted to imitate the gentile monarchs who personally officiated in their temples. He sincerely intended to show honor for the worship of God. He maintained that even though he was not from the priestly family of *Kohanim*, he still held a special status because he was from royalty. He thus rationalized his right to bring incense at the *Beis Ha-Mikdash*.

Azaryah the *Kohen* risked his life by ordering Uzziyah out of the Sanctuary. When Uzziyah heard the *Kohen*'s bold words, he turned in anger toward the *Kohanim*. Suddenly the mark of leprosy appeared on his forehead. He realized that God had stricken him. He rushed out of the Temple and out of the city, where he remained secluded until his death.

Yosam, son of Uzziyah (3167/594 B.C.E.), became king and reigned righteously for sixteen years. Because of the tragedy that had befallen his father in the Sanctuary, Yosam refrained from going there. This caused his descendants and his people to become estranged from the Sanctuary, and resulted in serious repercussions for his son, Achaz.

When Yosam was succeeded by his twenty-year-old son Achaz (3183/578 B.C.E.), the latter showed his disdain for the Temple by bringing back idolatry. He and his people were punished by God when the king of Aram (Syria) inflicted heavy losses upon them. To free himself from the king of Aram, he sent many treasures to the king of Assyria to induce him to help them. Achaz continued his evil ways, and during his reign, Yehudah sank to the lowest spiritual level in its history. He died an early death and was not buried with the other kings of Yehudah.

THE REIGN OF THE RIGHTEOUS AND PIOUS KING CHIZKIYAHU (3199/562 B.C.E.)

Chizkiyahu led the people in destroying all the altars and shrines of idolatry in the land. He invited the ten tribes to participate with him at the *Beis Ha-Mikdash* on Pesach. Most of them were too far estranged to heed his call. However, there were those who did respond to Chizkiyahu's invitation, and were eventually saved from being dispersed among the nations of the world when the ten tribes were sent into exile.

Chizkiyahu made sure to enforce the bringing of *terumos* and *ma'asros* for the *Kohanim* and *Leviyim*, for this would free them to become strong in the learning of Torah. Chizkiyahu was also very forceful in getting the populace to devote themselves wholeheartedly to the learning of Torah.

THE MIRACULOUS DEFEAT OF SANCHERIV

In the fourteenth year of Chizkiyahu's reign, Sancheriv, king of Assyria, set siege to Yerushalayim. This was eight years after the ten tribes were exiled. All neighboring kings and princes feared him, and even Chizkiyahu paid tribute to him until his treasury was empty. Then he claimed bankruptcy. This excuse was not adequate enough for Sancheriv, who mobilized his army for an invasion of Yehudah. Never before had the world seen such a mighty army — 45,000 gold and silver chariots and over half a million trained swordsmen. When they crossed the Jordan River, there was no water left, for the horses had drunk it all. With this large and mighty army, he easily captured all the fortified cities in Yehudah until he came to Yerushalayim.

At this point, Sancheriv boasted, "I could raze this city to the ground with only a few of my legions." Although his men were eager to fight, Sancheriv told them to rest from their weary journey. In the morning he commanded them, "Let every warrior bring me but one brick from the walls of the city." Sancheriv believed that if he destroyed Yerushalayim and the Temple, he would destroy God's power.

Up stood Ravshakeh, his leading general, who called out to the defenders of the city to surrender. "Do not let Chizkiyahu deceive you into thinking that God will save you." On and on Ravshakeh ranted arrogantly, finally demanding that the defenders revolt against Chizkiyahu and surrender the city.

When news of this reached Chizkiyahu, he went to the *Beis Ha-Mikdash* to pray to God. He also ordered all his people to observe a day of solemn prayer, for victory lay only in God's hands. Almost all remained loyal to the king, except for the traitor, Shevna the Scribe. He decided to make peace with the enemy at any cost. In the middle of the night, he led his men to the gates of the city and forced his way out. Suddenly the gates swung closed, and he found himself alone. When he was brought before Sancheriv, the king was furious. "Have you come to mock me? Where are your followers? I'll teach you, you deceitful traitor." Shevna was immediately put to a horrible death.

It was the first night of Pesach in Yerushalayim, but the holiday spirit was gone. All the Jews prayed to God for deliverance. Soon after their prayers, the Prophet Yeshayahu appeared before the king and brought God's message to him. It was a message of comfort and hope, of victory and triumph.

"God has heard your prayers. No enemy shall come into this city. God Himself will defend and save this city."

When midnight came, the Angel of Death smote thousands upon thousands in the Assyrian camp. When Sancheriv rose up early in the morning to storm the city of Yerushalayim, he found thousands of corpses in place of his mighty army.

In the land of Yehudah, the Festival of Pesach was an occasion for double rejoicing, both for the people of Yerushalayim and their King Chizkiyahu. It was as though the miracles of God which had saved and delivered their forefathers from Egypt many years before had been repeated again.

LESSON I

The Death of Sancheriv and God's Punishment of the Wicked

The commentaries state that Sancheriv was spared death along with his army in order to suffer disgrace in the wake of his return to Ninveh after his defeat. He remained in Ninveh, never again to go out to battle. He did not even rate a hero's death on the battlefield with the rest of his army. Sancheriv asked his wise men what merit the Jews had that God saved them from sure defeat, and instead destroyed his camp. They replied that the Jews had many merits in their favor, especially those from their Patriarchs. The Patriarch Avraham had passed all of the

Almighty's tests, even the most difficult, when he had been called upon to sacrifice his son.

When Sancheriv heard this he replied, "If this is so, then I will offer my two sons to my god." When his sons heard this, they slew him while he was prostrating himself before his god. This harsh punishment of Sancheriv was a result of the fact that he believed in his own strength and thought that he could be victorious over Hashem.

At the time of the Egyptian enslavement of the Jews, Paroh also thought that he could be victorious over Hashem. Paroh lived to see the destruction of his entire army in the Red Sea. Only Paroh remained alive so that he could relate God's miracles that he had personally witnessed.

The wicked Roman Emperor Titus, who destroyed the Second *Beis Ha-Mikdash*, also thought that by doing so, he had defeated the God of the Jews. The Almighty punished him with one of the smallest creatures in creation; a gnat flew up his nostril into his brain, where it buzzed and drove him mad.

LESSON II

King Chizkiyahu's Greatness

Among the kings of Yisrael, Chizkiyahu is considered second only to David in greatness and righteousness. To understand the great spiritual level of the people during Chizkiyahu's reign, the Talmud[1] gives us an insight into the very high level of Torah learning at that time. It states that in his day, there was neither man nor woman, neither a young boy nor young girl to be found in all the borders of Yisrael who was ignorant of Torah law or who was not thoroughly versed in the laws of purity and impurity. It is also interesting to note that the outstanding Torah scholars of his day were known as the *Anshei Chizkiyahu* (Men of Chizkiyahu) because Chizkiyahu had encouraged them to learn Torah.

King Chizkiyahu made one crucial mistake: He neglected to sing *shirah* and praise Hashem after the great miracle that Hashem performed for the Jews. They had been on the brink of a major disaster when Hashem performed His miracles to destroy the enemy. Had King Chizkiyahu not been remiss in singing *shirah* and thanking Hashem, he would have become the *Melech Ha-Mashiach* and his generation would have ushered in the Messianic era.

King Chizkiyahu was known as a prince of peace, and carried his people to great spiritual heights. He was beloved by the prophets, and was considered worthy to be the final *Mashiach*. As the *Tanach* describes him, "He did what was righteous in the eyes of God, according to all that his father [ancestor] David did...He trusted in Hashem...There was none like him among all the kings of Yehudah...and he kept His commandments as God commanded Moshe."

❦ HISTORY

CHIZKIYAHU'S CRITICAL ILLNESS

King Chizkiyahu became deathly ill and was visited by the Prophet Yeshayahu (Isaiah), who informed him of his impending death. The reason for God's anger at Chizkiyahu was his failure to marry and have children. Although he was preoccupied with his kingdom and his service of Hashem, he was not exempt from the important mitzvah of having children.

Through *ruach ha-kodesh* (Divine revelation) Chizkiyahu foresaw in the future that he would have a very wicked son. To forestall this from happening, Chizkiyahu did not marry. God considered this a sin, and punished him with severe illness.

The Prophet Yeshayahu then told him, "Why do you meddle in God's mysteries? You must do what you are commanded to do, and the Holy One, blessed be He, will do what pleases Him." Ultimately, Chizkiyahu married the daughter of the prophet Yeshayahu.[2]

LESSON III

The Power of Prayer

Chizkiyahu, the pious and great king, prayed devoutly to Hashem to spare his life. He prayed from the bottom of his heart with great sincerity, and reminded Hashem of the merits of his great ancestors. Hashem listened to his prayers and promised that he would live fifteen additional years.

From Chizkiyahu's behavior, we learn how important and how potent are the powers of prayer. Even in a case where death had already been decreed, the power of prayer was able to save Chizkiyahu's life.

Prayer is the worshiper's appeal to God to judge him with mercy and compassion. As the Talmud[3] states, "Even if a sharp sword rests on a man's neck, he should not cease praying." When a person prays, he must pray sincerely and must picture himself as if God is in front of him.[4]

God said to the Jews,[5] "Be careful with prayer, since it is greater than sacrifices. Even if a person is not otherwise worthy of being answered, if he prays sincerely, God will be kind to him."

ETHICS I

The Consequences of Being Proud and Catering to the Gentiles

All the great miracles that happened to Chizkiyahu earned great prestige for his kingdom. Emissaries came from far and wide bearing gifts. Chizkiyahu was especially pleased by letters and gifts brought to him from the king of Babylonia. He received the Babylonian emissaries very warmly and showed them everything in the land, including the sacred objects. The *Tanach* records that Chizkiyahu displayed pride in showing off his kingdom and his great wealth. God's wrath at Chizkiyahu was expressed by the Prophet Yeshayahu: "'Behold, days will come when everything in your house and all which your fathers gathered up to this day will be carried off to Babylonia; not a thing shall remain,' said God. 'And from your sons who shall come out of you, whom you shall beget (this was before he had children) he shall take, and they shall be servants in the palace of the king of Babylonia.'"[6]

The pious King Chizkiyahu had acted out of his desire to gain the friendship of Babylonia in order to counteract the power of mighty Assyria. But for this, he was severely criticized by God. It was also an unnecessary closeness (as God saw it) to the gentiles. He did not realize that by catering to the gentiles, he would eventually cause his descendants to be enslaved by them.

Shelomo Ha-Melech put a tiny ant in his palm and asked, "Is there anyone in the world greater than I?"

The ant replied, "Yes, I am greater, since Hashem sent you to carry me."

The great Hillel said, "Do not be too sure of yourself until the day you die."

❦ HISTORY

THE PROPHET YESHAYAHU

It was during the reign of Chizkiyahu that the great Prophet Yeshayahu prophesied. He reprimanded the nation and urged them to do penance. He rebuked the people who deceived themselves into thinking that sacrifice and prayers could free them from punishment for sins for which they had not repented. Yeshayahu foretold the destruction of Yerushalayim. He also spoke about the *Mashiach* and *techiyas ha-mesim* (when the dead will be resurrected).

Yeshayahu is referred to by the Sages as the greatest of all prophets, second only to Moshe *Rabbenu*. He wrote prophecies of good tidings and consolation for Yisrael. Yeshayahu was of royal descent, a nephew of King Amatzyah. He lived for one hundred and twenty years, spanning the rule of four kings of Yehudah, the last being Chizkiyahu.

THE EVIL MENASHE

Chizkiyahu was succeeded by his son Menashe (3228/533 B.C.E.). The latter was only twelve years old when he assumed the throne. Consequently, he came under the evil influence of the wrong kind of advisors. Unlike his pious and righteous father, Menashe introduced all manner of idol worship and pagan sacrifice. He even went so far as to place an idol in the Temple. He imitated the abominations of the Kena'anites. He shed the blood of pious men who opposed him until he filled Yerushalayim from one end to the other with blood. Among those who were slaughtered was his own grandfather, the saintly prophet Yeshayahu.

In response to Menashe's wickedness, God informed His prophets that He would bring terrible punishment upon the nation and upon Yerushalayim. The period of his wickedness was so destructive that the fate of Yerushalayim was sealed. The land was to be laid waste and the Temple destroyed because of "the anger which Menashe had angered Him." Menashe eventually received his just retribution. He was captured by the king of Assyria and brought to Babylonia in chains. He was put into a copper vessel, and just as they were about to kindle the fire beneath it, he began to cry out and to pray to all of his gods. When he saw that no help was forthcoming, he returned wholeheartedly to the Lord, God of his fathers. He cried out in complete sincerity, and Hashem heard his prayers and he was saved. Menashe was succeeded by his son Amon, whose wickedness exceeded that of his father. After two years, he was slain.

LESSON IV
The Seeds of Destruction Cannot Be Removed

Menashe repented and removed the idols and altars that he had previously erected. Although he repented, he did not succeed in eradicating the evil that he had brought into existence. The darkness which Menashe cast over Yerushalayim would not lift for the fifty-five years of his reign. Although he personally repented, the actions and deeds that he had implanted in the Jewish nation could not and would not be eradicated, and were the cause of the eventual destruction of the Temple.

Many times an individual can affect the general populace. Whether he be a leader, writer, or scholar, his actions will leave an imprint that will be hard to erase. There have been times when an author has written books about Jews and Judaism which sowed a negative feeling toward Judaism in the minds of the readers. Although later the author regretted his action and felt remorse over what he had written, he could not alter the impact of what he had aready done. This also applies to actions of Jewish leaders who take it upon themselves to do things which are detrimental to the Jewish nation and religion. It is very difficult for them to rescind the action.

A man once came to his rabbi to beg forgiveness for the terrible lies he had spread about him. He asked the rabbi what he could do to correct his misdeeds. The rabbi responded, "Take this pillow, open it up, and shake it outside. Then come back to me."

The man did as instructed and came back for further instructions. The rabbi then told him, "Now go outside and gather together all the feathers that flew out of the pillow."

"But Rabbi, that's impossible! You can't gather up feathers flying in the air."

"That's right, my son," said the rabbi. "Similarly, it is impossible to undo the evil that has already been done by your malicious words."

Even if this person's *teshuvah* was sincere, and it was accepted by God, the damage done was irreparable. Just as *teshuvah* could not undo the damage this person did, *teshuvah* could not eradicate the harm Menashe did.

❦ HISTORY

THE RIGHTEOUS YOSHIYAHU (3285/476 B.C.E.)

Only eight years old when he assumed the throne, Yoshiyahu was a righteous person who unswervingly followed the ways of his ancestor, David Ha-Melech. Just as a flame flickers most brightly right before it dies out, hope shone once more in Yerushalayim. Yoshiyahu rejected the evil and idol worship that had been introduced by his father and grandfather. With great enthusiasm, he set about to cleanse the land of the idolatrous filth with which it had been filled. His first major project was to repair the Temple.

Chilkiyahu the High Priest found a Torah scroll in the Temple and had it read to the king. The scroll was opened to that part in the Bible warning of the destruction that would befall Yisrael as a consequence of its straying from the righteous path. King Yoshiyahu heard the contents of the scroll and interpreted it as meaning that he and his people would be sorely punished for the idolatry that was rampant in the land. He dispatched officials throughout the land to seek out and destroy all remnants of idol worship. Despite Yoshiyahu's actions, God was unwilling to annul the decree against the Jewish people. Yoshiyahu was killed in the battle against Paroh Nechoh of Egypt. His life was extinguished at age thirty-nine, before his mission was completed.

THE EVIL THAT WAS RAMPANT PRIOR TO THE DESTRUCTION

Yoshiyahu was succeeded by his son Yehoachaz, who followed in the footsteps of his grandfathers, Amon and Menashe. After ruling three months, Paroh Nechoh replaced Yehoachaz with Yehoyakim, another son of Yoshiyahu.

Yehoyakim, too, was evil. He ruled for eleven turbulent years, during which time there was an ongoing power struggle between Nevuchadnetzar, king of Babylonia, and Egypt. Yehoyakim eventually died after having been taken captive to Babylonia. Yehoyakim actively sought to antagonize God, declaring that he was so self-sufficient that he had no need of the Creator. God sent the great Prophet Yirmeyahu to warn the Jews to repent and save their kingdom.

The text of the Book of Lamentations (*Eichah*) was revealed to the Prophet Yirmeyahu (Jeremiah) by God (3327/434 B.C.E.). It prophesied the impending destruction that was to befall the Jewish nation. When Yehoyakim and his advisors listened to the reading, the king rose up and tore the scroll from the hand of the reader, slashed it with a blade, and threw it into a fire. Thus, they destroyed Yisrael's last chance to do *teshuvah* and be saved.

Yehoyakim was succeeded by his son, Yehoyachin. He, too, was evil and God punished him by having him taken captive to Babylonia. While suffering there in a dungeon, Yehoyachin did complete *teshuvah* and returned to Hashem.

At the time that Yehoyachin was taken to Babylonia, many prominent Jewish leaders and scholars were taken there as well. Among them were the Prophet Yechezkel (Ezekiel), Daniyel, and Mordechai — future leaders of the Jewish people. Unknown to the Jews, God was already paving the way for the Jewish people to survive in exile, out of the land of Yisrael.

Nevuchadnetzar appointed Tzidkiyahu, son of Yoshiyahu, as the new king (3327/434 B.C.E.). Although Tzidkiyahu was generally a righteous and pious person, he was not strong enough to oppose the evil men who were in power. God called him 'a wicked prince of Yisrael.' He was unwilling to take a courageous stand against the evil which permeated the kingdom. He was, therefore, held responsible for the evil during his reign.

Tzidkiyahu broke his vow to Nevuchadnetzar, king of Babylonia, when he secretly entered into an alliance with Egypt. He did not listen to the Prophet Yirmeyahu, who warned him not to rebel against Nevuchadnetzar. On the tenth day of *Teves*, Nevuchadnetzar's army laid siege to Yerushalayim. Tzidkiyahu begged Yirmeyahu to pray for him. The prophet responded that the fate of Yerushalayim was sealed. Those who would not submit to the Babylonians would be slain. Tzidkiyahu refused to surrender, and paid no attention to Yirmeyahu's advice.

Yirmeyahu's repeated predictions of the fall of Yerushalayim and his pleas for surrender aroused the anger of some of the evil officers of the king. They had him thrown into a pit from which he was ultimately saved. Yirmeyahu continued to warn the people to repent to avoid the impending destruction, but his call went unheeded.

In the eleventh year of Tzidkiyahu's reign (3338/423 B.C.E.), during the month of *Tamuz*, the walls of Yerushalayim were broken through by the enemy. Despite a mutual assistance pact between Yisrael and Egypt, no help ever came from Egypt for the beleaguered Jewish nation.

King Tzidkiyahu fled through a secret tunnel, but was captured and brought to Nevuchadnetzar. There, the king's children were slain before his very eyes, and then his own eyes were put out. Thus was fulfilled the prophecy of Yechezkel, who resided in Babylonia and had predicted that King Tzidkiyahu would be carried off to Babylonia but would never see it.

Shortly before the destruction, Yirmeyahu was called away from Yerushalayim. On the seventh day of *Av*, Nevuzaradan, chief of Nevuchadnetzar's army, led the destruction of the city. At first, Nevuzaradan did not believe that he would be able to destroy the holy city and the Jewish people. However, there were certain signs from Hashem that these were inevitable. Nevuzaradan shot arrows in different directions, but each ended up in the direction of Yerushalayim. Also, Nevuzaradan measured the walls of the city every day, and noticed that they were gradually sinking lower into the ground. This, too, was a sign from the Almighty that the destruction was imminent.

LESSON V

Recognizing the Hand of Hashem

The wicked Nevuzaradan, who caused so much death and destruction in Yisrael, was still clever enough to realize that his successes were due to the fact that the God of Yisrael had turned His protection away from His people. He then reasoned that if God punished His own people so severely, how much more so would He be likely to punish someone like Nevu- zaradan for all the suffering and destruction that he caused to the Jewish people.[7] Nevuzaradan ran away from his great position of power and wealth, sincerely repented, and converted to Judaism.

Imagine! A gentile who was victorious in his battles was still able to perceive that it was not his own victory, but rather that God was punishing His people.

❦ HISTORY

THE DESTRUCTION OF YERUSHALAYIM (3338/423 B.C.E.)

The enemy looted all the gold, silver, and holy vessels in the *Beis Ha-Mikdash.* On the ninth day of *Av* the enemy set fire to the *Beis Ha-Mikdash,* and it continued burning on the tenth day as well. The *Kohanim* were either slain or threw themselves into the fire. Those who escaped the sword were led into captivity to Babylonia. When Yirmeyahu saw the fire raging, he rushed back to Yerushalayim. He sought to join his sorrowful brethren who were being led away in chains. Nevuchad-netzar had commanded his officers to take off Yirmeyahu's chains, and to allow him to choose between remaining in Yisrael or going to Babylonia as an honored guest.

Yirmeyahu asked Hashem what to do. Hashem told him that if he would go to Babylonia, then the Almighty would stay with the remaining Jews in Yisrael, or vice versa. Yirmeyahu agreed that it was best that the *Shechinah* (Divine Presence) go into exile with the Jews in Babylonia, and Yirmeyahu stayed with the small Jewish community that remained in the Holy Land.

THE PROPHET YIRMEYAHU

The prophet Yirmeyahu prophesied from the year 3298 to the year 3338. He spanned a period of four decades from King Yoshiyahu until the destruction of the First Temple. He was a great prophet who lived during the most crucial period of the existence of the Jewish kingdom. He forewarned the people of the coming destruction of Yerushalayim, and admonished them to repent before it was too late.

Unfortunately, the people did not heed his warning. He witnessed the destruction of Yerushalayim and the holy Temple. When the catastrophe finally overwhelmed his people, he wanted to go along with them into exile. He bitterly lamented Yisrael's terrible fate in *Eichah* (the Book of Lamentations) which is read on *Tishah B'Av.* It was Yirmeyahu's perfect faith in Hashem and in the ultimate redemption that elevated him from despair and infused him with hope and vitality so that he could still assist the rest of the nation. He thereby helped his stricken people to bear the blow with courage and dignity by pointing out to them the path that would lead to restoration and redemption.

Reasons for the Destruction

Yerushalayim and the *Beis Ha-Mikdash* were destroyed because of the three cardinal sins — idolatry, immorality, and murder. The Sages[8] tell us that Yisrael worshiped idols only as a means of permitting public immorality. Worshiping idols gave the people a rationale for a new morality. The Jewish religion imposes high standards of moral behavior. Idolatry condones immorality, and so it flourished. When righteous people tried to stop them, the idolators even resorted to murder. These three cardinal sins weakened the holiness and special status of the Jewish people. This drove the Divine Presence from the Holy Land and resulted in the destruction of the Temple and the exile of the Jewish people.

❦ HISTORY

THE REMAINING JEWISH COMMUNITY IN YISRAEL

Following the exile of the majority of the Jewish nation to Babylonia, only a small number of Jews from the poorest residents of Yerushalayim were permitted to remain. Nevuchadnetzar chose a righteous man by the name of Gedalyah to be the provisional governor over the surviving community.

Gedalyah was close to the Prophet Yirmeyahu and offered a ray of hope for the possibility of rebuilding the Temple. Under this pious ruler, the poor and the ignorant who had remained in the Land of Yisrael were now offered the opportunity of rebuilding, through repentance and good deeds, from the ruins of the nation.

Out of hostility toward Gedalyah and because of personal envy, Yishma'el ben Nesanyah planned to slay Gedalyah. When the governor was warned of the plot against him, his misplaced piety prevented him from believing this evil report. Since he did not listen to the warnings and advice, he was eventually slain. The Fast of Gedalyah, which is the day after Rosh Hashanah, is mentioned together with the fast days for the destruction of the Temple to teach us that the death of a truly righteous person is as important as the burning of the *Beis Ha-Mikdash.*[9]

Following the assassination of Gedalyah, the people fled to Egypt, for they feared the wrath of the king of Babylonia who had appointed Gedalyah as governor. Yirmeyahu warned them not to leave the land, but they did not listen to his warning. Eventually they perished as foreigners in Egypt.

The bad fortune of the Jews who were exiled to Babylonia was lessened because they were led by the great prophet Yechezkel (Ezekiel). He was born in Yerushalayim to a preistly family, and was exiled to Babylonia with the first group of exiles prior to the destruction of the *Beis Ha-Mikdash*. He first prophesied about the destruction of the Temple, and afterwards prophesied that Yisrael would be revived with new life and glory, and that a new Temple would flourish. Yechezkel encouraged the people to repent and inspired them to elevate their spiritual level.

Yechezkel came to his people as a strong preacher who admonished the nation to keep the mitzvos of the Torah or face dire consequences. When Yerushalayim was captured and destroyed, Yechezkel became a consoling father, bringing courage and hope to his people. He foretold the enemy's doom and assured the nation that they would survive all their enemies. He prophesied that the breach between the king of Yehudah and the Ten Tribes would be healed. There would be one united nation restored to its land. Under Yechezkel's influence, the exiles built synagogues and houses of learning. He led his people for twenty-two years. His prophecies are recorded in the *Tanach* in the Book of Yechezkel.

MITZVAH

Fast Days and Tishah B'Av

There are four days which remind us of the sins of our ancestors that led to the destruction of the Temple and loss of the Land of Yisrael. The destruction of the Temple (the center of religious life) was a disaster which resulted in the exile of the Jews among the nations. The history of the Jewish people is a chain of alternating periods of subjection and liberation. Just as we celebrate the liberations, so, too, we remind ourselves of the tragedies that have befallen the Jewish people. The manner in which the Jews remind themselves of these tragedies is through proclaimed days of fasting. On these days, we not only fast, but also meditate on the wrongdoings that caused these destructions and resolve to improve our ways.[10]

I. ASARAH B'TEVES (Tenth Day of *Teves*)

This fast day commemorates the beginning of the siege of Yerushalayim by Nevuchadnetzar, when the city was completely surrounded. This siege eventually led to the destruction of the First Temple.

II. SHIVAH ASAR B'TAMUZ (17th Day of *Tamuz*)

This day commemorates five sorrowful events in the history of the Jewish people:

1) On this day, Moshe descended from Mount Sinai, saw the Golden Calf, and then broke the Tablets of the Law.

2) The daily sacrifice in the Temple, known as the *korban tamid*, was abolished on this day.

3) Apostomus the Wicked burned the Torah on this day.

4) Menashe, the wicked King of Yehudah, placed an idol in the Temple.

5) The walls of the city of Yerushalayim were breached on this day by the enemy, which led to the destruction of both the First and the Second Temples.

III. TISHAH B'AV (Ninth Day of Av)

1-2) Tishah B'Av is the saddest day of the Jewish year, for it commemorates the destruction of both the First and Second Temples.

3) On Tishah B'Av it was decreed that the Jews would not go directly into the Land of Yisrael, but would travel for forty years in the wilderness. That was the night the spies returned to give Moshe a highly critical report of Yisrael, and the Jews cried without good cause. God then decreed that years later they would have reason to cry on that night.

4) The Temple Mount was plowed under by the Romans.

5) On this day, Beitar, the last stronghold in Yisrael after the destruction of the Second Temple, was captured and destroyed by the Romans. The sadness at this time was nearly comparable to that when the Temple was actually destroyed, because so many thousands of Jews were killed. To compound the terrible tragedy, the Romans denied burial to the Jews slain in Beitar. Miraculously, the bodies did not decay during the long time that they remained unburied.

The reason why we fast is not merely to inflict hardships upon ourselves, but rather to awaken our thoughts to repentance. Those who have no intention of improving themselves are not accomplishing much with their *ta'anis* (fast). The Mishnah states that the reason for a fast is to confess our sins, analyze our deeds, and improve our ways.

THE LAWS OF TISHAH B'AV

The three weeks between the fast of the Seventeenth of *Tamuz* and Tishah B'Av are a period during which certain laws of mourning are observed. Among the things prohibited during this time are: getting a haircut, celebrating weddings or other social parties, playing or dancing to music, and wearing or buying outer clothing that is brand new, such as an overcoat or suit.

The period from *Rosh Chodesh Av* starts the Nine Days which is a time of intensified mourning. If possible, court cases should be delayed. We refrain from swimming, from eating meat and drinking wine, and we don't wash or launder clothing (except for small children's clothing).

At the approach of sunset on the eve of Tishah B'Av, one should sit on the floor while eating the "final meal." It should consist of a piece of bread and a cooked item — usually a hard-boiled egg — dipped in ashes.

The same prohibitions that apply to Yom Kippur in terms of abstinence, apply to Tishah B'Av as well (fasting, washing, anointing, marital relations and wearing leather shoes).

Since it is a period of mourning, we do not greet one another on Tishah B'Av until midday. We sit on low stools. We do not even learn Torah (except those sections dealing with sorrow and telling about the destruction of the Temple) until midday. It is a very solemn day and we abstain from frivolity and jest.

IV. TZOM GEDALYAH (Third Day of Tishrei)

As mentioned above, Tzom Gedalyah commemorates the death of Gedalyah, governor of the remaining Jewish community in Yisrael. Following his murder, those Jews fled to Egypt, and the last hope of rebuilding the Temple and the Holy Land died out until many years later. This fast takes place on the day following Rosh Hashanah.

ETHICS II

Hatred: One of the Main Causes of the Destruction of the Second Temple

One of the causes of the destruction of the Second Temple was bitter hatred and animosity that one Jew showed for another.[11] Therefore, on Tishah B'Av Jews should seek peace and forgiveness from one another.

A rabbi was once visiting a certain town, and on Tishah B'Av he was informed of a bitter feud between two groups. He was asked to mediate between them.

"We assume, however, that you will not want to hear the two sides until tomorros, since it is a fast day," they told him.

"On the contrary," responded the rabbi, "The destruction of the Temple was caused by unwarranted hatred of one Jew for another. What is more appropriate than trying to promote peace and brotherhood on this very day?"

LESSON VII

Why Must We Always Remember the Destruction of Yerushalayim and the Beis Ha-Mikdash?

The dispersed Jews do not forget their homeland and remain ever loyal to it. As King David stated in his Psalms, "If I forget you, O Yerushalayim, let my right hand forget its cunning..."[12]

The Emperor Napoleon was once riding through a town of one of the countries he had conquered, and passed a synagogue. As he approached the shul, he became aware of much crying and wailing coming from within, and sent one of his officers to investigate.

The officer came back with the rabbi of the synagogue, who explained: "Almost two thousand years ago on this day, our Holy Land was conquered and our Temple was burned. Every year we spend this anniversary in deep mourning and prayer that we may return very soon."

Napoleon was amazed. "Almost two thousand years, and still you remember and pray! What a strong spirited people you are. You, who do not forget, will surely return to your land, for you have an unconquerable spirit!"

The Prophet Yeshayahu said:[13] "Rejoice with Yerushalayim and be glad with her, all of you who love her; rejoice with her with great rejoicing, all of you who mourn for her." This means that those who truly mourn our Temple, especially during the three weeks, and forego all pleasure and entertainment in memory of Yerushalayim, will be privileged in due time to rejoice in the rebuilding of Yerushalayim and the Temple. But why does the prophet say "Rejoice with great rejoicing"?

The Dubno Maggid explained this in the form of a parable:

A man embarked on a long sea voyage. After a few months, reports reached his home town that his ship had met with an accident and that he had drowned. His family grieved deeply for him; his friends were sorrowful. As time went on, however, the memory of the man dimmed in their hearts. But though the months passed, his immediate family never stopped mourning for him.

Then one day, the door of the man's house opened. There stood the man whom they had thought was dead, very much alive! The good news quickly spread through the town. Soon the house was crowded with friends who were happy to hear that he had returned safely. Those who were only acquainted with him were pleased for him and his family. But his intimate friends, who had felt genuine sorrow when he had been presumed dead, were more than pleased; they were overjoyed that their friend was still alive. His family members, of course, were beside themselves with happiness. Those who had mourned the most for him were the happiest now that he had returned.

The same is true of our own mourning for Yerushalayim and the *Beis Ha-Mikdash* and the happiness that will be ours when they will be rebuilt. The degree of our rejoicing will be directly proportional to the degree of our mourning. Those who genuinely mourned for Yerushalayim will indeed rejoice "with great rejoicing" at its rebuilding.

NOTES

1. *Talmud Sanhedrin*, 94b.
2. *Talmud Berachos*, 10.
3. Ibid.
4. *Talmud Sanhedrin*, 22.
5. *Talmud Berachos*, 32.
6. *Melachim* II, 20:16-18.
7. *Talmud Gittin*, 26.
8. *Talmud Sanhedrin*, 63.
9. *Talmud Rosh Hashanah*, 18b.
10. Rambam, *Mishneh Torah, Hilchos Ta'anis*, 1:2.
11. *Talmud Yoma*, 9.
12. *Tehillim* 137:5-6.
13. *Yeshayahu* 66:10.

❦ Key People, Places and Things

CHIZKIYAHU: a righteous king who wiped out idolatry and raised the spiritual level of the Jews.

GEDALYAH: the governor over the remaining Jewish community in Eretz Yisrael, following the destruction of the Temple. After his assassination, the Jews fled to Egypt, and the land remained desolate for seventy years.

MENASHE: Chizkiyahu's son, who was most wicked and brought idolatry into the land. He murdered all the righteous people who opposed him. His malevolent rule planted the seeds for the destruction of the Temple. Some are of the opinion that he did personal *teshuvah.*

NEVUCHADNETZAR: the ruler of Babylonia who destroyed the first *Beis Ha-Mikdash.*

NEVUZARADAN: Nevuchadnetzar's general, who carried out the destruction.

YECHEZKEL: Ezekiel, the prophet who headed the exiled community in Babylonia and prophesied about the future days of *Mashiach* (the Messiah).

YEHOYACHIN: a king who reigned for only three months. He was taken into captivity in Babylonia along with most of the prominent Jewish leaders and scholars.

YEHOYAKIM: a king who brought back evil and idolatry to the land.

YESHAYAHU: Isaiah, a great prophet who lived one hundred and twenty years, from the reign of Uziyah till Menashe. He prophesied about the future redemption of the Jewish People.

YIRMEYAHU: Jeremiah, the great prophet who exhorted the people to repent, and warned them of the destruction of the Temple and the impending doom.

YOSHIYAHU: a righteous king who tried to undo the evil of his father's and grandfather's reigns.

❧ *Glossary*

The following glossary provides a partial explanation of some of the Hebrew, Yiddish (Y.), and Aramaic (A.) words and phrases used in this book. The spellings and explanations reflect the way the specific word is used herein. Often, there are alternate spellings and meanings for the words.

AFIKOMAN: part of the middle matzah, eaten at the close of the Passover Seder.

AKDAMUS: an Aramaic liturgical poem which praises God, recited on Shavuos.

AKEDAH: the Biblical account of Avraham's willingness to offer his son to God, and Yitzchak's willingness to be sacrificed.

AL NETILAS YADAYIM: the blessing recited upon washing the hands.

AL SEFIRAS HA-OMER: the blessing recited before the counting of the Omer.

ALIYAH: lit., "ascent"; being called up to the Torah.

AM KADOSH: a holy nation (the Jewish Nation).

AM SEGULAH: a chosen nation (the Jewish Nation).

ANSHEI KNESSES HA-GEDOLAH: the Men of the Great Assembly.

ARAVOS: willow branches, one of the Four Species used on Sukkos.

ARBA KOSOS: the four cups of wine served at the Passover Seder.

ARBA KUSHYOS: (A.) the Four Questions traditionally asked by the youngest child at the Passover Seder.

ARBA'AH MINIM: the Four Species used on Sukkos.

AREI MIKLAT: the six "cities of refuge" in ancient Israel designated for those who had killed another.

ARON: the holy ark in which the Torah was kept.

ASARAH B'TEVES: the tenth of Teves, a fast day.

ASHERAH: a tree utilized for idol worship in ancient times.

ASHREI: the opening word of the psalm which is recited daily in our prayers.

ASSERES HA-DIBROS: the Ten Commandments.

ASSERES YEMAI HA-TESHUVAH: the Ten Days of Repentance between Rosh Hashanah and Yom Kippur.

AVERAH GORERES AVERAH: one sin prompts another.

AVODAH: worship.

AVODAH ZARAH: idol worship.

AVADIM: slaves.

BA'AL: a Kena'anite deity.

BA'AL TEFILLAH: a cantor; one who leads the prayer services.

BA'AL TESHUVAH: a formerly non-observant Jew who returns to Jewish practice.

BAR MITZVAH: a Jewish boy of 13, the age at which he accepts religious obligations; the celebration held in honor of the occasion.

BARUCH ATTAH HASHEM: "Blessed are You, Hashem," the opening words of every blessing.

BAYIS: a home.

BEIN ADAM LA-MAKOM: between man and God.

BEIN ADAM L'CHAVERO: between man and his fellowman.

BEIS DIN: a court of Jewish law.

BEIS HA-KNESSES: the synagogue.

BEIS HA-MIDRASH: the house of study.

BEIS HA-MIKDASH: the Holy Temple.

BEMIDBAR: the Book of Numbers.

BECHIRAH: free will.

BECHOR: the firstborn son.

BECHOROS: one of the Ten Plagues, the death of the firstborn.

BEDIKAS CHAMETZ: the search for CHAMETZ conducted on the night before the Seder.

BERACHAH ACHARONAH: a concise form of the grace after meals.

BERACHOS: blessings.

BERESHIS: the Book of Genesis.

BESAMIM: fragrant spices.

B'EZRAS HASHEM: "With the help of God!"

BIGDEI KEHUNAH: priestly garments.

BIKKUR CHOLIM: the mitzvah of visiting the sick.

BIMAH: the table in the synagogue upon which the Torah is read to the congregation.

BIRKAS HA-MAZON: the grace after meals.

BIRKAS KOHANIM: the priestly blessing.

BIRCHOS YA'AKOV: the blessings of Ya'akov to his sons.

BITACHON: faith and trust in God.

BITTUL CHAMETZ: the renunciation of one's title to CHAMETZ, performed on EREV PESACH.

BI'UR CHAMETZ: the destruction of CHAMETZ in one's possession.

BOREI PRI HA-ADAMAH: the blessing recited over vegetables.

BOREI PRI HA-ETZ: the blessing recited over fruit.

BOREI PRI HA-GEFEN: the blessing recited over wine.

BOREI MINEI MEZONOS: the blessing recited over food made from grains, like cake and noodle products.

BNEI TORAH: learned, observant Jews who are devoted to Torah.

BNEI YISRAEL: the Children of Israel; the Jewish People.

BRIS MILAH: the ritual of circumcision.

CHAG HA-ASIF: the Festival of Sukkos, the holiday of the ingathering of the harvest.

CHAG HA-BIKKURIM: the Festival of Shavuos, the holiday of the first fruits.

CHALLOS: loaves of braided Sabbath bread.

CHAMETZ: leavened food.

CHANOCH LA-NA'AR AL PI DARKO: "Educate the child according to his ways" (*Mishlei* 22:6).

CHAROSES: a mixture of nuts, apples, and wine that is one of the traditional Passover foods on the Seder plate.

CHASAN: a bridegroom.

CHASSIDEI UMOS HA'OLAM: righteous gentiles.

CHATAS: the sin offering.

CHAZERES: horseradish, one of the traditional foods on the Seder plate.

CHAZZAN: a cantor.

CHESED: lovingkindness.

CHESED SHEL EMES: lit., "true kindness," that is, rendering services in connection with burial of the dead.

CHEVRAH KADDISHA: (A.) a Jewish burial society.

CHILLUL HASHEM: the desecration of God's Holy Name.

CHOL HA-MOED: the intermediate days of the Festivals of Pesach and Sukkos.

CHUKIM: Torah precepts whose purpose is not stated.

CHUMASH: (one of) the Five Books of Moses.

CHUPAH: the wedding canopy.

DAM: blood.

DAN L'KAF ZECHUS: to judge others in a favorable light.

DAVEN: (Y.) to pray.

DEVARIM: the Book of Deuteronomy.

DOR HA-PELAGAH: the generation of the Tower of Bavel.

DUCHAN: the platform from which the KOHANIM give the priestly blessing.

ECHAD: the number one.

ED: a witness.

EFOD: a priestly garment.

EGEL HA-ZAHAV: the Golden Calf.

EICHAH: the Book of Lamentations.

ELOKIM: one of the names of God.

EMOR ME'AT V'ASE HARBEI: "Say little but do much" (*Pirkei Avos* 1:15).

EMES: truth.

EMUNAH: faith in God.

ERETZ YISRAEL: the Land of Israel.

EREV PESACH: the day before Passover.

EREV SHABBOS: the day before Shabbos (Friday).

ERUV: a halachic arrangement which permits carrying within limits or walking a certain distance outside a city on the Sabbath.

ERUV TAVSHILIN: a halachic arrangement when a Festival falls on the eve of the Sabbath, in which some food is set aside before the Festival, to be eaten on the Sabbath, thereby enabling preparations of food on the Festival for the Sabbath.

ESAV SONEH ES YA'AKOV: (The nation of) Esav hates (the nation of) Ya'akov.

ESH TAMID: the fire that burned night and day on the altar in the BEIS HA-MIKDASH.

ESROG: a citron, one of the Four Species used on Sukkos.

ESER MAKKOS: the Ten Plagues with which Hashem punished Egypt.

EZRAS NASHIM: the women's section in a synagogue.

GABBAI TZEDAKAH: a charity collector in a Jewish community.

GADOL: a great Torah sage.

GAM ZO L'TOVAH: "This too is for the best."

GAN EDEN: the Garden of Eden.

GAON: a very learned man.

GEMILAS CHESED: acting with kindness and compassion.

GEMARA: explanation and commentary on the Mishnah (together they comprise the Talmud).

GER: a convert to Judaism.

GER TZEDEK: a sincere and righteous convert to Judaism.

HACHNASSAS KALLAH: providing a dowry for poor brides.

HACHNASSAS ORCHIM: hospitality.

HADASSIM: myrtle branches, one of the Four Species used on Sukkos.

HADLAKAS NEROS: lighting the Sabbath or Festival candles.

HAGGADAH: the story of the Jewish redemption from Egyptian bondage, read during the Passover Seder.

HAKARAS HA-TOV: displaying gratitude.

HALACHAH: Jewish law.

HALLEL: a prayer of praise and thanksgiving, recited on Festivals and Rosh Chodesh.

HALVAYAS HA-MES: the mitzvah of attending a funeral.

HA-MOTZI: the blessing recited over bread.

HAR: a mountain.

HASHEM: God.

HASHGACHAH: Divine Providence.

HAVDALAH: the blessings recited at the end of the Sabbath and Festivals.

HESPED: a eulogy.

HOSHANA RABBAH: the seventh day of Sukkos.

IYAR: the Hebrew month corresponding to May/June.

KE'ARAH: lit., a plate; the Seder plate.

KADDISH: the prayer recited by mourners for the soul of the deceased.

KALLAH: a bride; a daughter-in-law.

KARPAS: lit., celery; greens or another vegetable (for instance, potato), one of the traditional Passover foods on the Seder plate.

KASHRUS: the Jewish dietary laws.

KEDUSHAH: part of the Eighteen Benedictions in the daily prayer services stressing the holiness of God.

KERIAS SHEMA: the recitation of the fundamental Jewish prayer declaring the unity of God.

KERIAS YAM SUF: the miraculous splitting of the Red Sea.

KESUVIM: the third of the three divisions of the Holy Scriptures.

KIBBUD AV V'EM: honoring one's father and mother.

KIDDUSH: sanctification of the Sabbath and Festivals usually recited over wine.

KIDDUSH HASHEM: the sanctification of God's Holy Name.

KINIM: lice, one of the Ten Plagues in Egypt.

KITTEL: (Y.) a white robe worn by men on Rosh Hashanah, Yom Kippur, the Seder, and other occasions symbolizing purity and humility.

KLAL YISRAEL: the Jewish Nation.

KOHELES: the Book of Ecclesiastes.

KOHEN (KOHANIM): member(s) of the priestly tribe.

KOHEN HA-GADOL: the High Priest.

KOL NIDREI: the opening prayer of the Yom Kippur prayer service.

KORBANOS: sacrifices, offered when the Temple stood.

KORBAN PESACH: the Passover sacrifice.

KOS SHEL ELIYAHU: the special cup set aside for the Prophet Elijah at the Passover Seder.

KOSHER: food that is halachically permissible for a Jew to eat.

KVATER: (Y.) the man who has the honor of carrying the baby in at the BRIS MILAH.

LAG BA'OMER: the 33rd day in the counting of the Omer, marking a break in the period of semi-mourning between Pesach and Shavuos.

LAMED-TES MELACHOS: the thirty-nine categories of labor prohibited on the Sabbath.

LASHON HA-RA: evil gossip; slander.

LASHON HA-KODESH: lit., the holy tongue; Hebrew.

LECHEM MISHNEH: the two loaves of bread on the Sabbath table.

LEVAYAH: a funeral.

LEVI(-YIM): Levite(s).

LEHADLIK NER SHEL SHABBOS: the blessing recited upon lighting the Shabbos candles.

LICH'VOD SHABBOS: in honor of the Sabbath.

LILMOD TORAH: to learn Torah.

LULAV: a palm branch, one of the Four Species, used on Sukkos.

MA'ARIV: the evening prayer service.

MA'ASER: a tenth; a tithe of one's income or produce set aside to give to a KOHEN or LEVI.

MABUL: the Flood sent by God to destroy the world.

MALACH(IM): angel(s).

MALCHUS: kingship.

MAROR: a bitter vegetable (for example, horseradish or romaine lettuce), one of the traditional Passover foods on the Seder plate.

MASHAL: a parable.

MASHIACH: the Messiah.

MATAN TORAH: the giving of the Torah at Mount Sinai.

MATZAH: unleavened bread.

MATZAH SHEMURAH: matzah made from wheat especially guarded from the time of its harvest.

ME'ARAS HA-MACHPELAH: the Tomb of the Patriarchs in Hebron.

MECHIRAS CHAMETZ: selling of the CHAMETZ before Passover.

MEGILLAS RUS: the Book of Ruth, read on Shavuos, that tells the story of the convert Ruth.

MENORAH: a candelabrum; the seven-branched candleabrum that stood in the Holy Temple.

MERAGLIM: spies; those who were sent out to scout the land before BNEI YISRAEL entered Eretz Yisrael.

MES MITZVAH: a deceased person who has no relatives and for whom it is therefore a great mitzvah to arrange proper burial.

MESIRAS NEFESH: self-sacrifice; dedication.

MIDDAH (-DOS): positive character trait(s).

MIDBAR: desert; wilderness.

MI-D'RABBANAN: (A.) according to the ruling of the Sages.

MIDRASH: a collection of non-literal interpretations and homiletic teachings of the Sages.

MIKVEH: a pool for ritual immersion.

MINCHAH: the afternoon prayer service.

MINYAN: a quorum of ten Jewish males over the age of 13, the minimum necessary for congregational prayer.

MISHLEI: the Book of Proverbs.

MISHNAH: the codification of the Oral Law.

MITZRAYIM: Egypt.

MITZVAH: a commandment of the Torah.

MODIM: "We thank," the opening word of one of the Eighteen Benedictions recited daily.

MOHEL: one who is qualified to perform the ritual of circumcision.

MUSAF: the additional prayer which follows Shacharis on Sabbaths, Festivals, and Rosh Chodesh.

NA'ASEH V'NISHMA: "We will observe and we will hear," the words with which BNEI YISRAEL accepted the Torah at Mount Sinai (*Shemos* 24:7).

NER TAMID: the eternal light which burned continuously in the MENORAH in the Holy Temple.

NES (NISSIM): miracle(s).

NESHAMAH: the soul.

NEVI'IM: prophets; Prophets, the second of the three divisions of the Holy Scriptures.

NISSAN: the Hebrew month corresponding to March/April.

NUSACH ASHKENAZ: the arrangement and versions of prayers according to the custom of Ashkenazic Jews.

NUSACH SEFARAD: the arrangement and versions of prayers according to the custom of Sefardic Jews.

OLAH: the burnt offering.

OLAM HA-BA: the World to Come.

PARAH ADUMAH: a red heifer, whose ashes were used for ritual purification.

PARASHAH: a section of the Torah read on the Sabbath.

PAREVE: (Y.) food that is neither a dairy nor a meat product.

PESACH: the Festival of Passover.

PIDYON HA-BEN: the ceremony of redemption of the firstborn son.

PIDYON SHEVUYIM: the redemption of Jewish captives.

PIRKEI AVOS: Ethics of the Fathers, a tractate of the Mishnah.

RACHMANUS: mercy; pity.

RASHA: a wicked person.

RAV: a rabbi.

RIBBONO SHEL OLAM: Lord of the Universe.

ROSH CHODESH: the first day(s) of the new Hebrew month.

ROSH HASHANAH: the Jewish New Year.

RUACH HA-KODESH: Divine revelation.

SANDAK: the person who is honored by holding the baby during the circumcision.

SANHEDRIN: the Supreme Court of Jewish Law in the time of the Holy Temple.

SECHACH: the leaves and branches, or woven matting that comprises the roof of a SUKKAH.

SEDER: the order of the Pesach night ceremony recalling the Exodus from Egypt and liberation from bondage.

SEFER: a book; a holy book.

SEFER YEHOSHUA: the Book of Joshua.

SEFIRAS HA-OMER: the counting of the forty-nine days between Pesach and Shavuos.

SEMICHAH: rabbinical ordination.

SEUDAS HAVRA'AH: the mourner's meal, eaten upon returning from the funeral.

SEUDAH SHELISHIS: the third Shabbos meal.

SHABBOS: the Sabbath.

SHACHARIS: the morning prayer service.

SHALOM ALEICHEM: "Peace be with you," a traditional greeting; the opening words of the song sung upon returning from the synagogue on Friday night.

SHALOM BAYIS: marital harmony.

SHALOSH REGALIM: the three Festivals (Pesach, Shavuos and Sukkos) for which Jews made a pilgrimage to the Temple in ancient times.

SHAVUOS: the Festival celebrated seven weeks after Pesach, which commemorates the giving of the Torah, as well as the bringing of the first fruits.

SHECHINAH: the Divine Presence.

SHE-HA-KOL: the blessing recited over foods that are not fruits, vegetables, or grain products.

SHEKER: a lie; a falsehood.

SHELOMIM: the peace offering.

SHELOSHES YEMEI HAGBALAH: three days' preparation prior to Shavuos.

SHEMINI ATZERES: the eighth day of Sukkos.

SHEMIRAS HA-LASHON: lit., guarding one's tongue; refraining from gossip.

SHEMITTAH: the seventh, Sabbatical, year when land must not be worked in Eretz Yisrael.

SHEMONEH ESREH: the Eighteen Benedictions, or Amidah prayer.

SHEMOS: the Book of Exodus.

SHEVA BERACHOS: the seven blessings recited at a wedding; one of the festive meals held during the week following the wedding in honor of the bride and groom, at which the seven blessings are recited.

SHEVET: a tribe.

SHIBUD MALCHIYOS: domination by a foreign government.

SHIR HA-SHIRIM: the Song of Songs.

SHIRAH: song; poetry.

SHIVAH: the seven-days period of mourning.

SHIVAH ASAR B'TAMMUZ: the fast of the 17th day of Tammuz.

SHMUEL HA-NAVI: Samuel the Prophet.

SHOFAR: a ram's horn.

SHOFTIM: the Book of Judges.

SHOMER SHABBOS: one who observes the Sabbath.

SHUL: (Y.) a synagogue.

SIDDUR: a prayer book.

SIMCHAS TORAH: the Festival of rejoicing with the Torah, on the final day of Sukkos, when the Torah-reading cycle is completed and begun again.

SIVAN: the Hebrew month corresponding to June/July.

TA'ANIS: a fast day.

TALLIS: a prayer shawl.

TALLIS KATAN: a small fringed garment worn by males.

TALMID CHACHAM: a Torah scholar.

TAMMUZ: the Hebrew month corresponding to July/August.

TANACH: a Hebrew acronym for the Holy Scriptures, consisting of TORAH, NEVI'IM, and KESUVIM.

TANNA(-IM): (one of) the Sages of the Mishnah era.

TASHLICH: a ceremony on the first day of Rosh Hashanah in which the crumbs from one's pockets are thrown into a body of water, symbolizing the elimination of one's sins, and a special prayer is recited.

TECHIYAS HA-MESIM: the resurrection of the dead.

TEFILLIN: phylacteries.

TEFILLAH (-LOS): prayer(s).

TEHILLIM: (the Book of) Psalms.

TERUMAH (-MOS): part of the produce set aside as an offering to the KOHEN.

TESHUVAH: repentance.

TISHAH B'AV: the Ninth of Av, a fast day commemorating the destruction of the First and Second Temple.

TISHREI: the Hebrew month corresponding to September/October.

TORAH: the Five Books of Moses, the first of the three divisions of the Holy Scriptures.

TORAH SHE-B'AL PEH: the Oral Law, e.g., the Talmud.

TORAH SHE-B'KESAV: the Written Law, e.g., the Holy Scriptures.

TORAH TZIVAH LANU MOSHE, MORASHAH KEHILLAS YAAKOV: "Moshe commanded the Torah to us, an inheritance to the community of Jacob" (*Devarim* 3:4).

TREI ASAR: (A.) twelve; the books of twelve of the prophets, which are grouped together as a section of NEVI'IM.

TREIF: (Y.) non-kosher.

TUMAH: ritual impurity.

TZADDIKIM: righteous, pious men.

TZEDAKAH: righteousness; charity

TZEFARDE'A: the plague of frogs, one of the Ten Plagues of the Egyptians.

TZOM: a fast.

TZOM GEDALYAH: the fast of the Third of Tishrei, commemorating the death of Gedalyah.

TZARA'AS: a Biblical skin disease.

VAYIKRA: the Book of Leviticus.

YAHRTZEIT: (Y.) the anniversary of a person's death.

YEMACH SHEMAM: "May their names be obliterated!"

YETZER HA-RA: the evil inclination.

YIDDEN: (Y.) Jews.